The Structure of Detachment

Kuki Shūzō, courtesy of Konan University, Kobe

The Structure of Detachment

The Aesthetic Vision of Kuki Shūzō

with a translation of

Iki no kōzō

HIROSHI NARA

with essays by J. Thomas Rimer
and Jon Mark Mikkelsen

University of Hawai'i Press

Honolulu

Support for the publication of this book was provided by the
Japan Iron and Steel Federation Endowment publication subvention fund
and the Richard D. and Mary Jane Edwards Endowment Publication Fund
of the University of Pittsburgh.

Library of Congress Cataloging-in-Publication Data
Nara, Hiroshi.
[Iki no kōzō. English]
The structure of detachment : the aesthetic vision of Kuki Shūzō /
Hiroshi Nara ; with essays by J. Thomas Rimer and Jon Mark Mikkelsen.
p. cm.
Includes index.
ISBN 0-8248-2735-X (hardcover : alk. paper)—
ISBN 0-8248-2805-4 (pbk. : alk. paper)
1. Kuki, Shūzō, 1888–1941. I. Title.
B5244.K844N3713 2004
181'.12—dc22
2003020075

Jacket illustration: *The Flirt*, woodblock print
from the series *Ten Examples of Female Physiognomy*,
c. 1792–1793, by Kitagawa Utamaro (1753–1806).
British Museum, London.

Typeset in Quadraat by Tseng Information Systems, Inc.

Printed by The Maple-Vail Book Manufacturing Group

To Erika J. Nara
for keeping us busy
—H.N.

Contents

Acknowledgments

The project represented in this volume began as part of a workshop investigating the relationship between modernity and aesthetics in Japan, organized by J. Thomas Rimer and Brenda G. Jordan at the University of Pittsburgh several years ago. Thus the essays contained in this volume partly represent the authors' efforts to answer questions about this topic. Compiling this volume presented special challenges that demanded skills beyond my formal academic training. The translations pushed me to look in two principal directions—ethnography of Edo and Western philosophy—so that I might situate the text in the larger Western philosophical tradition. In conducting research for and writing the translation and the essay, I owe special thanks to J. Thomas Rimer, who first suggested that I do a translation of Iki no kōzō. After I completed a portion of the translation, it lay dormant for some years. Tom's continued enthusiasm for this project persuaded me to revive it. Without his generosity of knowledge and time (he was gracious enough to read much of the manuscript many times), I could not have brought this project to fruition. I also want to thank philosopher and friend Jon Mark Mikkelsen for clarifying many difficult philosophical concepts and for reading drafts of my essay, especially materials regarding Heidegger, with sharp scrutiny. Corresponding with Mikkelsen on aspects of Kuki's text and Continental philosophy was both helpful and intellectually stimulating. In addition, I would like to express my gratitude to the following colleagues at the University of Pittsburgh: Mae Smethurst for help with Kuki's references to classical studies including Greek mythologies and for commenting on an early draft of my essay; Richard Smethurst for offering valuable comments on an early draft of my essay; Cecile Sun for her assistance with Chinese classical literature; and Keiko McDonald for discussing with me aspects of iki and locating difficult-to-find sources on iki. I am indebted to John Singleton of the University of Pittsburgh, David Plath of the University of Illinois, and Ōtsu Shinsaku of Konan University for helping me gain access to the Kuki Memorial Library; to Uemura Kuniko, director of the Konan University Library, for granting permission to use images held in the Kuki Memorial Library; to Noguchi Sachie,

Japanese bibliographer of the University of Pittsburgh's East Asian Library, for her expert help in locating library materials and in obtaining copyright permissions; to John Partridge of Johns Hopkins University for his help with Kuki's interpretation of Plato's *Phaedrus;* to John Lomax of Ohio Northern University for his help with Latin; to Paula Locante for her clerical assistance; and to Arine Kaar Studios for their expert illustrations that appear in the translation. Earlier drafts of my essay were presented at a colloquium of the Department of East Asian Languages and Literatures and in a talk to the members of the Japan Council at the University of Pittsburgh. My gratitude goes to the participants of these occasions who made me sharpen some of my arguments. I would like to thank the members of the aforementioned aesthetics workshops who commented on my presentations substantively and brought to my attention ideas and sources for further pondering. In addition to Tom Rimer and Brenda G. Jordan, the list of members in the workshop includes Miki Hirayama, Jon Mark Mikkelsen, Joshua Mostow, Reiko Tomii, and Toshio Watanabe.

A lengthy project such as this could not have been completed without financial assistance from a number of resources. I wish to acknowledge the Griffith Way Foundation for making workshops on Japanese aesthetics possible at the University of Pittsburgh in 1996 and 1998. Grateful acknowledgments are due the Japan Iron and Steel Federation Endowment, the Hewlett International Grant Program of the University Center for International Studies, the Faculty Small Grants Program of the Asian Studies Center, the Faculty of Arts and Sciences of the University of Pittsburgh, and the Department of East Asian Languages and Literatures of the University of Pittsburgh.

I gained a great deal from the comments of two anonymous readers of this manuscript, for which I am grateful. I would like to express my gratitude to Joseph Brown and Jan-Paul Malocsay for patiently and expertly editing the translation and my essay for style and clarity. Lastly, I should not spare words about the helpful editors for this book. I want to make special mention of Patricia Crosby for pointing out shortcomings of initial drafts and suggesting ways to improve them. Above all, Pat oversaw this project from birth to publication with a kind heart, encouragement, and professionalism. I am very much grateful to Karen Weller-Watson for scrupulous and uncompromising editing and her ability to flush out long-buried oversights and to managing editor Cheri Dunn and the production staff of the University of Hawai'i Press for their usual expertise. Finally, special thanks go to my wife, Brenda G. Jordan, for supporting me throughout this endeavor.

Introduction

The sensibility of *iki*, for which I adopt the gloss "urbane, plucky stylishness"
for this introduction, is somewhat similar to that of dandyism in the West.
But while both sensibilities maintained tacit codes of dress and behavior, and
flourished around the same time, the dandyism of the late eighteenth and
early nineteenth centuries was a trademark of indolent and socially irrespon-
sible men who put on not only clothing that made a statement but an air of superiority, and *iki* shared little of this type of decadence. In contrast to dandies,
who were often sexually inert men, the men and women who cultivated *iki*
sensibility in its original form pursued romantic liaisons with the opposite
sex. Unlike dandyism, which was not practiced widely in a particular locale or
by a certain class of people, *iki* constituted one among the aggregate characteristics that made the inhabitants of Edo, today's Tokyo, true Edokko (Edoites). Not everyone could become an Edokko. Besides being born in the city —
preferably reared in the city center — other essential traits were the ability to
resign oneself quickly to inescapable destiny, an embodiment of *iki*, and a
type of spiritual tension called *hari*. Some unflattering characteristics were
essential as well, such as bravado, boastfulness, and spendthrift habits that
could squander a fortune overnight. These traits, Edokko *katagi*, were proudly
and mockingly put into use to draw a contrast between Edokko and those
lacking this "sophistication" — those not from the city, such as merchants
from the Kyoto-Osaka area, house servants, and samurai from outlying prov-
inces. The *iki* sensibility, first cited in literature in the Meiwa era (1764–1772),
was sharpened in the pleasure quarters of Fukagawa, in a southeastern part
of Edo. By the beginning of the nineteenth century, Fukagawa was one of the
major not-officially-sanctioned brothel areas of the city that had become a
trendy place for rich merchants and townsmen to spend an evening, while
its competitor Yoshiwara had declined due in part to the Kansei Reform of
1787, which had instituted austerities. Fukagawa courtesans differed from

their Yoshiwara counterparts in that they prided themselves on being more masculine in disposition, even affecting male attire to attend their entertainment engagements. Presenting themselves as strictly geisha, women of Fukagawa took customers on the side only when they felt inclined to do so, while Yoshiwara women never pretended to be other than ladies of the night. Fukagawa courtesans were thus more selective about their bedmates, and the ideal customer displayed wit, pluck, and, most of all, iki.

A man or woman in pursuit of iki would employ a certain cool, elegant, and flirtatious demeanor, backed by pluck, to win over the object of desire. Like a good Edokko, though, a successful pursuer was able to recognize a relationship destined to fail, and thus retreat quickly. This spiritual tenet became sublimated in the psyche of the common people of Edo, and by the beginning of the eighteenth century, the townspeople there identified themselves very closely with iki and strove to cultivate and embody this spirit. Iki became such a rarefied, creedlike code of behavior that it was said to be detectable in every facet of life, including patterns of speech, choices in food, furniture, and other household items, not to mention courting behavior and clothing colors and patterns.

Iki is arguably the phenomenon of a specific time and place in Edo, but its roots derive from the Kyoto-Osaka sensibility of sui, which in fact describes very similar, perhaps identical, sensibilities in Kyoto-Osaka from the late eighteenth century onward. The origins of iki and sui can be found in such traditional Japanese aesthetic sensibilities as miyabi (elegance), wabi (rustic simplicity), sabi (elegant simplicity), and yūgen (mystery; profundity), which were primarily found in the center of high culture, then the Kyoto-Osaka area. The exact combinations of sensibilities contributing to the various aspects of iki and sui are difficult to determine, but it is fairly certain that as the center of popular culture moved from the Kyoto-Osaka area to Edo, the once high-class aesthetic sensibilities gave birth to the sensibility of iki. We can still find in iki the simplicity, lightness, suggestiveness, sincerity, transience, and spontaneity, that comprise the basic components of traditional Japanese aesthetics. This discussion of iki through the vision of a philosopher not only reveals much on the lifestyle of late Edo's townspeople but facilitates further understanding of Japanese aesthetics, long an integral part of the culture of Japan. In fact, the predominance of aesthetics in the conceptualization of Japanese culture may be unmatched elsewhere.

In this context, then, it is natural for modern Japanese writers to reflect upon this tradition and to ponder how Japanese aesthetics might be treated in a philosophical idiom comprehensible in the West, a quest that began in earnest in the Meiji period (1868–1912). During this time, Japanese intellectuals learned of Western concepts of aesthetics and the arts, both through studies at Japanese universities and through research in Europe. From later Meiji until the late 1940s, a number of these important thinkers sought to explain centuries-old literary, aesthetic, and artistic concepts in Japan, to place them in an international framework.

In premodern Japanese culture, discussions concerning aesthetic principles were limited to those among the artists themselves, sometimes giving rise to secret treatises. More frequently, trade secrets were tacitly passed down through a succession of master-apprentice relationships. In the modern period, however, the Japanese aesthetics nexus came to be identified as a privileged means of defining the significance of Japanese society and culture for international and domestic audiences. The wider public, increasingly familiar with Western intellectual systems, also sought explanations concerning Japanese aesthetics. Kuki's attempt to recast traditional understanding within the context of Western aesthetic theory was to answer this need for explanations, and to assert afresh the centrality of Japanese aesthetic sensibilities.

Kuki Shūzō (1888–1941) was a philosopher of considerable prominence in Japan during the first half of the twentieth century. He was the fourth son of Kuki Ryūichi, a successful politician with special influence on government policies dealing with the arts. Kuki's education and training were on a par with any young man of financial means and intellectual promise—he was educated at the First Higher School and at the Tokyo Imperial University, graduating from the latter in 1912 with a degree in philosophy. Not much is known about what kept Kuki busy for the next several years, but in 1921, at the age of thirty-three, he embarked for Europe, accompanied by his wife, Nui, intent on studying Western philosophy in situ. Kuki traveled around in Europe for the next seven years, crisscrossing Switzerland, France, and Germany, staying in one city for a few months, and another city for a year, just long enough to nibble at the academic offerings there. These offerings included private readings from Rickert and Herrigel, talks by his fellow countrymen, studies with Husserl, lectures by and conferences with Heidegger, and visits to Bergson in Paris. During this time, Kuki wrote some of his most important philosophical thought, completing, for example, a draft of The Structure of Iki, in Paris, in December of 1926. He also gave public lectures, and in 1928 he spoke on the oriental notion of time and the expression of infinity in Japanese art.

While traveling, he divided his time between work and pleasure. He spent weeks collecting plant specimens in the Swiss Alps to satisfy his boyhood interest in botany. Paris particularly seemed to have agreed with Kuki. When he was not dining at the most exquisite restaurants and visiting houses of pleasure in the French capital, he was meticulously recording his private ruminations through poetry. One might say that he lived his philosophy and then recorded it on paper. Nonetheless, Kuki's scholarly cultivation impressed Nishida Kitarō (1870–1945), a prominent philosopher and department chair at Kyoto Imperial University until 1928. Just a few months before leaving his position as department chair, Nishida wrote a letter to his successor, Tanabe Hajime, in December 1928, recommending Kuki for a position in the university's philosophy department.

Kuki returned to Japan in 1929 via the United States. He then joined the department of philosophy at Kyoto and began teaching courses on French philosophy, Husserl, Heidegger, the problem of contingency, and the history of Western philosophy, among others. Kuki published *The Structure of Iki* in the year after he returned to Japan, first as a series of two articles in the philosophy journal *Shisō* (Thought), and then as a book, from the publisher Iwanami shoten. In this work, Kuki analyzed *iki* using new theoretical frameworks in the Continental tradition. He concluded that *iki* could be understood only through "lived experience." In other words, *iki* is not the sum of conceptual analyses of objective expression; its full signification cannot be determined by identification of generic concepts that pervade its manifestations. *Iki* should be defined, Kuki argued, in terms of "a mode of being" as localized in Japanese ethnicity. In this way, Kuki brought to the fore this quintessentially Japanese sensibility, which was in danger of being forgotten during the wave of modernizing in interwar Japan, and gave it an elegant analysis, situating it in a system of other Japanese aesthetic sensibilities.

There is a good deal of scholarly interest in Kuki's role in the formation of so-called Japanese national aesthetics in the 1930s, when the military Japanese government was grappling with defining and asserting Japan's identity to the rest of the world. Thus, the ideas proposed in Kuki's 1930 publication have been the subject of considerable discourse among historians and art historians, especially since the 1970s in Japan and more recently in the United States. Two critical books on Kuki have been written in English—Stephen Light's *Shūzō Kuki and Jean-Pierre Sartre* (Southern Illinois University Press, 1987) and Leslie Pincus' book *Authenticating Culture in Imperial Japan: Kuki Shūzō and the Rise of National Aesthetics* (University of California Press, 1996). The study of an aesthetic vision achieved by a Japanese thinker such as Kuki should shed light on the ways in which modern Japanese have defined their own culture. Through the translation comprising part 1 of this text, we hear a Japanese thinker speaking on aesthetics, a subject dear to the Japanese heart, not through paraphrase and summary, but in his own voice. We learn how he tackled the recondite sensibility of iki using the prevailing Western philosophical methodology. We see where the philosophical fit between methodology and phenomenon was perfect and where judicious trimming was needed. And through this analysis of iki, we feel the author's yearning to make this sensibility relevant to modern life.

Part 2 of this book presents in its three essays three distinct but clearly interlaced perspectives. The authors arrive at a similar intellectual locus about Kuki, which is that a more productive—and arguably more balanced— strategy for understanding Kuki's writing in his *Structure of Iki* is not wedding it to the view from Heidegger's philosophical window.

In the first essay, Hiroshi Nara presents a glimpse of Kuki as a man who expended considerable energy formulating scrupulous judgments on where to use which facts to argue for his own brand of philosophical analysis of iki and who was quite methodical in underscoring the fundamental thesis of his book. What emerges is that Kuki was a less than careful scholar, at least in writing this book. Nara argues that when judged in the context of Kuki's other writings, this shaky scholarly footing is uncharacteristic of Kuki and that adding in the 1930s sociopolitical and personal contexts, we gain a new perspective on the political roles of Kuki and his writing during the interwar years.

J. Thomas Rimer's essay compels us to reexamine the inclination to analyze Kuki's *Structure of Iki* as a work in philosophical aesthetics. Rimer sees this work in the celebrated literary tradition of casual writings (*zuihitsu*), much like the works of Kamo no Chōmei or Yoshida Kenkō. Though the tone is muted and clearly more philosophical, Kuki's easygoing writing style on a matter so abstruse supports Rimer's viewpoint well. Rimer points out, too, that Kuki's French connection—both in style of presentation and outlook—is undeniable. To be sure, Kuki begins with a quote from Biran and cites both Stendhal and Baudelaire to support some of his pivotal arguments.[1] If Kuki's French connection is shown to be more than merely tangential than his connection to the beleaguered German philosopher, we have good reason to orient future Kuki scholarship in this direction.

Jon Mark Mikkelsen questions the validity of the link between Kuki and Heidegger, arguing that although Heidegger's view of art is consistent both historically and conceptually with his political involvement with the Nazis, the same cannot be said about Kuki. Mikkelsen asks if Kuki's conceptualization of art and political conviction is manifest in his Structure of Iki. First comparing the role of the sensibility of iki in Kuki's work with that of Hölderlin's poetry in Heidegger's, Mikkelsen then attempts to find in Kuki's writing any suggestion that Kuki saw history as destined to achieve a political goal. Mikkelsen uses this analysis to remark on the role that Kuki might have played in the formation of the cultural landscape of Japan in the 1930s.

Evidence presented in these essays points to the validity of the thought that Kuki was unlikely to have been a willing and active conscript in serving the ideology that fueled Japan's imperialism. At least, the essays show that an incontrovertible basis to inculpate Kuki is lacking. A more rewarding vantage point for interpreting Kuki's Structure of Iki may be to consider this Japanese philosopher a man seeking to make organic connections between the world of ideas and the pleasurable and sometimes unsavory complications of life. During the 1920s and 1930s, a time of looming uncertainties when tradition was relinquishing its role to modernization, Kuki must have felt an urgent desire to return spiritually to the unfaltering bedrock of history and tradition. In this search, Kuki found the sensibility of iki to be a fitting means to sound the clarion message that tradition has a place in modernity; that is, one cannot move forward into modernity without keeping one's sight squarely on tradition.

Notes

1. Kuki's fascination with Alain was apparently more than speculative: In 1928, on his way back to Japan, Kuki stopped over in Washington, D.C., to meet French-poet-turned-diplomat Paul Claudel (1868–1955), a known admirer of Baudelaire, in order to discuss the aesthetic philosophy of Alain.

PART I

Iki no kōzō
(The structure of iki)

The Actor Nakamura Utaemon III (1778–1838), n.d., woodcut
on paper, 13¾ × 9⅝ in. (34.93 × 24.45 cm), by Utagawa
Kunisada (1786–1864). Carnegie Museum of Art,
Pittsburgh. Bequest of Dr. James B. Austin.

Translator's Preface

Kuki Shūzō's writing on *iki* in the form most familiar to us originally appeared as *Iki no kōzō* (The structure of *iki*) in a series of two articles in the philosophy journal *Shisō* (Thought) in 1930. These articles were then published in book form by Iwanami shoten that same year, with a few minor editorial changes; the book has since been reprinted many times. This translation of *Iki no kōzō* is based on the book in the twelve-volume complete works *Kuki Shūzō zenshū*, hereafter referred to as KSZ, and on a twenty-third printing of the book in the Iwanami bunko series. Kuki's handwritten notes, his scribbles in the margins of the books he consulted, and his manuscripts themselves were enormously useful in preparing this translation. Kuki's manuscripts were written in fountain pen on boxed manuscript paper, with a great amount of rewriting and rearranging of sentences. His thinking on *iki* changed over the years he devoted to this project, and some of his personal musings and notes on *iki* are now published as "Iki ni tsuite" (Concerning *iki*) in KSZ. "Iki no honshitsu" (The essence of *iki*), a draft of *Iki no kōzō*, was completed in December of 1926, in Paris, which brought together in coherent prose for the first time his thinking on *iki*. These manuscripts are stored in a special collection at the Kuki Memorial Library at Konan University, Kobe.

I have tried to maintain Kuki's easygoing style, as far as possible, and instead of always translating Japanese words into their closest English equivalents (e.g., *iki* to "chic"), I have left untranslated certain pivotal words in Kuki's argument when they carry heavy semantic burdens and cultural connotations. This is in keeping with Kuki's central thesis that words do not have translation equivalents in another language. Thus, in this translation, these words are given in transliteration, followed by a short semantic gloss in single quotation marks. Fuller connotative and denotative meanings, if pertinent, appear in the notes.

The modified Hepburn romanization system is used throughout for Japanese words. Unlike the standard system, the *n* is maintained even when followed by homorganic consonants (e.g., *shinbun*, not *shimbun*). In addition, vowel lengths are indicated with a macron, and the nasal mora followed by a vowel or the letter *y* is marked by an apostrophe. This system of romanization is used for all Japanese words, except for those few judged to be English words (e.g., Tokyo, Osaka, Kyoto, kimono).

Japanese words and phrases quoted in the original text in Japanese quotation brackets are given their romanized equivalents in italics, followed by English equivalents in double quotation marks. In some cases, however, the Japanese in romanization was judged to be more appropriate than providing its gloss in English, because it would otherwise be disruptive to the prose or not easily translatable parsimoniously to English. In such cases, the quoted item is not translated and is given in romanized Japanese and set in italics.

Kuki's own notes as well as the translator's notes appear as endnotes. The translator's comments are enclosed in square brackets and end with "—trans." Any comments regarding the contents of Kuki's notes are added at the ends of these notes, again enclosed in square brackets and followed by "—trans." When Kuki's bibliographical citation in his notes is incomplete, I have added information to complete it.

Titles of woodblock-print series and essays appear in double quotation marks, sometimes followed by their English translation in parentheses, where needed. Names of books enclosed in Japanese quotation brackets in the original are given in italics and in the original language (in romanization if Japanese).

Kuki placed single or double circles next to words in the original edition, and dots *(bōten)* in later paperback editions, to indicate emphasis. In this translation, the emphasized text appears in bold type. Three works proved useful in translating Kuki's works. One is a German translation of *Iki no kōzō* by Emi Schinzinger, with her own commentary, entitled "Die Structur des 'iki' von Kuki Shūzō," published as a part of her master's work at the University of Tübingen in 1985, kindly brought to my attention by Jon Mark Mikkelsen. The other two are John Clark's 1978 draft translation and his more polished 1997 translation published as *Reflections on Japanese Taste: The Structure of Iki*. When published translations of passages that Kuki quoted were available, they were used and cited herein; otherwise the translations of these passages are this translator's.

Works of literature from the Edo period to which Kuki refers in the text are cross-referenced to their locations in the series *Nihon koten bungaku taikei* (abbreviated as NKBT) published by Iwanami shoten in Tokyo beginning in 1957 such as: NKBT, 23:34. Kuki's references to *Morisada mankō*, an encyclopedic compilation of Edo customs and culture written beginning in 1852 by Kitagawa Morisada, are cited with respect to their locations in the 1992 reprint edited by Asakura Haruhiko and Kashikawa Shūichi (Tokyo: Tōkyōdō, 1992) and will appear as MM, such as: MM, 3:96. Also used was *Nihon koten bungaku zenshū* (abbreviated as NKBZ) published in 1971 by Shōgakukan in Tokyo, if NKBT was not available for a particular literary work. I have used the following translations for various subparts of the popular romance novel *(ninjōbon)* referred to in the text, i.e., *hen* 編 'section'; *kan, maki* 巻 'volume'; *kai* 回 'episode'; *shō* 章 'chapter'; *jō* 條 'article'; *kugiri* 齣 'scene'.

The Structure of Iki

KUKI SHŪZŌ

Translated by Hiroshi Nara

Le pensée droit remplir toute l'existence.
—Maine de Biran, *Journal intime*

FOREWORD

This is a revised version of a paper published in the journal *Shisō*, issue numbers 92 and 93 (January and February issues of Showa 5).

A living philosophy must be able to understand reality. We know there is a phenomenon called iki. What is the structure of this phenomenon? Is it not, after all, a way of "life" that is particular to our people? Comprehending the reality as it is and expressing logically the experience one undergoes are the tasks of this book.

October, Shōwa 5
Kuki Shūzō

I   INTRODUCTION

How is the phenomenon of iki structured?[1] How can we make clear the structure of iki and grasp its being? There is no doubt that iki has certain meaning; neither is there any question that iki exists as a word in the Japanese language. Can we then state that the word iki is found universally, in all languages? We must first look into this question; and if it turns out that what is meant by iki exists only in the Japanese language, then it follows that iki bears a specific ethnicity. If that is the case, what methodological approach should we take to treat this meaning, with its specific ethnicity, or, alternatively, its specific cultural being? Before we embark on the analysis of the structure of iki, we must answer some preliminary questions.

Let us begin by asking what general relationship language has to an ethnic group.[2] What relationship binds the meaning in language and its being of an ethnic group? The question of whether the meaning of a cultural phenomenon is captured cannot by any means make useless the question of whether meaning exists. On the contrary, we venture to say that the question of being is often more fundamental. We must therefore start with the concrete given us. What is given directly is "ourselves" and the "ethnic group," a collection of ourselves. When a mode of being of an ethnic group is central to that ethnic group, it reveals itself as a "meaning," which is made accessible through "language." For that reason, a meaning or a language represents none other than the manifestation of an ethnic group's past and present modes of being and, hence, is self-revealing of a particular historical culture. Thus the relationship between meaning and language, on the one hand, and the being of an ethnic group's consciousness, on the other, is not that the former come together to constitute the latter but that the "being" of an ethnic group, supported by experience, creates meaning and language. The relation between these two structures is not a mechanical one, in which parts take precedence over the whole, but an organic one, in which the whole determines its parts. For this reason, a particular meaning or language of a particular ethnic group cannot help but manifest its specific colorings of the experience of that ethnic group, as the expression of the being of that group.

Of course, meaning and language attached to so-called natural phenomena have a certain universality. That universality is, however, never absolute. For instance, if we compare the French ciel or bois to the English sky and wood and the German Himmel and Wald, the meanings of these words are not necessarily identical. This is a fact that anyone who has lived in one of these countries would readily comprehend. The meanings of the words ciel in Le ciel est triste et beau, and sky in What shapes of sky or plain? and Himmel in Der bestirnte Himmel über mir are all constrained by the people and their land in specific ways. If words describing natural phenomena already differ in this way among languages, we cannot hope to find precise counterparts in one language for words describing specific social phenomena in other languages. For instance, each of the Greek words πόλις 'polis' and ἑταίρα 'hetaira' has a different meaning from the French ville or courtisane. Even if two words share the same etymological origin, their realizations in different languages have distinct meanings. For example, the meanings of the Latin *caesar* and the German *Kaiser* are clearly different.

The same can be said about meaning and language concerning abstractions. Even when a specific mode of being of one ethnic group reveals the kernel of that ethnic group through meaning and language, it is obvious that certain meaning and language may not exist for another ethnic group when it does not possess that same experience at its core. For instance, the meaning of *esprit* reflects the personality and the entirety of the history of the French people. The meaning of this word and the French language presuppose the being of the French people, and if we were to look for a word with the same meaning in the languages of other ethnic groups, we would not find it. *Geist* is ordinarily substituted for *esprit* in German, but the specific meaning of *Geist* as expressed in Hegel's use of it is distinct from that of the French term. The word *geistreich* does not have the exact semantic shading that *esprit* does. If it did, it would be only in a case in which *geistreich* was intentionally used to translate *esprit*. In such cases, the word has been forced to take on yet another shade of meaning in addition to its original meaning. This would then be a case of introducing a new, different meaning into a language. The people did not create the new meaning organically; it was brought in artificially from abroad. None of the English words *spirit*, *intelligence*, or *wit* is equivalent in meaning to *esprit*. The first two are too specific, while the latter seems excessive in meaning. Another example is the German word *Sehnsucht* "longing, yearning," a word to which the German people gave birth and to which they possess an organic relation. *Sehnsucht* conveys the feeling of longing for a bright, happy world, harbored by the people who were disturbed by a melancholy climate and military conflicts. This longing to escape to the land where lemon flowers bloom is not a mere homesick sentiment of Mignon.[3] It is rather an earnest longing of Germans as a whole for the bright south of Germany in general. It is a longing for flight "away into distant futures which no dream had yet seen, into hotter souths than artists ever dreamed of, where gods in their dances are ashamed of all clothes" and what Nietzsche calls *flügelbrausende Sehnsucht*, both equally held dear by all German people.[4] The penchant for agonizing longing eventually gives rise to metaphysical sentiments that constitute the presupposition that underlies the world of *noumenon*.[5] The English *longing* or the French *langueur*, *soupir*, *désir*, et cetera cannot capture all the nuances of *Sehnsucht*. In his essay "La psychologie du mysticisme," Boutroux says of mysticism that "its starting point is a mental state which is difficult to define, which the German word *Sehnsucht* aptly describes,"

implicitly recognizing that there is no French word with meaning equivalent
to that of *Sehnsucht*.[6]

The Japanese word *iki* is one with meaning that is rich in ethnic coloring.
Suppose we look for synonyms in European languages. First, in English and
German all words similar in meaning to *iki* are borrowings from French. If
that is the case, can we find a counterpart for *iki* in that language? Let us begin
with *chic*. This word is borrowed by both English and German from French,
and it is often translated into Japanese as *iki*. There are essentially two theo-
ries as to the etymology of this word. One holds that *chic* is an abbreviation
of *chicane*, which refers to being adept at the "intricate trickery" that wreaks
havoc with court cases. The other holds that the original form of *chic* is *schick*,
a word from the German *schicken*, and that, like *geschickt*, *schick* meant "skillful"
in various matters, moving closer to that of *élégant* when imported into French
and used to describe aesthetic taste. Later, *chic* in its new sense was borrowed
by German from French. If we ask what this word means at present, it is by
no means as specific as *iki*. The semantic extension of *chic* is much wider. It
subsumes both meanings of *iki* and *jōhin* 'elegant, high class' as equally important elements of its meaning, and it can also express *senkō* 'delicateness
and skillfulness' and *takuetsu* 'excellence' of taste, as opposed to *yabo* 'boorish' and *gehin* 'crude, low class'.[7]

Then there is *coquet*. This word comes from *coq* and describes what happens when a cock is surrounded by a number of hens. It, therefore, corresponds to the Japanese *bitaiteki* 'coquettish'. The word *coquettish*, too, carries
the same sense in both English and German. In eighteenth-century Germany,
the word *Fängerei* was proposed to replace *coquetterie* but it never gained cur-
rency. This very "French" word does indeed symbolize one of the many facets
of *iki*. But unless we add additional definitions to the meaning of *coquetterie*, it
cannot encompass the entire range of meanings of *iki*. Depending how these
defining elements are combined, however, it could come to mean *gehin* 'crude,
low class' or *amai* 'sweet, undisciplined'. Carmen, singing the Habanera, be-
witching Don José, is precisely *coquetterie*, but it is definitely not *iki*.[8]

Let us take another example, the French *raffiné*. It comes from the word *re-
affiner*, meaning to "make something even finer," and *raffiné* corresponds to
the Japanese *senren* 'refinement'. An equivalent is also used in both German
and English. *Raffiné* also expresses one of the many facets of *iki*. But, again, it
still lacks something very important to encompass the entire meaning of *iki*.
In certain combinations of defining elements, *raffiné* can be said to be equivalent in meaning to *shibumi* 'understated, astringent', which is opposed to *iki*
in certain situations. In summary, words that carry meaning similar to that

of iki can be found in European languages, but none has the same semantic value of iki. It then follows that iki can be safely considered to be a distinct self-expression of an oriental culture or, no, more precisely, a specific mode of being of the Yamato people.[9]

Of course, it is not impossible to search for words having similar meanings to iki in the Western culture and, through formal abstraction, find some common elements among them. If we wish to understand the cultural being as a mode of being of an ethnic group, however, this is not the correct methodological approach. Even if we were to engage in what is referred to as *Ideation* in a domain of the possible by freely making changes to a phenomenon, the being of which is ethnically and historically determined, we would only gain in the end abstract general concepts containing that phenomenon as a part.[10] The important thing to bear in mind in the understanding of a cultural state of being is that one must grasp the living form of it, as it is, without altering its actual concreteness. Bergson states that when we recall the past as we smell roses, it is not that the fragrance triggers the memory. Rather, we smell in the fragrance the memory of the past. Immutable objects, such as the fragrance of roses, or, equivalently, general concepts that are universal for all men, do not exist in reality. Rather, there are individual fragrances having differing olfactory contents. According to Bergson, explaining experience by means of the combination of a general object, such as the fragrance of roses, and a specific object, such as a memory, would be much like trying to produce sounds specific to a language by arranging letters of the alphabet commonly used in many languages.[11]

Attempting to find, through formal abstraction, common ground between iki and similar phenomena in the Western culture is analogous to the foregoing example. Every time we attempt such a methodological examination for understanding the phenomenon of iki, the very question of *universalia* arises. Basing his opinion on the idea that general concepts do exist, Saint Anselm supported the orthodox belief that the Trinity was, after all, the manifestation of one god.[12] In contrast, Roscelin, couching his opinion on nominalism, a position which held that a general concept was no more than a name, asserted that the Trinity of Father, Son, and Holy Ghost represented three independent gods; as a result, he was highly criticized as a proponent of tritheism.[13] If we are to understand iki, we must find a nominalist solution to this problem of *universalia*—and therefore also resign ourselves to being branded heretics. In other words, we cannot attempt to "intuit the essence" of iki, that is, treat it as a specific concept and attempt to discover abstract universals among general concepts that subsume iki. The understanding of iki as an experience of meaning must be a concrete, factual, and specific "compre-hension of being."[14] Before questioning the *essentia* of iki, we should instead question first the *existentia* of iki. In short, a study of iki cannot be "eidetic"; it should be "hermeneutic."[15]

What structure does iki have as its meaning that is experienced concretely by an ethnic group? We must first comprehend the mode of being of iki that obtains as a **phenomenon of consciousness** and then reach the understand-ing of the mode of being of iki that has taken shape as **objective expression.** If we ignore the former or confuse the order of examination between the former and the latter, our attempt to understand iki will end in failure. In fact, when scholars have attempted to clarify iki, they have almost always made this mis-take. Because they first analyzed objective expressions of iki and then sought general characteristics from this domain, they have failed to grasp the ethnic specificity of iki, even in the area of objective expression. Further, having once obtained an understanding of objective expression, they erroneously assumed as well that they have obtained a comprehension of the phenomenon of con-sciousness. Thus, the explanations of iki as a phenomenon of consciousness have tended to be abstract and eidetic, and scholars have not been able to explain concretely and hermeneutically the mode of being, determined both ethnically and historically. We must set out on an opposite path and begin with an examination of the concrete phenomenon of consciousness.

II THE INTENSIONAL STRUCTURE OF *IKI*

To comprehend iki which manifests itself as meaning as a phenomenon of consciousness, we must first recognize the **intensional features** constituting the meaning of iki and **clarify** their semantic content. We will then explicate **extensionally** the distinction between the meaning of iki and the meaning of related words in order to **differentiate** the meaning of iki. In this way, that is, by giving balanced explanation to both the intensional and extensional struc-tures of iki, we can comprehend the complete being of iki as a phenomenon of consciousness.

In the intensional analysis of iki, we notice that the first distinguishing fea-ture of iki is **bitai** 'coquetry' directed at a person of the opposite sex. From the fact that *ikigoto* (lit. 'iki affairs') means *irogoto* (lit. 'romantic affairs'), we know that this relationship with a person of the opposite sex constitutes the fundamental being of iki. If we speak of iki *na hanashi* (lit. 'stories that represent *iki*'), the phrase invariably refers to stories about relationships between men and women. Furthermore, *iki na hanashi* and *iki na koto* 'matters that are *iki*' both connote relationships that are out of the ordinary. For instance, the short story by Chikamatsu Shūkō entitled "Iki na koto" (An *iki* matter) concerns "having a mistress."[16] In fact, we cannot imagine a relationship out of the ordinary that way without presupposing coquetry. And the essential condition of *iki na koto*, in some sense of the words, is coquetry. What then is coquetry?

Let us say that coquetry is a dualistic attitude; that it puts a person of the opposite sex in opposition to the monistic self; and that it posits a possible relationship between that person and the self. *Iki* ranges through meanings like *namamekashisa* 'lusciousness', *tsuyapposa* 'eroticism', *iroke* 'sexiness', and so forth, and these arise precisely from the tension implicit in the dualistic possibility. *Jōhin* 'elegant, high class', however, indicates a lack of this dualistic opposition. This dualistic possibility is the fundamental determinant for the being of coquetry, and coquetry disappears on its own accord when the opposite sexes unite totally and lose that source of tension. This is because the hypothetical goal of coquetry is conquest, destined to disappear when this goal is fulfilled. As Nagai Kafū says in his novel *Kanraku*, "there is nothing more pathetic than having a woman after trying to have the woman." He must surely have in mind the "boredom, despair, and aversion" arising from the disappearance of coquetry that once played such an active role in both sexes.[17] For that reason, the main concern of coquetry—and the essence of pleasure—is maintaining a dualistic relationship, that is to say, protecting the possibility as a possibility.

The intensity of coquetry, however, does not decrease in proportion to the physical proximity. On the contrary, a shorter distance increases its intensity. We find the following description under the section "Bitai" in Kikuchi Kan's *Fue no Shiratama*: "Mr. Katayama . . . tried to walk as fast as possible in order to allow more distance from Reiko. But Reiko, with slender long legs, . . . came closer and closer to Katayama, walking stride for stride at his heels, as he tried to put in more distance from her."[18] The essence of coquetry is to come as near as possible, and at the same time making certain that nearness stops short of actual touch. Coquetry as a possibility is only possible as a dynamic possibility. Achilles may attempt to come infinitely close to the tortoise "with long slender legs," but he should not forget to make valid the paradox of Zeno.[19] After all, coquetry, in its perfect form, must represent the dualistic and dynamic possibility that is made absolute only in the form of a possibility. A vagabond who maintains the "continual finitude," an evil person who finds joy in the "infinity of evil," and Achilles, who would not succumb to fatigue from "eternal" pursuit—only these kinds of people know true coquetry. And this type of coquetry defines *iropposa* 'coquet', a basic theme for iki.

A second distinguishing feature of iki is iki 意気, that is, **ikiji** 意気地 'pride and honor'. A moral ideal of Edo culture is manifestly reflected in iki, a mode of being as a phenomenon of consciousness. In this word, the spirit of Edokko "Edoites" is contained as a pivotal moment.[20] The *true* Edokko were proud of the fact that people who were *yabo* 'boorish' and apparitions did not live east of Hakone.[21]

True Edokko praised firefighters, who risked their lives to fight the "Flowers of Edo"; carpenters working high up on scaffolds wearing no more than white work socks; and *otokodate* 'neighborhood dandies', who sported only thin coats even in the middle of winter.[22] In iki, one must have *the stubborn pluck of Edo* and *the manliness of southwest Edo*.[23] To personify iki, one must possess an inviolable dignity and grace, commonly expressed in words such as *inase* 'dashing, spirited', *isami* 'chivalry', and *denpō* 'show-off bravado'. As has been said, "Leave *yabo* outside the hedge; what's iki is the competition of erotic allure of three thousand courtesan houses, vying for trade in a contest involving ikiji and pluck."[24] Iki here means more than just coquetry. It also includes a rather aggressive range of sentiments directed toward the opposite sex, showing a bit of resistance.

The Kabuki character Sukeroku, who wears "a blue purple headband," symbolizing a connection to iki, would make a sharp retort and pick fights by calling out "Hey you, young man! I dare you to come closer to take a good look at my face!"[25] Agemaki of Miura-ya, whose complexion was praised as being as beautiful as light pink cherry blossoms, showed resolute courage by reprimanding bearded Ikyū: "Excuse me, please, but you don't know who I am. I am Agemaki. How would I even mistake you for Sukeroku, even in the dark?"[26] This is precisely what is meant by *iro to ikiji o tatenuite, kidate ga sui de* "a woman's temperament, when she is upholding passion and ikiji, is *sui*."[27] Accordingly, Takao and Komurasaki shared the same qualities of iki.[28] The sprightly ideal of *bushidō* 'the way of the samurai' still **lives** in iki.[29] The sentiment expressed by "A samurai uses a toothpick even when he has not eaten" speaks for the pride of the Edokko's credo "Spend all the money on making merry for a single night." This pride nourished a gallant spirit that despised *kekoro* 'unlicensed prostitutes' and *mizuten* 'geisha who prostitute on the side'. Brothels aspired to a similar high standard: "Courtesans are not to be bought with money; it is ikiji that buys them." A high-ranking Edo courtesan would be pleased to be characterized as someone who "disdains the touch of money, dirty as it is; someone who has no idea of prices of any kind; a woman who lives free of complaint, as if she were truly a daughter of the imperial or *dai-myō* family."[30] Prostitutes of Yoshiwara would "give a cold shoulder to rich but *yabo* 'boorish' men over and over again," as if spurred on by saying such as "treating them in any other way would be a shame of Gochōmachi,[31] a disappointment to Yoshiwara."[32] These prostitutes lived according to a saying: "If I am not swept away by love, then I am shamed" and contemplated a love suicide "guided by (the ulterior motive of) the gods that tie the knots of their undergarments."[33] We observe that a special characteristic of iki that distinguishes itself is that coquetry is spiritualized by way of ikiji 'pride and honor', which is, in turn, born of idealism.

A third distinguishing characteristic of iki is **akirame** 'resignation, acceptance'. This word refers to a disinterest which, based on the knowledge of fate, permits us to detach ourselves from worldly concerns. To have the quality of iki, one must be sophisticated, possessed of a frame of mind that is light, fresh, and stylish. How did this deliverance come about? The existence of a special subculture that serves as the conduit between men and women is prone to inflict the pain of disappointment that comes with fulfillment in affairs of love. "We see each other only on occasion. Your appearance is Buddha's, but now that you tell me we must part: I have to ask; Dear Seishin, are you in fact a demon?"[34] A lament such as this would not only be that of Izayoi's. The sincerest heart, callously betrayed often over time, is tempered by that repeated pain and ceases to pay attention to deceitful targets. A heart that has lost its innocent trust in the opposite sex can hold to its resolve to love no more. But this result comes at a cost. "Ukiyo, where what we wish is not easily realized, refers precisely to that element of impossibility, which we are resigned to accepting."[35] On the other side of this sentiment lies the experience gained from earthly emotions. That experience teaches us that men are "unsympathetic, capricious, and, regardless of whatever some say about them, ill-natured." This teaching is flanked by the fate of all things that "the karmic relation is thinner than thread; easily frayed and severed."[36] Moreover, the sensibility of iki skeptically concludes that "man's heart is like the river Asuka; going with the changes is the nature of the profession." It also sanctions this pessimistic conclusion: "professionals like us don't have anyone to care for and customers who would care for us in turn are likewise few in this wide world."[37] It is probably for this reason that iki is found in older, not younger, geisha.[38]

In short, iki arises from the "world of suffering" in which "we are scarcely able to keep afloat, carried down on the stream of ukiyo."[39] *Resignation* or disinterest in iki represents the state of mind that has suffered through hard ukiyo's tough and merciless tribulations and shed worldly concerns; in other words, the state of mind that is free of grime, unclinging, disinterested, and free from obstacles, and that has removed itself from any egotistical attachment to reality. The saying "Yabo turns into iki, after so much suffering" refers to this situation and no other.[40] When we detect a trace of seductive and ingenuous tears behind a charming lighthearted smile, we have finally been able to grasp the truth about iki. Perhaps the sentiment of resignation in iki is the fruit of decadence. It may very well be that the experience and critical knowledge that iki embodies have been socially inherited rather than individually acquired. It could be either. Whatever the case, this undeniable fact remains: iki contains the sense of resignation to fate and the freedom from attachment based on that resignation. Two views of life and the universe undoubtedly lie behind this definitive moment in iki, both serving to intensify and purify it. One is especially Buddhist, with its regard for ruten 'transmigration' and mujō 'transience' as forms of differentiation, and for kūmu 'emptiness' and nehan 'nirvana' as principles of equality. The other, more generally religious view of life preaches resignation to a relationship never meant to be fulfilled and teaches us to let fate run its course.[41]

Let us summarize what we have examined thus far. The structure of iki exhibits three moments: bitai 'coquetry', ikiji 'pride and honor', and akirame 'resignation'. The first, bitai, constitutes the basic tonality of iki, while the following two—ikiji 'pride and honor' and akirame 'resignation'—define a people's ethnic and historical coloring. At first glance, the second and third distinguishing characteristics appear to be inconsistent with the first, bitai. But is that really the case?[42] The fundamental determinant of being for bitai, as explained above, lies in a dualistic possibility. Thus, the second distinguishing characteristic ikiji represents the strong state of mind that idealism has brought about. That state of mind brings increased tension and endurance to the dualistic possibility of coquetry; it also attempts to maintain the possibility as a possibility to the bitter end. That is to say, ikiji reinforces the existentia of coquetry, lending it luster and sharpening its edge. Limiting the dualistic possibility of coquetry by means of ikiji is tantamount to advocating the protection of a kind of freedom.

Akirame, the third distinguishing characteristic, is not incompatible with coquetry either. Because it does not achieve the hypothetical final objective, coquetry remains faithful to itself. Consequently, it is by no means irrational for coquetry to embody akirame in attempting to reach the final objective; akirame forces the fundamental state of being of coquetry to reveal itself. Unifying coquetry with *akirame* means that fate forces us to return to freedom and that positing of this possibility is determined by necessity. In other words, affirmation is reached by way of negation. In sum, in the mode of being we call *iki*, *bitai* is brought to its perfection of being by *ikiji*, a sentiment based on the idealism of *bushidō*, and by *akirame*, a state of mind that presupposes the unrealism of Buddhism in the background. For this reason, *iki* is the "very essence" (*sui*)[43] of coquetry. *Iki* ignores a careless positing of reality. It boldly brackets everyday life, and engages in autonomous play in a manner disinterested and purposeless, as it breathes a neutral air, transcending all of life around.[44] In one word, *iki* is coquetry for the sake of coquetry.

Seriousness and attachment to love go counter to the being of *iki*, because, in such a case, love has been actualized and is no longer a possibility. *Iki* must transcend the bonds of love to maintain its free and flirtatious spirit. The phrase "I prefer darkness to a moonlit night" describes the heart of darkness, lost in love.[45] "Stating a preference for the moon" is the "spirit of *sui*," maddening to a lover.[46] "Falling in love sincerely, in good faith, I lead a *yabo* 'boorish' life for love, in a *sui* floating world." This declaration clearly shows the opposition between the realistic inevitability of love and the transcendent possibility of *iki*.

When "a loving pair, thought to be *sui*,"[47] lose the spirit of lightheartedness and stylishness "because of the capricious spirit of an unrequited love" over time, they would have to find a way to excuse themselves. They would have to explain why they have fallen prey to a situation wherein "the deeper they are in love, the closer they are to *yabo*."[48] When the affair is "a freespirited flirtation, like a lotus leaf floating freely on the water," it is still in the domain of *iki*. When "a couple becomes inseparable, *yabo* rules." Their relationship has left the domain of *iki* far behind. A woman may become an object of ironic ridicule when her lover can be seen in such a light: "how *yabo* he is, living a life in the samurai quarters, hardly the place for a woman with *iki* like hers." Her heart may be described as smoldering "more than the kiln that fires roof tiles," a disposition considered "most unbecoming in a woman with the *iki* of Koume."[49] The intoxication of so-called *amour-passion* in Stendhal is a complete departure from *iki*. He who lives for *iki* must have reached a state of detachment. There he is said to live off the land, free from attachment, picking fern heads for nourishment, as he breathes the rarefied air of *amour-goût*. *Iki* is not a picture we often see in rococo period paintings in which "everything including shadows are **rose-colored.**"[50] The color of *iki* is probably **pale brown** in "a man of high fashion far in the past, dressed in pale brown *hakama*."[51]

Again, summing up, we can say that iki is coquetry, the material cause of iki, that perfected its existence as a being. This state was made possible by formal causes that characterize Japanese culture—moral idealism and religious unrealism.[52] That being the case, we see how iki exercises supreme authority and commands exquisite charms. The power of iki is attested by a sentiment like this: "Charmed by his iki heart, I ended up believing his love was real when it was not," which straightforwardly describes it.[53] In *Ein Spaziergang in Japan*, we find Kellermann describing a Japanese woman as "playing the coquet in a manner whose power to charm was far and away superior to anything we have seen in European women."[54] One would guess that Kellermann was responding to the allure of iki.

Finally, this question: is it not possible to propose a definition of iki? We would have to begin by taking note of its two forms. The first form will figure as a phenomenon of consciousness itself, with rich, diverse colorings. The second form would be a kind of coquetry that realizes itself by means of an idealism and unrealism. That done, could we not combine both forms into a definition of iki as **sophisticated** (arising from *akirame* 'resignation') **coquetry** (*bitai*) with **pluck** (arising from ikiji 'pride and honor')?

III   THE EXTENSIONAL STRUCTURE OF *IKI*

In the preceding chapter, we have attempted to clarify the meaning of iki by distinguishing the intensional characteristics. In this section, we will clarify the extensional meaning of iki by examining and distinguishing other terms related to it.

The primary meanings related to iki are *jōhin* 'elegant, high class', *hade* 'flashy', *shibumi* 'understated, astringent', to name a few.[55] If we look for the criteria of classification by examining the determinants of their beings when these words became established, they naturally fall into two categories. The domain of the public in which *jōhin* and *hade* exist as modes of being differs in character from the one in which iki and *shibumi* exist as modes of being. Of these two domains of the public, it would be safe to conclude that the one to which *jōhin* and *hade* belong is the **general human being,** while the one to which iki and *shibumi* belong is the **particularized heterosexual being.**[56]

Most of these words have their corresponding antonyms. *Jōhin* has as its opposite, *gehin*. *Hade* has as its opposite, *jimi*. The opposite of iki is *yabo*. Only *shibumi* does not have an obvious opposite. We customarily contrast *shibumi* and *hade*, but *hade* is already a counterpart of *jimi* 'quiet'. Incidentally, the word *shibumi* probably comes from the tannin taste of unripe persimmons. But since persimmons can be ripe and sweet as well, it seems safe to assume that *amami* 'sweet' is the opposite of *shibumi* 'understated, astringent'. Such pairs of related opposites abound. Examples could include *shibucha* 'strong tea' and *amacha* 'hydrangea tea', *shibukasu* 'spent persimmon seeds' and *amakasu* 'sweet lees of sake'. This sense of opposing difference is also served by *shibukawa* 'astringent epidermis [of a chestnut]' and *amakawa* 'epidermis'.[57] What, then, do such oppositions signify? What is their relation to *iki*?

Jōhin and Gehin

The distinction of **jōhin-gehin** is one that pertains to the self and is based on value judgment; in other words, it is a distinction that is based on the quality of the object itself. As it is clear from how these words are written in kanji, *jōhin* 'elegant, high class' refers to those that are of high quality, as opposed to low quality *gehin*.[58] The meaning of *hin*, however, is not uniform. *Jōhin* and *gehin* can be used to distinguish objects and goods. In addition, this distinction extends to the sphere of human activity. When we use the phrase *jōbon ni kanmon nashi, gebon ni seizoku nashi* "there are no poor families from the upper class, no powerful families from the lower class," *jōbon* and *gebon* seem to pertain to human relationships, particularly with regard to social class.[59] We see this in Utamaro's series of prints entitled "Fūzoku sandan musume" (Three ranks of young women according to their fashions). Using cues of appearance and manner, the artist depicts women at three levels of social status—*jōbon no bu* 'high class', *chūbon no bu* 'middle class', and *gebon no bu* 'low class'.[60] Sometimes the kanji character 品 *hin* can be read in the Wu dynasty pronunciation referring to the class system of Pure Land Buddhist paradise, but I consider this use to represent also a type of human relationship in a broad sense of the word.[61] The opposition of *jōhin* and *gehin* was based on human relationships and then it began to acquire a new sense denoting the property of human taste itself. Thus *jōhin* has taken on the meaning of highly refined, and *gehin*, of crude and unsophisticated.

What then is the relation between *iki* and these meanings? It is thought that *jōhin* belongs to the domain of the public of general human being and, as such, does not interact with coquetry. There is a phrase *samo jōhin naru sono idetachi* "a look that exudes high class" describing the mother of Tōbei in *Shunshoku umegoyomi*.[62] The mother had not only become widowed already but was "a Buddhist nun of about fifty years of age." Further, she makes a wonderful contrast to the coquetry of Oyoshi, the mistress of Tōbei. It follows that, since iki encompasses aspects of *ikiji* 'pride and honor' and *akirame* 'resignation', iki is understood as a superior form of taste. When we look into the relation between iki and *jōhin*, we find they have superior taste and positive value in common, even as they differ with respect to coquetry. Similarly, *gehin*, like *jōhin*, does not itself imply coquetry, even as it has characteristics that tend to put it in a predetermined relationship with coquetry. Consequently, when we think about the relationship between iki and *gehin*, we generally understand the existence of coquetry as a common feature, and the difference in superiority and inferiority in taste as a differentiating feature. *Iki* has positive value, while *gehin* has negative value. We would expect that the coquetry common to them both would manifest itself differently, depending on whether the taste involved is superior or inferior. The relation between iki and *gehin* can be seen in descriptions of someone as *iki ni shite iyashikarazu* "iki and not vulgar"[63] or as *iki de hitogara ga yokute gebita koto to ittara koreppakari mo nai* "iki and a wonderful personality, without the slightest whiff of vulgarity."

Hence, when we consider how iki relates to *jōhin* 'elegant, high class' and *gehin* 'crude, low class', we see why iki is commonly thought of as occupying the middle ground between *jōhin* and *gehin*. There are those who maintain that if a certain element is added to *jōhin*, we obtain iki, and if too much of it is added, we obtain *gehin*. *Jōhin* and iki both represent a positive value, but are distinguished by the presence or absence of this certain attribute. Moreover, this attribute is also shared with *gehin*, which represents a negative value. *Iki* is therefore viewed as signifying a middle ground between *jōhin* and *gehin*. Viewing these three concepts in terms of a linear relation like this, however, is secondary and not fundamental to the basic determinants of being.

Hade and Jimi

Hade 'flashy' and **jimi** 'quiet' offer a distinction that is based on their modes of relationship to the other. The distinction may depend on the strength of self-assertion; or it may depend on the presence or absence of self-assertion in relation to the other. *Hade* means *ha de* "leaves come out."[64] This is the literal meaning of 葉出 *hade*. *Jimi* 'quiet' means that the root tastes the earth, the literal meaning of 地味 *jimi*.[65] The former refers to the mode of being that comes out from the self and goes to another; the latter denotes sinking back into one's given temperament. It follows that an outgoing person prefers pomp and dresses flashily. In contrast, a person who sinks into himself dresses quietly, having no one in mind to impress. Toyotomi Hideyoshi, an unreserved man who wished to assert himself in Korea, brought about the opulence and splendor of the Momoyama period.[66] In contrast, Ieyasu lived modestly, guided by secret maxims such as the five- and seven-character phrases "do not be ambitious" and "know thy place." He reproved those in his retinue who wore beautiful clothing, and ordered that imperial processions be simplified.[67] The difference in taste is revealed in these men's attitudes. In summary, the opposition of *hade* 'flashy' and *jimi* 'quiet' is one that is value-neutral in itself and does not embody value judgment. The significance of this opposition derives from the distinction between active and inactive.

Let us now consider the relation of *hade* 'flashy' to *iki*. As is evident in the phrase *hade na ukina ga ureshūte* "happy to have a rather flashy reputation," *hade*, like *iki*, is capable of expressing coquetry to others. *Urahazukashiki hade sugata mo mina kore otoko o omou yori* "rather embarrassingly flashy attire; I wear it only to captivate my man" also indicates a possible relation between *hade* and coquetry.[68] But the flashy, show-off character of *hade* is totally incompatible with the *resignation* of *iki*. Take, for instance, a *senryū* that reads: *Hade musume Edo no shita yori Kyō o mise* "What a showy girl! She flashes Kyoto from underneath Edo."[69] This woman is showing her slip on purpose—the Kamogawazome undergarment from under her Edozuma kimono.[70] The mind-set of this *hade musume* "flashy girl," is all about splendor and charm displayed without regard for harmony or unity. It is quite different from the mind-set of a woman with *iki*, one whose kimono "does not show much of the pale violet lining on the collar and sleeves, who is clad in lusterless Yūki kimono, with a stripe design in which a red thread has been woven in."[71] For this reason, when the quality of goods is examined carefully, *hade* items are often branded as *gehin*, tainted by conspicuous bad taste. *Jimi* cannot have the coquetry that *iki* possesses, because it inherently stands in an inactive relation to the other. Instead, *jimi*, always simple and understated, exhibits a certain type of *sabi* 'quiet elegance' and embodies a possible link to the *resignation* of *iki*. When the quality of goods is examined closely, *jimi* attaches itself to things that are notable for being refined, things whose design speaks for the modesty of the elegant but simple outlook that *jimi* represents.

Iki and Yabo

The pairing **iki-yabo** signifies a distinction in relation to the self. This distinction is based on a value judgment in the domain of the public of the pecu-

liarity of the heterosexual being. Since the determinant of the being origi-
nates in the peculiarity of the heterosexual being when it first took shape, iki
expresses a certain supposition about the opposite sex.

However, the objective content of what is emphasized in this iki-yabo opposition does not represent the intensity of the relation to the other or whether
or not such an opposition exists; rather, it represents a value judgment on the
relation to the self. That is to say, the presence or absence of a special kind of
refinement explains the opposition of iki and yabo. Iki, as I said before, is literally iki 意気 'pride and honor'; it corresponds to kishō 'disposition, nature'.
Iki refers to kishō no seisui 'the purity of disposition', and as such came to mean
"being thoroughly familiar with worldly affairs and human emotions," "being
well-versed in matters pertaining to the special society of the opposite sex,"
and "being sophisticated."

Yabo 'boorish' is said to be a phonetic mutation of yabu 'field hand'. In contrast to people who possess iki, this word refers to crudely mannered workers
of the land, who do not possess broad experience with worldly affairs or
qualify as connoisseurs of complex human emotions. Hence the meanings
"rustic" and "unsophisticated." The author of *Harutsugedori* describes himself as "yabo by nature and ignorant of worldly matters . . . I have never even
dreamed of pleasure quarters. Hence I have been criticized time and again by
connoisseurs in that arena."[72] In *Eitaidango*, a woman is quoted as saying "I
have heard that you would not like a woman if she were not a geisha from
Fukagawa. Why would you fancy me? I am just a yabo girl, who works for a
samurai retainer."[73]

Often when someone says "I am yabo," he expresses a sense of conceit
about being yabo. He takes pride in not having gone through the refinement in
the domain of the public of the peculiarities of the opposite sex. Here exists
something that is worthy of pride and conceit. Whether to favor iki or choose
yabo is a matter of taste. Here we do not see the objective, absolute value judgment. However, when one of a pair of opposites that constitutes a determinant of cultural being expresses a meaning positively while the other does so
negatively, we can do two things. First, we can judge which meaning came
first and which is derived in turn. Secondly, we can speculate on the relative
value of the words in the domain of the public in which the meanings arose.
The words gōri 'rational' and fugōri 'irrational' can be seen as taking form in
the public domain of rational discourse. Shinkō 'religious' and mushinkō 'irreligious' would spring from the domain of religion. Further, these words carry
a value judgment in each of the domains of the public where they belong.
Now, both iki and sui are expressed in the affirmative.[74] On the other hand,

yabo, and its synonyms *buiki* and *busui,* are expressed with a negative prefix.[75] From this evidence, we are able to learn that *iki* is the original word and then *yabo* was born from the need for an antonym. We can also surmise that *iki* is judged to possess a positive value and *yabo* a negative value in the domain of the public of the peculiarities of the opposite sex.

To a professional in any field, an amateur appears to be *busui* 'boorish'. *Machifū* 'ways of the town, townsmanlike' is allowable as *iki* to someone close to it, but *yashikifū* 'ways of the samurai and their servants' is *yabo,* since it is rather unfamiliar. A naïve love is also *yabo.* So is a homely woman's layering heavy makeup on her face. Consider the phrase "Pray not to pretend to be *busui;* you are not so *yabo* as to not know what really goes on in the red-light district." Here, too, a negative value is shown through the words *busui* and *yabo,* which come about as a result of a value judgment in the domain of the public of the peculiarities of the opposite sex.[76]

Shibumi and Amami

In the pair **shibumi-amami,** we find a distinction based on the relation to the other. This pair does not offer any value judgment in itself; that is, this pair only expresses whether or not the relation to the other is active or inactive. *Shibumi* 'understated, astringent' signifies an inactive relation to the other. This can be likened to the fact that persimmons contain tannin to protect themselves against crows. Chestnuts protect themselves against insects by means of an astringent inner skin. People fend off moisture by wrapping things in tannin-treated paper, just as they wear a sullen face to avoid human interaction.[77] *Amami* 'sweet', in contrast, denotes an active relation to the other. An active path always exists between the dependent and the provider.[78] Similarly, when we want to get on the good side of someone, we use sweet words; if we have ulterior intentions, we try to offer sweet tea.[79]

Shibumi and *amami,* in which the distinction is made on the type of relation to the other, do not offer characteristics open to value judgment. Value-loaded meanings arise only when we know the background in each individual case. The *shibukawa* 'astringent skin, tannin skin' represents a negative value in the *senryū* that reads *Shibukawa ni mā daisoreta Edo no mizu* "Her complexion is so unrefined. And yet she dabs on Water of the Edo River—preposterous!"[80] *Shibumi* takes on a positive meaning value in *shibuuruka,* where *uruka* praises the agreeable sensation of a bitter taste.[81] Sweetness, too, has a positive value; as when *gyokuro* tea is said to impart a "sweet, elegant taste." Other examples include the saying "If the country is well-governed, sweets will fall from Heaven,"[82] and the use of the word *kandaku* 'sweet acceptance' to refer to swift, uncontested acceptance. But, in words like *amatcho* 'chick', *amattarui mono no ii kata* "plebeian way of speaking," and *amai bungaku* "shallow literature,"[83] we learn that sweetness does indeed reveal a negative value in some cases.

If we understand *shibumi* and *amami* to represent inactive and active modes of being in terms of how they relate to the other, we can think of their essential meanings as belonging to the domain of the public of the peculiarities of the opposite sex. The usual assumption is that sweetness in this domain may be seen in a positive light, as in expressions like *amaete sunete* "purring and pouting" and *amaeru sugata iro fukashi* "a woman cooing at a man is so coquet."[84] *Shibumi* is the negation of sweetness. Nagai Kafū, in *Kanraku*, writes about a man meeting "a *shibui* woman, known locally as *nēsan* plain and simple," who turned out to be the geisha Kogiku, who had promised to die with the man ten years earlier.[85] In this case, the woman's sweetness once upon a time was negated and turned into *shibumi*. *Shibumi* is often used as the antonym of *hade* 'flashy', but this definition hinders our attempt to grasp the being of *shibumi*. As the opposite of *hade*, we encounter *jimi* 'quiet'. Contrasting *shibumi* and *jimi* against *hade* equally results in a confusion of *shibumi* and *jimi*. *Shibumi* 'understated, astringent' and *jimi* 'quiet' are similar in that they both stand in an inactive relation to the other, but with an important difference. At the outset in its development in the domain of the public of human nature, *jimi* had no relevance to *amami*. Such was not the case with *shibumi* 'understated, astringent'; it originated from the negation of *amami* 'sweet' in the domain of the public of the peculiarities of the opposite sex. As a result, *shibumi* reveals a richer past and present than *jimi* does. To be sure, *shibumi* is the negation of *amami*, though this negation is enriched by possibilities of remembering as well as forgetting. Thus, paradoxical as it sounds, *shibumi* expresses *tsuya* 'erotic luster'.

That being the case, what relation do *shibumi* 'understated, astringent' and *amami* 'sweet' have to *iki*? All three express the modes of being specific to the opposite sex. As we move from the usual state of *amami* to the inactive end of the relation to the other, we mark a pathway that leads to *shibumi* by way of *iki*. In this sense, *amami*, *iki*, and *shibumi* stand in a straight-line relation. We see how *iki* stands midway between affirmation and negation.[86]

In the preceding section concerning the intensional structure of *iki*, we discussed how selfish, "sweet" dreams are broken, and *iki*, rich in critical knowledge, is born. We also mentioned how *iki* can take the form of "coquetry for the sake of coquetry" or the form of "autonomous play" by means of "affirmation by way of negation,"[87] an observation on the change of meaning from *amami* 'sweet' to *iki*. When the negation prevails and approaches its limit, *iki* changes into *shibumi* 'understated, astringent'. Kafū's woman embodying *shibumi* 'understated, astringent' must have changed from *amami* 'sweet' to *shibumi*, passing *iki* along the way. The *shibumi* taste found in Utazawa-bushi is, after all, a different manifestation of *iki* seen in Kiyomoto-bushi.[88] Under the entry of "shibushi," the dictionary *Genkai* explains that it means "*kusumite iki nari*" (iki, having become rather understated) and recognizes it as a modalized form of *iki*.[89] Furthermore, given this linear relationship, we can also conceive of a situation in which *iki* moves back toward *amami* 'sweet'. Here, the *ikiji* 'pride and honor' and the *akirame* 'resignation' components of *iki* are lost and, as a result, only the sugary sweetness remains, like that in the personality of an ordinary, pleasant person. The women of Kunisada from Kiyonaga and Utamaro came into existence in this way.[90]

In the foregoing, we believe that we have almost completely distinguished the meaning of *iki* from other major words with similar meanings. By comparing it to other similar meanings, we have suggested that *iki*, as an experience of meaning, not only takes on objectivity as a meaning, but also becomes both the subject and the object of value judgment as a **taste**. As a result, we can comprehend *iki* as a component in a system of taste and in relation to other components in that system. These relations are found in the following diagram.

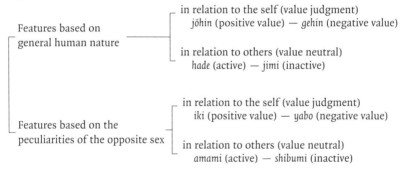

Needless to say, each individual instance of taste is normally accompanied by subjective value judgment. There are cases, however, in which the judgment is asserted clearly and objectively, and other cases in which the judgment remains within our subjective view and does not become any clearer. For the time being, we will characterize that difference as value judgment versus value-neutral.

Now, these relations can be expressed by means of a rectangular prism.

In the following illustration, the two squares at the top and the bottom, corresponding to the determinants for the various modes of taste with which we have dealt thus far, represent the two domains of the public. The bottom plane represents the human nature in general. The top plane represents the peculiarities of the opposite sex.

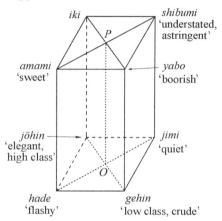

We place the eight words for taste at the eight vertexes. The terms placed at the vertexes of the top or bottom squares and connected by diagonal lines represent the tastes that oppose each other. There is no absolute a priori pairing of particular tastes. The vertexes of the top and bottom squares where the side planes intersect (*iki* and *shibumi*, for instance), the vertexes on the side surface that can be connected by a diagonal line (*iki* and *hade*, for instance), the vertexes connected by the line formed by two side planes (*iki* and *jōhin*, for instance), and the vertexes opposite each other on the rectangular prism (*iki* and *gehin*, for instance) all represent some kind of opposition. In other words, each of the vertexes can stand in opposition to another vertex in some way. In the square on the bottom or at the top, the vertexes that oppose each other diagonally stand out most in the degree of opposition. As the principle for that opposition, we considered two properties—an opposition to the self and an opposition to the other—in each of the domains of the public. The opposition embodied in the former was based on value judgment, where the opposing elements revealed a contrast between positive and negative values. The opposition to the other was irrelevant to value judgment and it could be either active or inactive. In the rectangular prism, two rectangles represent the opposition of values that relates to the self and the value-neutral opposition that relates to the other. To obtain these rectangles, we quadrisect the rectangular prism vertically along the two sets of diagonal lines formed by connecting the vertexes of the top and bottom squares. That is, the rectangle with jōhin, iki, yabo, and gehin as its vertexes represents the oppositions that relate to the self, and the rectangle with hade, amami, shibumi, and jimi as its vertexes represents the oppositions that relate to the other.

Suppose we let O represent the point where the two diagonal lines intersect on the bottom square, and similarly, we let P represent the point where the two diagonal lines cross on the top square, drawing a vertical line OP connecting these two points. This is the vertical line at which the rectangle representing relation to the self and the one representing the relation to the other intersect, a line which in turn symbolizes a person who is unbiased in any way in this system of taste. By means of inner development, the person will exhibit specific taste on the outer planes.

Now this perpendicular line OP divides two rectangles into equal halves, one corresponding to the relation to the self and another to the relation to the other. The rectangle with O, P, iki, and jōhin as its vertexes corresponds to a positive value, and the rectangle with vertexes O, P, yabo, and gehin a negative value. Further, the rectangle formed by O, P, amami, and hade represents activity, and one with O, P, shibumi, and jimi inactivity.

We can also think of this rectangular prism as containing points corresponding to various tastes of similar kinds on the surface or certain points in the interior of the rectangular prism. We list some examples here.

Sabi 'quiet elegance' is a term given to the triangular prism which has on one side a triangle formed by the points O, jōhin, and jimi, and, on the other side, another formed by P, iki, and shibumi. A characteristic of Japanese taste is the fact that this triangular prism currently exists in this shape.

Miyabi 'elegance' should be sought somewhere in the tetrahedron formed by connecting the point O and a triangle formed by jōhin, jimi, and shibumi.

Aji 'witty' refers to the triangle formed by amami, iki, and shibumi. Being able to posit amami, iki, and shibumi in a linear relationship, as manifestations of the particularized being of the opposite sex, is based on the fact that we can think of a movement from amami to shibumi via iki on the two right-angled sides of the right-angled triangle.

Otsu 'smart' is found in the tetrahedron formed from the same triangle mentioned above with the vertex at gehin.

Kiza 'affected' is located on the line that connects hade and gehin.

Iropposa 'coquet' is located on the top square but it sometimes projects a shadow onto the bottom square. On the top square are two points, obtained by, first, drawing a line that goes through P that is parallel to the line connecting amami and iki and, secondly, finding intersection points of this line with two sides of the square. We posit a rectangle by connecting these two intersecting points obtained above, *amami*, and *iki*, a shape that symbolizes *iropposa* 'coquet'. When a shadow is cast on the bottom square, *iropposa* is characterized by the rectangle formed in the following way. First draw a line that goes through O and is parallel to the line connecting *hade* and *gehin*. We obtain this rectangle by the intersecting points created by this line on the sides of the bottom square and connecting them to *hade*, and *gehin*. To consider *jōhin*, *iki*, and *gehin* in a linear manner means that we first posit the shadow of *iropposa* on the bottom square; that done, we can think of a triangle formed by the vertexes *jōhin*, *iki*, and *gehin*. Finally, we think of a movement from *jōhin* to *iki*, then to *gehin*. Often shadows have a way of being darker than the objects that cast them.

Chic points vaguely to the line in general that connects *jōhin* and *iki*.

Raffiné is the term given to the rectangle formed by the line that connects *iki*, *shibumi*, and the same line that moves toward the bottom of the rectangular prism and comes to rest in the middle.

In summary, the value of a graphic representation of this rectangular prism lies in the fact that a functional relation exists between the terms of various tastes like *iki* and in the fact that we can place these names on the surface or in the interior of this rectangular prism.

IV NATURAL EXPRESSIONS OF *IKI*

We have thus far examined *iki* as a phenomenon of consciousness. We must now turn our attention to that aspect of *iki* which takes the form of objective expression, a mode of being of *iki* that is our next goal of understanding. Grasping the meaning of *iki* depends on whether or not we can understand the objective form of *iki* on the basis of *iki* as a phenomenon of consciousness and, at the same time, on whether or not we can comprehend the structure in its entirety. Let us begin by categorizing objective expressions of *iki* in two ways: natural expression, that is, expression through **natural form;** and artistic expression, that is, expression in **artistic form.** There may be some question of whether these two categories will permit a clear distinction. It could be argued natural form is, in effect, identical to artistic form.[91] We must, however, put that intriguing question aside and press on. Let us follow a common custom and assume, for the sake of convenience, that natural and artistic form are distinct enough to consider separately.

Let us first turn our attention to the expression of *iki* as an expression of natural form. We see this as **symbolism in nature** in the form of "symbolic empathy," as when we sense *iki* in willow trees and slow steady rain. Even so, let us confine our search for natural form at present to **physical manifestations,** those that embody the notion of "true empathy."

When it comes to the **sense of hearing,** the natural form of *iki* as a physical manifestation shows in ways that language is used or certain words articulated. Examples come by way of situations described in terms like this: "The way she talks to a man is alluring, without a hint of sweet talk." Another example would be "No word or inflection is *yabo.*" This type of *iki* is also encountered in pronunciation or inflection at the ends of words.[92] A word said slowly, in a drawl, suddenly cut short with an inflection at the end—that is basic to *iki* in language use. In it, we see a dualistic opposition in rhythm come into being between the part articulated slowly and the part concluded quickly. It is this opposition that is understood to be the objective expression of the duality of coquetry in *iki.* The voice exhibits *iki* when it is pitched to convey an element of *sabi* 'quiet elegance'; a shrill, higher-pitched tone of voice would never do. When dualistic opposition in speech rhythm is created by a voice whose pitch is not quite the highest, the material and formal causes of *iki* are completely objectified. Still, the clearest and greatest variety of natural forms of expression in the physical realm come when *iki* is manifest in the area of **sight.**[93]

Natural form of expression pertaining to sight refers to expression in the broadest sense including posture and gesture, as well as to the physical body that supports the expression. Expression pertaining to the entire body can symbolize *iki* by means of a physical movement, namely, **relaxing the body slightly.** This mode of expression is captured with astonishing sensitivity in prints of all kinds by Torii Kiyonaga. This artist plays with variations using men and women, figures seen in a standing or sitting posture from every point of view. Coquetry, the material cause and part of the duality, expresses the activeness and receptiveness toward the opposite sex by disturbing the body's monistic equilibrium. But the unrealistic idealism—the material cause of *iki*—adds control and moderation to the breakdown of monistic equilibrium. Doing so curbs any unbridled tendency of duality. Nothing could be less like *iki* than sirens, "writhing salaciously in the branches of an aspen tree,"[94] or the crazed maenads "cavorting with satyrs and their cohorts"[95] at festivals in honor of Bacchus. Unabashed hip-waggling coquetry, Western-style, is also out of the question. *Iki* must be subtle, content with suggesting movement in the direction of the opposite sex. In an expression of *iki*, when the body's symmetry is broken, it is vital that the expression remain aware of iki's unrealistic idealism, as symbolized in the bending of the perpendicular line through the center of the body to form a curve.

An expression embodying iki that involves the entire body is the **wearing of very thin fabric.** Take for example this *senryū: Akashi kara honobono to suku hijirimen* "The scarlet crepe chemise from Akashi; how it shows through ever so subtly." Here, the reference is the fact that the undergarment made of scarlet Akashi crepe can be seen through the kimono.[96] The motif of wearing thin fabric is often found in *ukiyoe.*[97] There, the relation between material and formal cause is expressed in terms of fabric so translucent it opens a way to a woman by at once veiling her and revealing her. The Venus de Medici expresses coquetry specifically by means of the position of her hands on her naked body, but her gesture is too explicit to be said to represent iki. It goes without saying that the scantily clad ladies in the Paris revues have nothing whatever in common with iki.

Iki, however, can be used to describe someone **right after bathing.** Nakedness in such a case is consigned to the immediate past as a mere recollection. Coquetry and the formal cause consummate the sensibility of iki by means of a woman casually draped in a simple *yukata.* "Always stopping by after a bath, looking iki" is not limited to Yonehachi in *Shunshoku tatsumi no sono.*[98] The subject of looking *free of grime* right after bathing is frequently depicted in *ukiyoe.* Harunobu also portrayed bathers right after bathing. Furthermore, even during the *benie* period, artists such as Okumura Masanobu and Torii Kiyomitsu pictured people right after bathing, a fact that makes us realize the special value this theme offers.[99] Utamaro, too, did not forget to capture women after bathing, as in his series "Fujo sōgaku juttai" (Ten types in the physiognomic study of women).[100] In contrast, in the paintings of the West, while women bathing in the nude are often depicted, it is rare to find them immediately after bathing.

The body itself can be used as an objective expression of iki, as in the **svelte body** with its narrow "willow" waist. Utamaro's devotion to this ideal was almost fanatical. Beauties during the Bunka and Bunsei eras very much assert this quality in contrast to the Genroku era's more substantial ideal.[101] In *Ukiyoburo,* we encounter series of adjectives such as "svelte, pretty, and iki."[102] Since the formal cause of iki is unrealistic idealism, attempts to express unrealism and idealism in an objective way almost unavoidably take on a thin, slender shape. This svelte-body ideal goes beyond the obvious suggestion of declining physical power by speaking for power in the spiritual realm. El Greco, attempting to depict spirit itself, painted nothing but attenuated figures. Gothic sculptures also favored slender figures. We ourselves imagine ghosts as being slender. As long as iki remains spiritualized coquetry, figures that embody iki must also be svelte.

Thus far we have discussed iki in terms of the body as a whole. Iki is also expressed more specifically, as in two aspects of the face: its shape and its expressions. In terms of the structure of the face, that is, the basic facial features, a **long,** rather than round, face is generally more befitting iki. The ideal face was plump and round in the Genroku era. The playwright Ihara Saikaku, active in this period, stated "a fashionable face nowadays is a bit round." In contrast, the elegant face of the Bunka and Bunsei eras was distinctly oblong. Needless to say, the reason for this difference is based on the same principle as for the figure as a whole.

For facial expressions to possess iki, **both relaxation and tension are required of the eye, mouth, and cheek.** This, too, we understand in terms of reasons we have already considered, especially those that explain how the figures as a whole must undergo a slight breakdown in the equilibrium. As for the **eyes,** ryūben is the most common form of coquetry. Ryūben refers to the sideways glance, a motion involving the eyes alone, a coquettish signal sent to the opposite sex. It is modalized as yokome 'sideways glance', uwame 'upward glance', and fushime 'downward glance'. Looking askance at him alongside is coquettish, as is giving an upward glance to him in front. Fushime, too, is used as a means of coquetry, to suggest coquettish shyness. All these glances share a common trait. They alter the normal state of the eyes, upsetting equilibrium, in order to suggest a motion toward the man. But using simply a "coquettish gaze" in this way does not in itself signify iki. For the eyes to display iki, they must glisten, moist with remembrance. Pupils must speak openly, yet silently, of resolute detachment and taut tension.

The **mouth,** with its realistic function as a path between the sexes and its great possibility of movement, can express tension and relaxation required of iki in a notably clear way. The purposiveness of iki without purpose is objectified in tiny rhythmic movements of the lips.[103] Then too, painting the lips heightens their importance. The **cheeks** are important for expression because they rule the scale of a smile. The smile of iki is most often in minor key expressive of melancholy, shying away from cheerful major moods. Saikaku stressed the importance of "light cherry-blossom color" for the cheeks. Yoshii Isamu, however, described a woman more in the iki vein of sentiments appropriate to autumn: "Sayoko is a beautiful woman, a woman bewitchingly beautiful, much like the fall of the year."[104]

On the whole, the expressive face of iki is reticent, in marked contrast to the boorish face of the winking, pouting Western coquette "playing jazz with both cheeks."[105]

As for the makeup on the face, **thin applications** express *iki*. During the Edo period, women in Kyoto and Osaka applied thick, sensuous makeup, despised as boorish by the women of Edo. The term *ada* 'charming', used and valued by Edo prostitutes and geisha, also refers to light makeup. Shunsui wrote that "a thin application of makeup to the face, cleaned with powder and rubbed with Senjokō, is particularly alluring."[106] According to Nishizawa Risō, makeup in Edo "does not call for a thick layer of *oshiroi* used in the Kyoto-Osaka area; the preferred effect is notably understated, since the women in Edo are more inclined to possess a masculine disposition."[107] We can see the material and formal causes of *iki* both in this expression of *bitai* in applying makeup and in positing idealism that confines it to a mere suggestion.

Hairstyles, when **informal,** also speak for *iki*. The formal hairstyles of the Bunka–Bunsei eras were known as *marumage* and *shimadamage*.[108] The most common variant of the *shimadamage* style was *bunkin takamage*.[109] In contrast, the styles considered to illustrate *iki* were informal, like *ichōyui* 'gingko leaf style' or *gakuyayui* 'dressing room style' or styles thought to be deviant forms of *shimadamage*, like *tsubushi shimada* 'squashed *shimada*' and *nage shimada* 'thrown *shimada*'.[110] The connoisseurs of Fukagawa, famous for their sensibility of *iki*, preferred "water hairstyles," meaning those not styled with oil. *Sendō shinwa* describes a coiffeur that could be identified "at a glance" even outside of Fukagawa. It "tied the hair in back, using water to lift and pouf." The writer adds that "you could tell by the look of her hair alone that the woman had it done in Fukagawa."[111] The dualistic "coquetry" directed at the opposite sex is expressed in disturbing the formal equilibrium, departing from the conventional hairstyle. These deviations from the norm were made with a delicate touch, expressive of *akanuke* 'sophistication'. The same point of origin accounts for another effect of *iki*, namely, the sentiment expressed by "stray hair escaping its tie" or "the straggling hair from the night before on a woman's face." It stands to reason that we discern no quality that qualifies as *iki* in the spectacle of Mélisande at her window, loosing her abundant locks to fall on Pelléas below.[112] When it comes to *iki*, that gaudy show of golden blonde must yield to hair so black it shimmers blue.

Except in samurai households, a type of **décolletage** expressive of *iki* was seen in the Edo period.[113] It was coquettish emphasis on the nape of the neck. *Kinsei fūzokushi*, by Kitagawa Morisada, speaks of "accentuating the hairline at the nape by applying white makeup there, a practice called *ippon'ashi*." He adds that prostitutes and low ranking geisha "wear white makeup applied rather heavily on the neck."[114] This coquettish practice was to call attention to the nape laid bare. Décolletage symbolizes *iki* because it breaks the equilibrium of the garment slightly and suggests a possible pathway to the woman's flesh. This type of décolletage speaks for the contrast between *iki* and the boorish Western custom of exposing large areas of bosom, back, and shoulder.

Another expression of *iki* is **taking the kimono skirt in the left hand.**[115] Various writers describe effects that satisfy the conditions for *iki*. One describes a woman "showing glimpses of the crimson undergarment and the pale yellow crepe undersash when she walks." Another comments on "the beauty of showing the scarlet crepe undergarment that gives flickering glimpses between the white *yukata* and the snow white skin, as she picks up her feet."[116] In *Harutsugedori*, we find that "the charming woman who made an entrance" shows off her "white feet as she gathers her kimono skirt in her left hand."[117] *Ukiyoe* artists, too, employed various methods to expose women's lower legs. Hidden in the handling of the front of the kimono is a subtle symbolization of coquetry. "Taking the front of the kimono casually but elegantly" is a far more refined style of coquetry than the recent fashion in the West—the one hikes the hemline up, almost to the point of exposing the knees and, furthermore, anticipating the effect of illusion by wearing flesh-colored stockings.

Bare feet, too, can become an expression of *iki*. The geisha of Edo often complained of this, crying out: "My bare feet would dearly love socks, that would be *yabo*. Oh, how cold it is!"[118] Yet even in winter, they did without socks. Apparently some imitated geisha in this respect. Going without socks was proof of studied elegance. Exposing just the feet, in contrast to the rest of the body clad in kimono, most certainly displays the duality of coquetry. The relationship between the kimono and the bare feet, however, is the direct opposite of the naked vulgarity seen in the West where women disrobe completely, wearing only shoes or stockings.[119] Therein lies another reason why bare feet embody *iki*.

The hand has much to do with coquetry. *Tekuda*, or a disinterested play of *iki* that mesmerizes men, is often found simply in women's hand movements. Hand movements of *iki* are subtly nuanced, as when the **hand is curled or bent back slightly.** In the works of Utamaro, there are pictures in which the focal point is the hand. We go one step further and contend that the hand, next to the face, displays the personality and tells of past experience. We must reflect on why Rodin often sculpted only hands. Palmistry is no nonsense. One can judge the soul of a man through the lingering reverberation still left in the fingertips. And the possibility that the hand can be an expression of *iki* depends, after all, on this point.

In the foregoing, we have examined physical, especially visual, manifestations[120] of *iki* as they concern the entire body, face, head, neck, lower legs, feet, and hands. We found that *iki*, as a phenomenon of consciousness, originated in coquetry as a dualistic supposition directed at the opposite sex, which was perfected by the idealistic unrealism. The crucial point of the natural form of *iki*, an objective expression, was explained by the fact that *iki* takes a form that suggests duality, one achieved by breaking elegantly and lightly the monistic equilibrium. In this way, coquetry, the material cause of *iki*, is expressed in the act of breaking the equilibrium and hypothesizing duality. Further, we recognized the idealistic unrealism, the formal causes, found in the ways in which this equilibrium is broken.

V ARTISTIC EXPRESSIONS OF IKI

We must now move on to examine the artistic forms of *iki*. When it comes to expressions of *iki* in art, the relationship varies considerably, depending on whether the art in question is objective or subjective. In general we can distinguish between spatial and temporal as well as objective and subjective arts. The former distinction is based on the means of expression and the latter on the type of the object of expression. We call art objective when its content is constrained by concrete representation. Subjective art, in contrast, is realized when its formative principles work freely and abstractly. Examples of objective arts would be painting, sculpture, and poetry. Design, architecture, and music exemplify subjective arts. The objective are sometimes referred to as arts of imitation; the subjective as "free" arts.

In objective art, *iki*, as a phenomenon of consciousness or as a natural expression of objective art, forms the content of art in concrete form. In other words, painting and sculpture are able to express the natural form of the expression of *iki* as content. This is why we were able to cite a number of examples from *ukiyoe* in our earlier discussion of physical movements and expressions embodying *iki*. By defining poetry in the broad sense, as including literary production in general, we can describe not only expressions and physical movements that constitute *iki* but also *iki* as a phenomenon of consciousness. This would explain our use of examples drawn from literature in our previous discussion of *iki*. However, the fact that objective art can be used to treat *iki* as content in this way interferes with the complete establishment of *iki* as a pure artistic form. This is because, figuratively speaking, objective art senses neither the interest in nor the demand for objectifying *iki* as a form of artistic expression, because it already embodies concrete expressions of *iki* as content. Since the distinction between objective and subjective art is, to begin with, made for the sake of convenience and cannot be made precisely, artistic form of *iki* may exist as a formative principle even in objective art. For instance, the use of contour lines as primary in paintings, along with light colors, simple composition and so on—all can satisfy the formal requirements of expressions of *iki*. The same can be said of poetry, that is, literary production. There it may be possible to find artistic expression of *iki* in the nature of rhythm, especially in reference to poetry in a more restricted sense. Hence it is possible for us to examine the relationship between the rhythms in *haiku* and *dodoitsu* singing and the expression of *iki* as an issue worthy of investigation.[121]

In objective art, however, artistic expression of *iki* does not exhibit itself in one clear monosemous manner. In contrast, because subjective art does not hold out much possibility of treating concrete *iki* as content, subjective art relegates all the responsibility of expression to abstract form. As a result, artistic expression of *iki* is actually exhibited more saliently in it. Therefore, the artistic form of *iki* expressions must be sought mainly in the formative principle of subjective art, that is to say, in "free" art.

First of all, as free art, **design** enjoys an intimate relationship to expressions that represent *iki*. That being the case, what form does the objectification of *iki* take with respect to design? First, it must embody some aspect of the duality of "coquetry." Secondly, this duality in question must possess certain attributes which objectify *ikiji* 'pride and honor' and *akirame* 'resignation'.

When it comes to geometric design, nothing expresses duality better than parallel lines. Parallel lines are the purest visual objectification of duality, extending on forever, eternally equidistant. It is no coincidence that stripe designs are considered to be *iki*. According to *Mukashi mukashi monogatari*, prostitutes are said to have worn striped garments in the old days, when ordinary women wore the *kosode* type of kimono with foil embroidery.[122] It was not until the Tenmei era that samurai households were officially permitted to wear stripes.[123] Then too, fashionable customers in the pleasure quarters of the Bunka and Bunsei eras favored striped crepe over everything else. The description of "the clothing of a customer visiting a courtesan" we find in

Harutsugedori tells us that "the overcoat is dark brown . . . made from **striped** crepe from Nanbu . . . the haori coat is of tōzan in black and white **stripes** with fine dots . . . and other accessories, too, are just as iki as these garments, as you should know."[124] In Shunshoku umegoyomi, the clothing of Yonehachi, who was visiting Tanjirō, was described as being "of gray broad **stripes** woven with fat threads in the Ueda weave and a **striped** belt made from black silk satin and crepe in purple and white stripes."[125] Well may we ask, what kind of stripe symbolizes iki best?

To begin with, we can say that vertical stripes embody the sentiment of iki more than do horizontal stripes.[126] As striped garments, only horizontal stripes were available until about the Hōreki era.[127] In fact, the word "stripes" itself, then called orisuji, literally "weaving lines," referred exclusively to horizontal stripes. The horizontal stripes called noshime, woven in the waist of a kimono, and those in the torizome 'spot-dyed cloth' were both fashions prevalent before the Hōreki era.[128] In time, however, vertical stripes gained popularity in the Hōreki and Meiwa eras. By the time of the Bunka and Bunsei eras, only vertical stripes were preferred, exclusively.[129] Vertical stripes, therefore, expressed the iki taste in the Bunka and Bunsei.

But why were vertical stripes more iki than horizontal ones? One reason for this is that vertical stripes appear to the eyes as parallel lines more easily than horizontal ones. The fact that our eyes are lined up horizontally right and left, makes it easier for us to follow the parallel set up by a design of vertical stripes running side by side, so that a design that embodies the fundamental parallel relationship horizontally appears to the right and left of one another. Somewhat more effort is required to perceive horizontal stripes, where the fundamental of the parallel relationship is defined vertically by two lines — one below the other. In other words, because our eyes are placed horizontally, spatial relationships of objects can generally be more clearly expressed when they are in horizontal orientation. Thus, in the case of parallel vertical lines, our eyes clearly perceive the discrete opposition of two lines. The opposite is true of parallel horizontal stripes. There, our eyes perceive the side to side successive continuity of a line. This explains why vertical stripes are more suitable for expressing duality.

Perhaps we should consider how the effects of gravity come into play as well. Horizontal stripes suggest the weight of geologic strata at rest brought about by gravity.[130] In contrast, vertical stripes represent light rain brought down by gravity, and the lightness of "willow branches." Related to this is the fact that horizontal stripes make an object look wider by directing our gaze from side to side. Vertical stripes do the opposite, narrowing objects by directing our gaze up and down. In sum, we can say that vertical stripes express iki better than horizontal lines for two reasons: first, because they symbolize the duality of parallel lines more clearly; and secondly, because they express a lighter, more refined relationship.

This is not to say that horizontal stripes cannot embody *iki*. They can, though only under certain carefully circumscribed conditions. The first requirement has to do with horizontal stripes used in relation to vertical ones. In these special cases, horizontal stripes may express *iki* when they are used to hem fabric in vertical stripes. A horizontally striped sash may be worn with a kimono whose stripes run vertically. The straps of wooden sandals may have horizontal stripes to go with vertical stripes in a wood grain or a lacquered design.[131]

The second circumstance in which horizontal stripes exemplify *iki* is in relation to the shape of the whole object. For instance, when a slender woman is wearing a garment with horizontal stripes, they are particularly expressive of *iki*. Horizontal stripes tend to make objects appear broader, hence, our aversion to the sight of heavy women wearing horizontal stripes. Slender women, on the other hand, can look very becoming in them. Even so, this is not to say that horizontal stripes embody in principle more *iki* sensibility than vertical ones. The *iki* of horizontal stripes depends, first and last, on context, as in the case of a wearer who already embodies *iki* characteristics lending a background to horizontal stripes.

Thirdly, situations in which horizontal stripes represent *iki* have to do with sustaining sensual and emotional appeal. This occurs only when senses and emotions are jaded, insensitive, say, to vertical stripes; then we may perceive horizontal stripes as being particularly *iki*, imparting a refreshing taste. It is mainly for this reason that a resurgence of horizontal stripes in the fashion world of late allows us to perceive the sense of *iki* in them.

In order to examine the relationship of vertical and horizontal stripes to *iki*, we must detach ourselves from these particularized constraints and assign some enduring general values to various striped designs. A number of such designs vary widths too freely to serve expressions of *iki*, lacking as they do the clarity of duality inherent in parallel lines. Examples would be designs using very thin stripes as in *sensuji* 'thousand stripes', *mansuji* 'ten thousand stripes', *komochijima* 'broad and narrow stripes together', and *yatarajima* 'stripes in random widths'.[132] For stripes to exhibit *iki*, they must be designed with appropriate width and simplicity, so that we can grasp duality with perfect clarity.

Intersecting vertical and horizontal lines create striped patterns accordingly. Such patterns are, on the whole, not as iki as vertical or horizontal stripes since they diminish the ease of perception of parallel lines. The checkerboard pattern created by the widest of all intersecting stripes can be an expression of iki. For this to occur, however, the eye must pursue the duality in vertical parallel lines without interruption, unhindered by the horizontal parallels. A checkerboard pattern rotated right or left at a 45 degree angle to the perpendicular, that is, when vertical and horizontal parallel lines both lose their respective verticality and horizontality and create two systems of inclined parallel lines, the checkerboard pattern then loses its inherent iki characteristic. This is because the eye can no longer pursue the duality in parallel lines without hesitation, and so long as the pattern is viewed straight on, the eye perceives only the intersections of the two different systems of parallel lines. When the squares in the checkerboard pattern change into rectangles, they become a pattern called kōshijima 'rectangular stripes'. Due to the length of these rectangles in kōshijima, it can represent iki more effectively than intersecting-stripe patterns.[133]

When some part of a pattern of stripes appears to be rubbed out in a comparatively small area in relation to the whole, the effect is one of design added to stripes. But when this effect is applied to a larger area, a design called kasuri emerges.[134] The affinity of this type of design to iki depends on how much the partial existence of the stripes that have not been rubbed out can suggest the infinite duality of parallel lines.

A pattern of stripes radiating out from a single point does not express iki. Examples of this occur in patterns inspired by the converging ribs of an umbrella or ribs of a fan that run toward its pivot as well as the radiating lines of a spiderweb or rays of light from a rising sun. None of these are expressions of iki. In order to express iki, a design must be visually disinterested and purposeless. Radiating stripes, having a center, have achieved their goal; hence, they cannot be felt to represent iki. An iki sensibility can be found in this type of stripes only when the point of origin is concealed, deceiving us into seeing the radiating lines as parallel.

The further a design deviates from parallel lines, the further removed it is from iki. Patterns such as masu 'square boxes', meyui 'boxes in a box', rai 'thunderbolt pattern', and genjikōzu can sometimes be perceived as consisting of parallel lines.[135] This is especially true of such designs connected vertically, in which case they can be considered to embody iki. In contrast, kagome 'woven basket', asa no ha 'hemp leaf', and uroko 'fish scale' designs are based on triangles and thus are even more distant from iki.[136]

Complex patterns in general do not represent iki. The kikkō pattern, a design made from a combination of three pairs of parallel lines, is a six-sided polygon, making it too complex to exemplify iki.[137] Manji 卍 'reversed swastika', in which the tips of a cross—a combination of vertical and horizontal lines—are bent at right angles, imparts an impression of complexity. Thus, *manjitsunagi*, a chain of *manji*, does not constitute iki. The so-called *a* pattern, consisting of a series of the Chinese character *a* 亞, is even more complex. This pattern is used on the clothing of ancient Chinese officials and is said to "take on the meaning of royal subjects turning their backs on evil, facing good, as well as coming together and parting company, and also taking leave and staying behind." However, ideas of encouraging the good and chastising evildoers, and of meeting and parting are too meticulously made into an abstraction. There is nothing stylish about the character 亞. Its strokes turn at ninety degrees as many as six times and result in a shape whose sides "show their backs to one another."[138] The 亞 pattern exhibits the bad side of Chinese taste and is the complete opposite of iki.

Next, patterns containing curves do not normally become a pure expression of iki. If *kōshijima* rectangular stripes contain curved lines clinging to them in spirals, the stripes lose much of their iki character. We also rarely detect iki in wavy vertical stripes. When the *waribishi* pattern, usually made of straight lines, is drawn with curved lines and turned into a *hanabishi* pattern, the design itself becomes *hade* 'flashy', losing every vestige of iki.[139] Likewise, the fan motif can embody iki, so long as the design is *tatami ōgi* 'folded fan' made from straight lines. But as soon as the fan is open, drawn with arcs, not even a whiff of iki remains.[140] The *karakusa* 'arabesque' pattern, in use since before the Nara period, is far removed from iki sensibility. Its design is derived from the unfurling curve of the fern fiddlehead, as is the *karahana* pattern often seen in the Tenpyō era; both fail to express iki because of their curved lines.[141] Other examples of curvilinear disqualification would be the *wachigai* 'intersecting circle' pattern of the Fujiwara period and the *maruzukushi* 'circle pattern' popular in the Momoyama period through the Genroku era.[142]

Curved lines are said to be more in tune with the motions of seeing itself and therefore being more easily seen, offering the eyes a more pleasurable sensation. Such is the reasoning of those who expound on the absolute beauty of curved lines. Even so, such lines are not suitable for clear-cut expressions of iki embodying *ikiji* 'pride and honor'. Someone once said that "all warmth, all movement, all love is round, or at least oval, and goes in spirals or other curved lines! Only the cold, immobile, worthless, and hateful is straight as string stretched taut or something bent at an angle. If soldiers were found in rings instead of ranks, they would dance and not attack one another."[143]

Still, there is something severe about *iki*, something characterized by these lines from a Kabuki play: "Excuse me, please, but you don't know who I am. I am Agemaki." Such an unyielding sentiment cannot be expressed by curved lines. *Iki* embodies cold disinterest. It is evident from this quality that artistic form representing *iki* tends to go in the opposite direction from "Beautiful Objects Small."[144]

Representational design, as opposed to geometric, never characterizes *iki*. *Harutsugedori* speaks of someone who "is wearing a *yabo* collar that has butterfly designs stitched on with gold and silver threads."[145] I have seen a design in which the artist runs three vertical lines up from a *shamisen* pick at the bottom past three weeping willow branches off to one side. Several cherry blossoms dot the willow.[146] Judging from the content and from the application of parallel lines, we might consider this design as expressive of *iki*, but such is not the case. The impression is one of *jōhin* 'elegant, high class', not *iki*. Representational design by its very nature cannot express the straightforward duality available to geometric design. This explains why representational design cannot suggest *iki*. The same may be said of Kōrin and Kōetsu patterns.[147] It is in geometric design that *iki* is objectified as design. Furthermore, geometric design is, in the true sense of the word, design. That is, as far as the realm of design is concerned, the meaning of free art—art in which form is created freely and is not restricted by representational expression of the real world—is found only in geometric design.

Design not only has form but color as well. Intersecting stripe patterns become the so-called *ichimatsu* design when boxes in the checkerboard pattern are filled with two alternating colors.[148] When are the colors of a pattern to be considered *iki*? To begin with, fabrics having myriad colors cannot express *iki*. An example from the Genroku era and later would be the "folded obi in twelve colors" that Saikaku mentions, fabrics dyed with *dandara zome* or Yūzen dyeing techniques.[149] There are two relationships between form and color. One expresses through color a duality in form by means of two or three contrasting colors. The other works with colors at different levels of saturation or with a certain tonal saturation; in either case, color plays its role by endowing the dualistic opposition with a special sentiment.

Which colors are used in this way? The answer is that the colors expressive of *iki* cannot be *hade* 'flashy'.[150] Colors, to be *iki*, must speak to duality in a subdued manner. In *Shunshoku koi no shiranami*, the author describes an overcoat in which the weave "incorporated a small and delicate checkerboard pattern with **deep orange** thread against **gray** in a formal crepe material. The obi was sewn from two pieces, one is an old-fashioned domestic weave, the other in a **navy** weave from Hakata without the iron club design of two **dark brown** lines woven in." He adds that over- and undergarments were "perfectly tailored, both with satin cuffs in **grayish navy** reminiscent of **green pine needles.**"[151] The colors that emerge in this description belong to three groups. The first group is comprised of grays. The second includes browns like *kigara cha* 'deep orange' and *kobi cha* 'dark brown'. The third group is made up of blues like *kon* 'navy' and *onando* 'grayish navy'.[152] The author of *Harutsugedori* describes an apron "done in *tazunazome* pattern with half-inch stripes, dyed in **onando** blue, **kobi cha** brown, and **nezumi** 'mouse' gray." "How iki the whole thing is," he adds.[153] We safely conclude that colors that embody iki are those belonging to grays, browns, and blues.

Grays emblematic of iki call to mind the oft-quoted phrase: "Fukagawa *nezumi* gray colors are in fashion at Tatsumi." The *nezumi* 'mouse' colors, or grays, represent stages of noncolor transition from white to black. Furthermore, when the tonalities of all colors are least saturated, they turn into gray. Gray, therefore, represents reduced saturation, that is, diminished brightness of a color itself. If we were to express the *akirame* 'resignation', a component of iki, in color, nothing would be more appropriate than gray. For this reason, gray has been valued as a color that exemplifies iki, occurring in variations like Fukagawa gray, silver gray, navy gray, brownish gray, and reddish gray. However, if we consider colors only in the abstract, gray certainly lacks "coquetry" and cannot express that aspect of iki. As Mephistopheles says, gray may be a color of "theory" that turns its back to "life."[154] But in actual design, gray always accompanies a form that asserts duality. And in many such cases, the form embodies the dualistic coquetry, the material cause of iki, with the gray expressing its formal cause, its idealistic unrealism.

It may well be true that no color group favors iki more than tans, that is, browns. This sentiment is expressed in the phrase *omoi some cha no edozuma ni* "edozuma design in brown your newfound lover wears."[155] There are no end of names that specify subtle variations on the color brown. Some of those used in the Edo period named for color's abstract property are *shira cha* 'pale brown', *onando cha* 'blue or reddish brown', *kigara cha* 'dark brown', *fusube cha* 'smoked dark brown', *koge cha* 'burned brown', *kobi cha* 'dark brown', and *chitose cha* 'greenish brown black'. Other color names derive from things around us that possess the colors, as in *uguisu cha* 'bush warbler brown; a dark greenish brown', *hiwa cha* 'siskin color; a light greenish brown', *tobi iro* 'kite color, or auburn', *susudake iro* 'drab bamboo brown', *gin susudake* 'silvery drab bamboo brown', *kuri iro* 'the color of chestnut', *kuriume* 'the color of reddish chestnut', *kurikawa cha* 'chestnut brown', *chōji cha* 'clove brown', *sumiru cha* 'violet brown; a dark bluish brown', *aimiru cha* 'indigo brown', *kawarake cha* 'bisque clay brown', to name but a few. Some names come from actors known to be partial to particular shades of brown. A sample of these would include *shikan cha* 'reddish deep brown', *rikan cha* 'dark brownish blue', *shikō cha* 'reddish brown', *rokō cha* 'bluish brown', and *baikō cha* 'brownish light brown'.[156]

What color exactly is the color brown? It is a *hade* 'flashy' color that has lost its saturation, taken on a black hue in the transition from red to yellow, passing through orange. Thus, it is a color that results from loss of brightness. Browns embody *iki* because the opulent characteristic of a color and the loss of saturation express a sophisticated sensuality and a coquetry that knows resignation.

Blues make up the third group of colors expressive of *iki*. Why? First, we must consider another question, namely, which bright colors that have not lost saturation exemplify *iki*? I would say they must be colors that go well with dark colors. As to the question of what these colors are, we cannot but imagine colors that match those at dusk in accordance with the so-called Purkinje phenomenon.[157] Reds, oranges, and yellows do not adapt to decreasing amounts of light striking the retina. A darkening heart will lose touch with such colors. In contrast, greens, blues, and violets remain in contact with the twilight vision of the soul. Consequently, with regard to hues, greens and blues, which tend to assimilate, can be said to embody more *iki* than reds and yellows, which tend to dissimulate. Further, cool colors like blues can be said to characterize *iki* more effectively than warm colors like reds. Thus, indigo and navy blue can exemplify *iki*. Among purples, *edo murasaki* 'bluish purple' is considered to embody *iki* more than *kyō murasaki* 'reddish purple'. The degree of saturation determines whether greenish colors can exhibit *iki* more than bluish ones. Those with lower levels of saturation can prevail. One example of this would be the color described as "*onando* blue, with a hint of the green of pine needles." Other examples would be *tokusa iro* 'dark green' and *uguisu iro* 'dark brownish green', which exhibit *iki*.

In sum, we can say that colors expressive of *iki* offer inactive afterimages that accompany a luscious experience. *Iki* **lives** in the future, holding the past in its arms.[158] A coolly discerning knowledge based on personal or social experiences rules *iki*, whose existence depends on maintaining possibility as a possibility. The soul that has tasted the last drop of sizzling excitement of warm colors draws on the quietude in cool colors that offer complementary afterimages. *Iki* embodies in its sensuality the gray of color blindness. *Iki* allows for being tinged by another color without being muddled by it. *Iki* shelters a dark negation concealed within its sensual affirmation.

To summarize the preceding, when iki is objectified in design and contains the two moments of form and color, parallel lines are used to express duality, the material cause of iki. When it comes to color, the formal cause of iki, its unrealistic idealism, is served by cool colors or dark colors low in saturation.

Next, what artistic form does iki take in **architecture,** a form of free art like design? Here we must look to teahouses. First let us examine the teleology of formation of interior space and exterior form.[159] In the most basic sense, the peculiarity of the opposite sex is founded on the duality that excludes plurality. Interior space created for the sake of duality, especially for the sake of secluded meditation about duality, must embody exclusive completeness and centripetal intimacy. "The shoji screens of a small four-and-a-half-mat sitting room with a small verandah outside" sever all connection to the outside world; this offers the dualistic transcendental being a place that is an "iki four-and-a-half-mat sitting room for lovers."[160] In a teahouse, a four-and-a-half-mat room is considered typical, a model not usually subject to much, if any, deviation. Since the exterior is determined indirectly by formative principles of interior space, it must not exceed a certain size constraint. With this fact as a basic premise, how does the construction of a teahouse show the objectification of iki?

In a construction that suggests iki, irrespective of the interior or exterior of the building, the dualistic relationship of coquetry is expressed by the choice of materials and the method of partitioning space. The dualistic relationship of material is most often expressed through the contrast between wood and bamboo. In Edo geijutsuron (Theory of Edo art), Nagai Kafū makes the following observation. "The house has only two rooms, a kitchen and a sitting room, separated by shoji screens of lacquered panes above wooden panels. It would seem that there is a small garden beyond a **bamboo** verandah, with vines climbing up from the edge of a stone washbasin into the spaces between the slats of a **bamboo** fence. Potted plants are placed on a shelf hung high off the ground. On the outside of the house we see small spaces around the eaves above the entryway, the closet for the sliding storm doors, and wood siding of the house, each decorated with wickerwork, wooden planks, and **bleached bamboo.**"[161] Further, he notes that "a most intriguing discussion is opened up by the scope of the use of bamboo and its artistic value as well."[162]

Bamboo embodies an intensely lyrical sensuality. We see this expressed in haiku. Take no iro Kyoyū ga hisago mada aoshi "The color of bamboo! As green as Kyoyū's calabash." Umerareta ono ga namida ya madaradake "I see my tears buried in it. O, mottled bamboo."[163] The use of bamboo as the expression of iki is significant when it is used in contrast to wood. Incidentally, along with bamboo, cryptomeria bark is also a preferred material for structures representing *iki*, contributing to one side of the dualistic opposition. The beginning section of *Shunshoku tatsumi no sono* speaks of "straight cryptomeria pillars with the bark left on. No decoration has been added to them, but they are certainly a stylish construction that matches the local ambience."[164]

Where duality calls for partitioning interior space, a difference in materials accentuates the opposition of ceiling and floor. The chief function of a bamboo ceiling is to call attention to that opposition, either with poles in the round, spaced out side by side, or with a covering of spliced bamboo. Lining the ceiling with dark brown cedar bark underscores an interest in its contrastive relationship to the fresh tatami floor.[165] Furthermore, the ceiling itself is often used to express duality. For instance, it might be divided into two unequal areas, the larger done in suspended ceiling (*saobuchi tenjō*), the smaller covered with bamboo wicker (*ajiro tenjō*).[166] We may further stress duality by using a plain stuccoed ceiling in one area *kakekomi tenjō* in the other.[167] The floor, too, should attempt to represent duality. The *tokonoma* alcove and the tatami mats must clearly manifest the dualistic opposition. Thus, placing tatami or tatami matting on the raised floor of the alcove is not *iki*. Doing so diminishes the strength of opposition between alcove and room. For the alcove to embody *iki*, its floor should be of wood, clearly opposing the floor of the rest of the room. That is to say, in order for the alcove to satisfy the constraints of *iki*, its flooring cannot be the same as the tatami used in the rest of the room. For that difference, we should choose a *kekomidoko* or *shikikomidoko* floor.[168]

In a room that embodies *iki*, we must also show the dualistic opposition between alcove and shelving next to it. For instance, we may use dark brown flooring for the alcove and pale yellow crushed bamboo on the floor in front of and below the shelving. At the same time, it is preferable to show, for example, a contrast of bamboo basket weave and flat wood paneling for the ceilings of alcove and shelving. The existence of the shelving on the side often speaks for the difference in sensibility between the *iki* construction of a teahouse and the *shibumi* 'understated, astringent' quality of a tearoom. Further, there is a customary distinction in structure between a teahouse and a tearoom in the degree of dualistic opposition between the alcove pillar and *otoshigake* beam.[169]

However, these assertions of duality in *iki* architecture clearly cannot succumb to complexity. Architecture that embodies *iki* exhibits similar characteristics to design that embodies *iki* in that they both generally require stylishness. For instance, one such characteristic is avoiding curved lines. It is utterly impossible to imagine a round room or ceiling that embodies iki. Architecture exemplifying iki does not accommodate the curved lines of katō mado or mokkō mado window types.[170] As for the ranma, designs with straight lines are preferred to kushigata making use of curved lines.[171] In this respect, however, architecture is more accepting of certain design elements than independent, abstract designs embodying iki. Round and half-moon windows are acceptable. So are curved lines on alcove pillars, and wisteria twining as it clings to bamboo of shitajimado windows.[172] This is perhaps because we would like to see any kind of building free to soften the otherwise rigid straight lines that are a natural tendency of architectural construction. In other words, unlike abstract designs, architecture possesses a concrete meaning in relation to the whole.

The duality of coquetry embodied in architectural form is modalized by idealistic unrealism in several ways: through the color of materials, the method of bringing outdoor light indoors, and the choice of artificial light. Architecture that is iki shares color principles with iki design in general, sharing that range of blues and grays and browns. Architecture can assert duality strongly in form precisely because of the quality of sabi 'quiet elegance' in these colors. If architecture asserts duality in form too strenuously, prizing the use of flashy colors, it will surely deteriorate into the kind of boorishness we might see in Russian interior decoration.

Outdoor light brought indoors and light from an artificial source both must work in consort with the colors of materials used. We should not desire to see a four-and-a-half-mat room flooded with light. Instead, we should interrupt its flow appropriately with eaves, low fences on either side of the main entryway, through garden trees. Indoor lighting at night should follow suit. The oil-lit paper lantern was best suited for this purpose. The present-day machine age invites us to substitute incandescent light glaring through translucent glass or to use indirect lighting, with light reflected in various ways. The so-called "blue light and red light" effects do not necessarily satisfy the conditions of iki.[173] The lighting of iki is subdued; the color of its radiance is that of a paper lantern.[174] Iki lighting must allow one to sink into the depths of the soul, its subtlety inspiring one to inhale the scent of perfumed sleeves.[175]

To sum up, iki in architecture manifests duality, the material cause, by means of the difference in materials used and the method of partitioning space. It expresses unrealistic idealism, the formal causes, primarily in the color of materials used, in the ways outdoor light is brought indoors, and in the use of artificial lighting.

Architecture is called frozen music; music, in turn, can be called flowing architecture. How does *iki* manifest itself in **music,** a type of free art? According to an essay by Tanabe Hisao entitled "Nihon no ongaku no riron fu sui no kenkyū" (A theory of Japanese music and a study of *sui*),[176] *iki* in music appears in melody and rhythm. Two types of musical scale are used as the basis for melody in Japan: the *miyakobushi* scale and the *inakabushi* scale. The former underlies the main melodic device called *ritsu* melodic scale (*rissenpō*), which governs almost all technical music composed in accordance with traditional rules. For instance, if we take *hyōjō* as the tonic, the *miyakobushi* scale sounds this series of notes: *hyōjō*—*ichikotsu* (or *shinsen*)—*banshiki*—*ōshiki*—*sōjō* (or *shōsetsu*)—*hyōjō*.[177]

In this scale, *hyōjō*, the tonic and *banshiki*, its fifth, maintain an ordered relation as the crucial interval of the scale. In contrast, other notes on the scale in actual practice do not always correspond to theory. They tend to diverge somewhat from the set relationships prescribed by the scale. In other words, these notes deviate somewhat from the ideal. *Iki* depends to a certain degree on this deviation. If the deviation is too small, it imparts a sense of *jōhin* 'elegant, high class'. If it is too large, the sense imparted is *gehin* 'crude, low class'. For example, a melody that ascends the scale from B (*banshiki*) through D (*ichikotsu*), to E (*hyōjō*), the pitch of D (*ichikotsu*) may be somewhat lower in practice than it is in theory. The amount of deviation is not so large in *nagauta* music, but in Kiyomoto and Utazawa, it may be as large as three-quarters of a whole tone. In some kinds of vulgar music like *hauta*, the pitch may vary a whole tone or more.[178] Limiting our discussion to *nagauta* only, pitch doesn't vary much in narrative parts, though the deviation is greater where the part represents *iki*. When the deviation is excessive, it imparts a sense of *gehin* 'crude, low class'. Incidentally, this drift in pitch is also apparent in the tone of A (*ōshiki*), when the melody goes from F (*shōzetsu*) through A (*ōshiki*), to B (*banshiki*). It also occurs in the tone of G (*sōjō*) when the melody goes from E (*hyōjō*) through G (*sōjō*) to A (*ōshiki*). The same deviation can also occur in the tone of C (*shinsen*) when a melody descends the scale from E (*hyōjō*) through C (*shinsen*) to B (*banshiki*).

We now turn our attention to rhythm. We recognize that the instruments accompanying a melody establish the rhythm, and the melody thus sustains the rhythm. In Japanese music, in many cases, melodic rhythm and rhythm of accompanying instruments are not in step with one other, thus causing a certain amount of variation between them. In *nagauta*, where narration is accompanied by *shamisen*, both rhythms do match. In other instances in which both parts match rhythms, the melody imparts a sense of monotony. In music considered to represent *iki*, melody and accompaniment often deviate by as much as a quarter beat.

The foregoing account outlines the views of Mr. Tanabe. In sum, we may conclude that *iki* in melody mounts to breaking the monistic equilibrium of the idealism of a scale and, by doing so, positing duality by means of deviation. By supposing duality, tension is created, and this tension becomes the expression of *iropposa* 'coquet', the material cause of *iki*. The formal cause of *iki* is objectified because the degree of deviation is not excessive, limiting itself to about three-quarters of a whole tone. We can say the same about *iki* in rhythm. There, the formal and material causes of *iki* serve objective expression by breaking the monistic equilibrium of singing and *shamisen* music. Again, duality is created by deviation careful not to exceed a certain limit. It is in this fact the material and formal causes of *iki* are expressed objectively.

The form of a musical movement may also express *iki* under certain circumscribed conditions. A musical passage often becomes *iki* when a phrase is repeated several times, beginning suddenly on an extremely high note that slows as it descends through lower ones. An example of this comes on the phrase *murasaki no yukari ni* in a song called "Niimurasaki" of Utazawa.[179] This passage is divided into four units—*murasaki*, *no*, *yukari*, and *ni*—each of which begins with a sudden high note and descends. Then too, the part that serves the text *ne ni hodasareshi en no ito* is separated into six phrases—*ne ni ho*, *da*, *sare*, *shi*, *en no*, and *ito*. Another example comes from the Kiyomoto song for a play *Izayoi Seishin*. There, the text reads: *umemigaeri no fune no uta, shinobu nara shinobu nara, yami no yo wa okashanse*.[180] This can be thought of as having seven parts— *umemi*, *gaeri no*, *fune no uta*, *shinobu nara*, *shinobu nara*, *yami no*, and *yo wa okashanse*. This type of musical movement can exhibit *iki* because the initial high pitch of each phrase contrasts with the low pitch of a preceding phrase. This effect imparts sensual duality. Each phrase also evokes loneliness through diminishing dynamics combined with downward progression of notes on the scale. The relation between the duality expressed by the initial tone of a passage and the descending progression in the passage may resemble one between stripe patterns and subdued colors in a design that embodies *iki*.

In this way, the art form of the objective expression of *iki*, a phenomenon of consciousness, not only exhibits itself spatially in two-dimensional design and three-dimensional architecture, but also temporally, in music, a form of art without tangible form. Both types of expression presuppose duality and follow through by exhibiting prescribed characteristics consistent with that supposition. Furthermore, when we compare these art forms with natural forms, we notice an unmistakable correspondence between the two. We can understand these artistic and natural forms as objective expressions of iki, a phenomenon of consciousness. That is, the supposition of duality observed objectively is constructed on the foundation of *bitai* 'coquetry', the material cause of iki as a phenomenon of consciousness. And, certain characteristics that accompany the way duality is posited are established on *ikiji* 'pride and honor' and *akirame* 'resignation', the formal causes of iki. Thus, we believe that we have reduced the objective expressions of iki to iki as a phenomenon of consciousness, clarified the relationship between these two modes of being, and elucidated the structure of iki as meaning.

VI CONCLUSION

In order to understand the being of iki and elucidate its structure, we attempted, first, a concrete grasp of the experience of its meaning. We did so for methodological reasons. Yet that method of contemplating iki has its unavoidable limitations. We were forced to approach the subject by way of conceptual analysis. Hence, on the other hand, it is the same with ethnic groups as it is with individuals: the particularized, lived experience cannot be described by means of conceptual analysis alone. Even if such experience is assigned a certain meaning, some part of it will elude analysis. Strictly speaking, meaning rich in the concrete is to be sensed through intuitive understanding. Maine de Biran points out that language cannot convey what it means to toil to paralytics who have never made a voluntary movement. He adds that the same applies to any hope of explaining color to someone blind from birth.[181] We can probably say with some certainty that the same applies to the meaning of taste. "Taste" begins with "tasting," with lived experience. We literally "learn the taste" of something. We make value judgments based on that experience. We rarely experience taste as pure taste. The expression *aji na mono* 'scrumptious things' suggests not just taste, but a certain scent in which the sense of smell itself takes part. It hints of fragrance faint and elusive. Moreover, it sometimes involves the sense of touch as well. The tongue itself is part of taste, with tactile sensations of its own. The sense of touch also extends to indescribable sensations, much like the idea of touching someone's heartstrings. In a very fundamental sense, the senses of taste, smell, and touch comprise "lived experience."

The less immediate, or so-called higher senses, separate aspects of the outside world from the self and may in fact endow them with some degree of opposition to the self. In this way, the sense of hearing can make us clearly aware of the pitch of a tone. Overtones may achieve a tonal coloring, as if to turn their back, blurring clarity of perception. The sense of sight has its own equivalent. We create a system of colors by dividing them into groups of hues. Yet no distinction between colors, however finely drawn, eliminates the difficulty of capturing nuance. Sensory taste comes from learning, as lived experience, these fleeting tonalities in hearing and nuances in seeing that elude clear grasp.

Like sensory taste, taste in the aesthetic sense also answers to "nuances" of objects. When we talk about a person's, or an ethnic group's, taste, we are speaking about ethical and aesthetic judgments we see them making. Nietzsche asked: "Does one have to curse right away, where one does not love?" He answered: "That seems bad taste to me."[182] His own term for it was *Pöbel-Art (gehin)*. We do not doubt that taste has a meaning in the realm of morality. Even in art, where taste is concerned, we believe in the value of nuance. As Verlaine said: "Never the Color . . . always the nuance."[183]

After all, iki, too, was a taste determined by a people. It follows that appreciation of iki must be based on a *sens intime*, an "intimate sense" in the truest sense of the word. The abstract conceptual moments reached through analysis merely point to several aspects of concrete *iki. Iki* can be analyzed into individual conceptual moments, but this process cannot be reversed, bringing these conceptual moments back together to reconstitute the being of *iki. Bitai* 'coquetry', *ikiji* 'pride and honor', and *akirame* 'resignation' are not parts of *iki* per se; they are no more than its conceptual moments. Consequently, an unbridgeable chasm separates *iki* as a set of conceptual moments and *iki* as an experience of meaning. In other words, the potentiality of *iki* in terms of logical expression and the actuality of *iki* are subject to an uncompromising distinction. The reason why we think that we can constitute the being of *iki* by means of combining the abstract conceptual moments obtained by analysis is that *iki* lies at our disposal already as an experience of meaning.

If we assume that a disparate relationship indeed exists between *iki* as an experience of meaning and its conceptual analysis, then we face a problem. When we are trying to understand the structure of the meaning of *iki* from the outside as an experience of meaning, the conceptual analysis of *iki* will most likely not yield a result of practical value, except to offer an appropriate position of and occasion for grasping its being.

How, for example, would we explain the being of *iki* to a foreigner ignorant of Japanese culture? We will position him in a specific place according to the conceptual analysis of *iki*. Taking the opportunity, he must acquire the being of *iki* using his own "inner sense." In such a case, the conceptual analysis of the comprehension of the being of *iki* can only be a simple *causa occasionalis*.[184]

Even so, we have to ask if conceptual analysis is solely committed to practical value. The issue is whether evaluation, from the utilitarian point of view, of the conceptual effort that proposes to change potentiality of the logical manifestation of experienced meaning to actuality offers any practical value. And if so, how much practical value does it offer? No. None at all. The worth of an intellectual being hinges on whether he can show the way to conceptual awareness from meaningful experience. Whether or not there exists a practical value or, if so, how much value it amounts to is not an issue.

The significance of scholarly investigation resides in *eternally* pursuing the *task* of actualizing logical expression. At the same time the scholar must be clearly mindful of an incommensurable discontinuity between meaningful experience and its conceptual recognition. I believe that an understanding of the structure of *iki*, too, will have significance in this sense.

As we have seen, it is a grave error to base one's understanding of the structure of *iki* on its objective expressions. For *iki* does not necessarily exhibit all the nuances available to that expression. Objectification itself is subject to a number of constraints. That explains why *iki* that has been objectified rarely embodies, both in terms of breadth and depth, the entirety of *iki* as a phenomenon of consciousness. Objective expression is no more than symbolic of *iki*. Thus the structure of *iki* cannot be understood solely in terms of its natural and artistic form. On the contrary, objective form can only come to life, and be comprehended, by transferring the meaning of *iki* obtained from personal or social experiences of meaning. We can only begin to understand the structure of *iki* by asking the *quis* 'who' question first. That is done through immersing oneself in the phenomenon of consciousness. That done, then we can ask the *quid* 'what' question when we come into contact with objective expression.[185] Artistic form in general cannot be truly comprehended unless such an understanding is based on the mode of being of human nature in general or on the mode of being peculiar to the opposite sex.[186]

The Germans offer an example that shows how the mode of being is objectified in design. In their case, a type of inner unease manifests itself in a preference for irregularity in design. Some such designs survive from prehistoric times, when nations were still in process of migration. They also appear in forms distinctive of the decorative arts in the Gothic and Baroque periods.

In architecture, too, the relationship between lived experience and artistic form cannot be denied. In Paul Valéry's *Eupalinos ou l'architecte*, the architect

Eupalinos, who was born in Mégare, proclaims: "that little temple, which I built for Hermes, a few steps from here, if you could know what it means to me!—There where the passer-by sees but an elegant chapel—'t is but a trifle: four columns, a very simple style—there I have enshrined the memory of a bright day in my life. O sweet metamorphosis! This delicate temple, none knows it, is a mathematical image of a girl from Corinth, whom I happily loved. It reproduces faithfully the proportions that were particularly hers."[187]

In music, too, the trend that can be characterized as romanticism or expressionism aims at a formal objectification of lived experience. Speaking to his lover Péronne, Guillaume de Machaut wrote that "everything I have was made from your emotion."[188] Chopin himself admitted that the beautiful larghetto in the second movement of the F Minor Concerto was a result of giving melodic form to his affection for Konstancja Gladkowska.[189]

Artistic objectification of lived experience need not be a conscious endeavor, since artistic impulses often work unconsciously. Yet this type of unconscious creation is nothing less than an objectification of lived experience. That is to say, personal or social experience freely and unconsciously selects formative principles and completes self-expression as art. The same can be said about natural forms. Physical movements and other natural forms are often created in the unconscious. Whatever the case may be, the objectified expression of iki can be understood only if its understanding is based on iki as a phenomenon of consciousness.

Most of the scholars who have attempted to clarify the structure of iki by taking objective expression as their point of departure have fallen into the same trap. They have not gone beyond the abstract and eidetic understanding of iki and hence have not reached a point of grasping concretely and hermeneutically the determinants for the particular being of iki. For instance, an attempt has been made to explain the "feeling of iki" based on the observation of artistic objects as "objects that give aesthetic sensations."[190] The result is a limited grasp of general, abstract characteristics, such as "a mixing of unpleasant things." As a result, iki comes to have a meaning limited to a vague approximation of raffiné. It fails not only to establish the distinction between iki and shibumi 'understated, astringent', but also to capture the ethnic coloring so much a part of iki.

If we assume even for a moment that iki has no meaning beyond that vague and limited one, we should expect to discover iki in much of Western art. If that were the case, iki would be identified as no more than a sensibility that "people of today take a fancy to," no matter where, "in Japan or in the West." But do we see it, say, in paintings by Constantin Guys, Degas, or van Dongen?

Do they exhibit nuances that qualify as iki?[191] And what of certain melodies in the works of Saint-Saëns, Massenet, Debussy, and Richard Strauss? Are they, strictly speaking, iki? We probably can't say yes to any of these questions.

As we have pointed out before, it wouldn't be difficult to pick out features such works have in common with iki, thanks to a process of formalized abstraction. Choosing an eidetic approach, however, is not a methodological attitude suitable for grasping this type of cultural being. Those who attempt to elucidate the meaning of iki by taking its objective expressions as their point of departure often fall prey to this kind of eidetic method.

Let us sum up by saying that it is well-nigh fruitless to begin the study of iki by seeking to understand natural or artistic form as an objective expression of iki. Instead, we must first grasp the meaning of iki hermeneutically, as a phenomenon of consciousness, in terms of the ethnic concrete. That done, we can use that comprehension as the foundation for an appropriate understanding of the objective expression that has been exhibited in natural and artistic forms. In a word, the study of iki can exist only as a **hermeneutic study of ethnic being.**

A hermeneutic study of the being of a people, when attempting to demonstrate the ethnic peculiarity of iki, should not be misled by the fact that we happen to discover iki in artistic forms of Western art. Assuming that objective expression cannot express perfectly all the subtle, complex gradations in color of iki itself, then, even if we locate in Western art the identical artistic form to iki, we must not immediately regard it as an objective expression of iki arising from lived experience nor hypothesize the existence of iki in Western culture. Even when we can actually sense iki in a Western artistic form, such sensation presupposes our own ethnic subjectivity, with coloring specific to the ethnic group.

Whether or not the artistic form itself is an objectification of iki is a totally separate issue. It in turn raises a number of questions. For example, does iki exist as a phenomenon of consciousness in Western culture? Can we then find iki as a phenomenon of consciousness in Western culture? Careful assessment of structural moments of Western culture suggests that iki will not be found there. Does the meaning of "dandyism" really exhibit the same structure as iki in full and at all strata of concrete consciousness? Does it possess the selfsame fragrance and coloring? A volume from Baudelaire's *Les fleurs du mal* in places refers to emotions close to iki. His poem entitled "The Thirst for Extinction" expresses sentiments such as "Resign yourself my heart," "You find no joy in love," and "The spring is gone and all its odors fade."[192] All these are fully expressive of the sentiment of resignation. In "Song of Autumn," Baudelaire wistfully describes the speaker's declining years in terms of autumn's melancholy afterglow: "Regretting this torrid summer, let me bask / Awhile in autumn's gentle yellow rays."[193] In "Meditation," too, Baudelaire expresses transcendent emotion embracing the past.[194]

Baudelaire himself has much to say about dandyism:[195] "dandyism is the last spark of heroism and decadence; . . . Dandyism is a sunset; like the declining daystar, it is glorious, without heat and full of melancholy."[196] As a "doctrine of *élégance*,"[197] dandyism is "a kind of religion."[198] Dandyism no doubt has a similar structure to that of *iki*. But as an ideal, "Caesar, Catiline, and Alcibiades providing us with dazzling examples,"[199] dandyism is seen as a property almost exclusively male. *Iki* is notably different in that respect, since its "heroism" is also the life and breath of delicate women, even women reduced by circumstance to a "life of prostitution."

The "nobility" and "pathos of distance" that Nietzsche discusses are no doubt each a kind of *ikiji* 'pride and honor'. Originating in chivalry, these words have similarities that are difficult to distinguish from *ikiji*, which came out of *bushidō*.[200] However, as Western culture developed under the influence of Christianity's summary condemnation of carnal desire, sexual relations outside of holy matrimony were seen as leading straight to hell, along with materialism itself. As a result, we find hardly any instances in which *ikiji* 'pride and honor', which anticipates idealism, spiritualizes coquetry in its fullest extent, and forms a particular mode of being in Western culture. "You are going to women? Do not forget the whip." Such is the warning the old woman gives to Zarathustra.[201]

But let us say, for the sake of argument, that *iki* is found in certain hypothetical cases in Western culture, and that such cases represent actual personal experience in exceptional circumstances. Even then, the meaning is entirely different. In this case, *iki* is not manifested in the domain of the public as meaning of an ethnic group. For a word to have a consistent meaning and value to a people, a linguistic path must be always open there. The fact that the West has no word corresponding to *iki* is itself evidence that the phenomenon of consciousness that is *iki* has no place in Western culture as a certain meaning in its ethnic being.

Although *iki* as a meaningful experience exists in the peculiarity of the determinants of the ethnic being of the Japanese people, all too often we encounter mere ghosts of *iki* where it has decayed into the abstract, eidetic world of nothingness. Noisy loquacity and vacuous verbosity speak of illusions as if they exist. But, we must not be led astray by *flatus vocis* exchanged between *ready-made* general concepts.[202] When we encounter these illusions, we must recall "what **our** soul once saw"[203] in its concrete, clear shape. This recall is none other than the horizon that makes us recognize hermeneutically once more that *iki* is **ours**.

What must be recalled, we must keep in mind, is not the abstract universal of general concepts proposed by Platonic realists. It is rather an ethnic peculiarity, a type of individual peculiarity advocated by nominalists. Here, we must dare to seek a conversion of the Platonic epistemology by inverting its thought process. If such is the case, how can we tether ourselves to the possibility of *anamnesis* 'recollection' of this meaning? No way but this: by refusing to consign our spiritual culture to oblivion. Only then can we remain steadfast, true to the passionate eros of our idealistic and unrealistic culture. *Iki* stands in an inseparable internal relationship to the idealism of *bushidō* and the unrealism of Buddhism. *Iki* means that *bitai* 'coquetry' that has acquired *akirame* 'resignation' **lives** in the freedom of *ikiji* 'pride and honor'.[204] We cannot allow coquetry to take the form of *iki*, unless we as a people possess an unclouded vision of our destiny and an unabated longing for freedom of soul. We comprehend and understand completely the core meaning of *iki* only when we grasp its structure as a self-revelation of **the being of our people.**

Notes

1. [Although the word *iki* is a noun in Japanese, it is used sometimes attributively to mean "possessing the quality of *iki*" in the English text for the benefit of readability (e.g., "*iki* manners" means "manners possessing the quality of *iki*"). The same principle is applied to other words of aesthetic taste throughout this translation.—trans.]

2. [Here Kuki uses the word *minzoku*, which I translate as "ethnic group" or "people."—trans.]

3. [The reference here is to the first stanza of a famous poem by Johann Wolfgang von Goethe (1749–1832) included in his novel *Wilhelm Meisters Lehrjahre*. In it, Wilhelm Meister is speaking to his beloved, Mignon:

> Know you the land where lemons are in flower,
> Where the golden oranges glow in the dusky bower,
> A gentle wind descends from the azure sky,
> The myrtle is still and the laurel stretches high,
> Is it known to you?
>   Oh there, yes, there,
> Beloved, goes the way that you and I should share.

Translated by H. M. Waidson, *Wilhelm Meister's Years of Apprenticeship* (London: John Calder, 1978–1979), 127.—trans.]

4. Nietzsche, *Also sprach Zarathustra*, Teil III, Von alten und neuen Tafeln. [(Kuki's note 1, chap. 1 in original.) Pt. 3, chap. 12, "On Old and New Tablets," *Thus Spoke Zarathustra*, trans. Walter A. Kaufmann (New York: Viking Press, 1966), 197.—trans.]

5. [Both in Kant's philosophy and in Husserlian phenomenology, *noumenon* refers to the unchanging essence of an object, *phenomenon* to the object's appearance. —trans.]

6. [M. Émile Boutroux, "La nature et l'esprit," in *La psychologie du mysticisme* (Paris: Librairie Philosophique J. Vrin 1926), 177. (Kuki's note 2, chap. 1 in original.) The quote from Boutroux reads as follows:

> Le point de départ, le premier moment, c'est un état d'âme difficile à définir, que caractérise assez bien le mot allemand *Sehnsucht*. C'est un état de désir vague, inquiet, très réel et susceptible d'être très intense comme passion de l'âme, très indéterminé ou plutôt très inexplicable dans son objet et dans sa cause. C'est une aspiration vers un inconnu, vers un bien nécessaire au coeur et irreprésentable pour l'intelligence. Un état de ce genre peut, à vrai dire, se rencontrer chez des hommes très divers et avoir des significations très différentes. —trans.]

7. [These aesthetic terms, and all others in Japanese, will be fully defined later. —trans.]

8. [The heroine in Bizet's opera *Carmen* is under arrest, hands tied, in this famous scene. She uses the Habanera to seduce her guard, Don José, who sets her free and joins her in the gypsy life, with tragic consequences in the end.—trans.]

9. [The term Kuki uses, *Yamato minzoku* (the Yamato people), is an ancient one usually used to refer to the people of the Nara-Kyoto area, the heartland of Japan. Here, it is used to refer to the Japanese people as a whole.—trans.]

10. [Husserl used the term *Ideation* (also *ideierende Abstraktion*) to refer to the method of bracketing existence (or, equivalently, conducting phenomenological reduction), that is, suspending the question of whether the object under investigation actually exists. Husserl believed that this method was needed to ensure that the object under investigation is described completely, as we fully experience it, prior to making evaluative judgments about its causal nexus or ontological status. This method was also described in terms of the phenomenological reduction, a rigorous philosophical method intended to make it possible to intuit the essence of all objects. Kuki's phrase *"genshō o jiyū ni henkō-site"* (by freely making changes to a phenomenon) refers to the technique of free variation, a specific method recommended by Husserl for distinguishing essential from nonessential features of objects, thereby making it possible for us to grasp their essence *(eidos)*.—trans.]

11. Bergson, *Essai sur les données immédiates de la conscience*, 20e éd., 1921, p. 124. [(Kuki's note 3, chap. 1 in original.) The passage Kuki paraphrases is:

> I smell a rose and immediately confused recollections of childhood come back to my memory. In truth, these recollections have not been called up by the per-

fume of the rose: I breathe them in with the very scent; it means all that to me. To others it will smell differently.—It is always the same scent, you will say, but associated with different ideas.—I am quite willing that you should express yourself in this way; but do not forget that you have first removed the personal element from the different impressions which the rose makes on each one of us; you have retained only the objective aspect, that part of the scent of the rose which is public property and thereby belongs to space. Only thus was it possible to give a name to the rose and its perfume. You then find it necessary, in order to distinguish our personal impressions from one another, to add specific characteristics to the general idea of rose-scent. And you now say that our different impressions, our personal impressions, result from the fact that we associate different recollections with rose-scent. But the association of which you speak hardly exists except for you, and as a method of explanation. It is in this way that, by setting side by side certain letters of an alphabet common to a number of known languages, we may imitate fairly well such and such a characteristic sound belonging to a new one; but not with any of these letters, nor with all of them, has the sound itself been built up.

Henri Bergson, *Essai sur les données immédiates de la conscience* (Time and free will: An essay on the immediate data of consciousness), translated by F. L. Pogson (London: George Allen and Unwin, Ltd., 1910), 161–162.—trans.]

12. [Saint Anselm (1033–1109), archbishop of Canterbury, is typically credited with first formulating the ontological argument for the existence of the Christian god. —trans.]

13. [Roscelin, active in the latter half of the eleventh century, was a founder of early medieval nominalism.—trans.]

14. [For clarity, I have consistently employed *comprehend* and its variants for Kuki's *etoku-suru*. This usage is based on the fact that, in other published writings, Kuki was quite strict about the distinction between ordinary understanding, including the sort of knowledge possible in the natural sciences, and the sort of comprehension that makes it possible to understand historical and cultural phenomena, including ideas, intentions, and feelings. The latter sort of comprehension is what the Germans might refer to as the phenomenon of "lived experience" (*Erlebnis*). This usage is also consistent with Wilhelm Dilthey's (1833–1911) notion of *Verstehen*, a term typically translated into English as "understanding." Dilthey, however, believed that historical and cultural experiences could be comprehended only by employing methods appropriate to the *Geisteswissenschaften* (the humanities or cultural sciences) rather than the method of the *Naturwissenschaften* (the natural sciences). In this translation, such other terms as *grasp, understand, acquire,* et cetera, refer to types of understanding other than Dilthey's *Verstehen*. See H. P. Rickman's entry for Wilhelm Dilthey in *The Encyclopedia of Philosophy* (vol. 2, pp. 403–407) and Kuki's chart of terminological equivalencies for various philosophers in "Seiyō kinsei tetsugakushi kō," in *Kuki Shūzō zenshū* (hereafter KSZ) (Tokyo: Iwanami shoten, 1982), 6:13–15.—trans.]

15. See the following for the meaning of the terms *eidetic* and *hermeneutic* and the relationship between *essentia* and *existentia*.

[Edmund] Husserl, *Ideen zu einer reinen Phänomenologie* [(Halle a. d. S.: Max Niemeyer, 1913), 1:4, 12.].

[Martin] Heidegger, *Sein und Zeit* [(Halle a. d. S.: Max Niemeyer, 1927), 1:37.].

Oskar Becker, *Mathematische Existenz* [(Halle a. d. S.: Max Niemeyer, 1927), 1.].

[Note 4, chap. 1 in original.—trans.]

16. [Chikamatsu Shūkō (1876–1944) was a novelist most active in the Taishō era (1912–1925).—trans.]

17. [These two quotations can be found in "Kanraku," *Nagai Kafū zenshū* (Tokyo: Iwanami shoten, 1992) 6:29. (*Nagai Kafū zenshū* was originally published in 1920 by Shun'yōdō, Tokyo.) For an English translation, see "Pleasure," translated by Matsumoto Ryōzō in *Japanese Literature New and Old* (Tokyo: Hokuseidō, 1961), 31–74.—trans.]

18. [Kikuchi Kan (1888–1948), well-known playwright and novelist, wrote *Fue no shiratama* (The unsoiled gem), a novel serialized in *Tōkyō Asahi Shinbun* from 1929 through 1934. See *Kikuchi Kan zenshū* (Tokyo: Bungei shunjūsha, 1994), 8:453.—trans.]

19. [According to *Dictionary of the History of Ideas*, Zeno of Elea was a Greek philosopher in the fifth century B.C., whose well-known paradox against motion, "Achilles and the Turtle," is described as follows: "[I]n a race between a quick-footed Achilles and a slow-moving Turtle, if the Turtle has any head start at all then Achilles cannot overtake him, ever. In fact by the time Achilles has reached the Turtle's starting point the latter has moved on a certain distance; when Achilles has covered that distance, the Turtle has again gained a novel distance, etc. This gives rise to an unending sequence of distances; and the puzzle maintains Achilles cannot exhaust the sum of the distances and come abreast with the Turtle." Kuki brings this paradox, also discussed by Bergson in his *Time and Free Will*, to caution us against confusing space and motion.—trans.]

20. [Bona fide Edokko were said to be at least third-generation born and raised in Edo proper. Edo (present-day Tokyo) was the capital of the Tokugawa shogunate of Japan between 1603–1868.—trans.]

21. [The Hakone mountains, some sixty miles southwest of Tokyo, divide eastern Japan from western Japan. The word *true* here is a translation of the Japanese "kissui," written in a combination of kanji 生 "live, life" and 粋 "core, essence, the sensibility of iki."—trans.]

22. ["Flowers of Edo" refers to fires, which often ravaged neighborhoods in Edo. —trans.]

23. [In this phrase, "*tatsumi no kyōkotsu*," *tatsumi* refers to the direction southwest and in this context the southwest area of Edo, that is, the Fukagawa area of Edo known not only for the pleasure quarters but the roughness and stylishness of the men. *Kyōkotsu* "cheekbones" refers to the manliness of men. See Saitō Ryūzō, *Kinsei nihon sesōshi* (Tokyo: Hakubunkan, Taishō 15 [1926]), 895.—trans.]

24. [From *Kōtei nagautashū*, by Okamura Kiichirō and revised by Okayasu Nanpo (Tokyo: Fubunkan, 1916), 67. The quote is from a melody entitled "Tsui no amigasa" (A pair of braided hats). — trans.]

25. [In one version, this Sukeroku's line reads: ". . . this youthful Sukeroku, Agemaki's Sukeroku! Scum! Bow before this face!" James R. Brandon, *Kabuki* (Cambridge: Harvard University Press, 1975), 72. Agemaki was a historical figure as well as a name of a courtesan in a Kabuki play. — trans.]

26. [In another version, Agemaki's line directed to villain Ikyū reads: "I am Agemaki, of the House of Three Harbors. . . . but in her blackest life, in the blackest night, she could not mistake Sukeroku for Ikyū!" In this quotation, Kuki left out several lines between "I am Agemaki" and ". . . but in her blackest." For further detail, see Brandon, *Kabuki* 61. — trans.]

27. [See NKBT, 64:146 and Saitō Ryūzō, *Kinsei nihon sesōshi*, 735. As we will see later, Kuki regards *sui* to be semantically equivalent to *iki*. See Kuki's own note (note 43) below. — trans.]

28. [Takao was a famous courtesan who worked for the Miura-ya as well. It is also a name passed down from one courtesan to the next. Komurasaki was a popular early-Edo courtesan in the major brothel district Yoshiwara, in Edo. — trans.]

29. [By emphasizing the word *lives*, Kuki plays with the word *"iki"* with *ikite iru* "lives, is alive," which shares a homophonic component with *iki*. — trans.]

30. [Saitō Ryūzō, *Kinsei nihon sesōshi*, 481. — trans.]

31. [Gochōmachi (*go-* "five" plus *-chō* "city section, block") euphemistically refers to Yoshiwara. It was so named because it comprised five *chō* "city sections, blocks," which included Edochō itchōme, Edochō nichōme, Kyōchō itchōme, Kyōchō nichōme, and Sumichō. The source of the phrase is probably Saitō Ryūzō's *Kinsei nihon sesōshi*, 475. — trans.]

32. [Saitō Ryūzō, *Kinsei nihon sesōshi*, 483. — trans.]

33. ["*Shitahimo o musubu kami no shitagokoro*" ([the ulterior motive of] the gods that tie the ties of their undergarments) is a play on a common phrase "*enmusubi no kami*" (gods that tie the knots of a pair of lovers, gods of love). The play is on the word "*musubu*" (tie a knot, realize a romantic liaison) and its linguistic relative "*musubi*" (tying). "Double suicide" (Jap. *shinjūdate*) refers to a promise of eternal loyalty such that the lovers would be willing to commit suicide together, which on occasion led to a real love suicide (Jap. *shinjū*). The quotation can be found in a Katōbushi song called "Matsu no uchi" (New year) reportedly popular during the Tenmei era (1781–1789). Katōbushi was a style of *jōruri* singing founded by Masumi Katō during the Kyōhō era (1716–1736) and known for its elegance, which Edokko found particularly appealing. See Saitō Ryūzō, *Kinsei nihon sesōshi*, 476. — trans.]

34. [Izayoi's line to her lover Seishin comes from a singing part in the opening act of the Kabuki play *Satomoyō azami no ironui* (Love of Izayoi and Seishin, a.k.a. *Izayoi Seishin*). The play is a story about Seishin, a Buddhist monk, and the courtesan Izayoi, who in the end tragically take their own lives. For an English translation of this play,

see *Love of Izayoi and Seishin, A Kabuki Play*, by Frank T. Motofuji (Rutland, Vt.: Tuttle, 1966).—trans.]

35. [The phrase comes from a melody entitled "Kishō" (A contract), in *Kōtei nagautashū*, by Okamura Kiichirō and revised by Okayasu Nanpo, 280. "Ukiyo" (floating world) refers to the transient world of people, and of pleasures and sufferings. —trans.]

36. [The phrase comes from a Kabuki melody entitled "Kyōga no komusume Dōjōji" (Dance of Hanako), in *Kōtei nagautashū*, by Okamura Kiichirō and revised by Okayasu Nanpo, 160.—trans.]

37. [Katayama Yosankichi, *Gidayū hyakkashū* (Tokyo: Fubunkan, 1926), 207. This line comes from a *gidayū* melody entitled "Akegarasu yuki no akebono" (Crow in a snowy dawn).—trans.]

38. In vol. 7 of *Shunshoku tatsumi no sono* is the quote "*Sazo iki na toshima ni narudarō to omou to imakkara tanoshimi da wa*" (She will grow old to be iki and we are already looking forward to it). Also, in vol. 2 of *Shunshoku umegoyomi* appears the phrase "a woman in her late twenties whose unpainted face is very iki." Further, in vol. 1 of the same book, one finds: "I heard that you had a beautiful, iki wife, so thinking that I had made a mistake, I asked more closely about her, then I was told that she was older than you." The woman who is described as possessing iki here is older than the man. Generally, iki subsumes knowledge about the world as well, so the *wisdom that comes with age* is also presupposed. One who possesses the quality of iki must be a sophisticated person who has *experienced much of the world*. [(Kuki's note 1, chap. 2 in original.) The quotations can be found in NKBT, 64:345, 73, and 49, respectively.—trans.]

39. [*Kōtei nagautashū*, by Okamura Kiichirō and revised by Okayasu Nanpo, 211, 279. These fragments are found in a melody entitled "Takao zange no dan" (Confession of Takao).—trans.]

40. [*Kōtei nagautashū*, by Okamura Kiichirō and revised by Okayasu Nanpo, 109. —trans.]

41. [Buddhism holds that a being manifests itself in various life forms as it transmigrates and that things in the world are therefore endowed with different forms; things are in this sense all differentiated (*shabetsusō*). The opposing and complementary concept is *byōdōsō*, which affirms that objects in the world around us are equal in the eyes of Buddha and thus all laws apply equally to all beings.—trans.]

42. [Kuki's writing in the margin of his own copy has corrected this sentence to read: "The second and third distinguishing characteristics may appear to be inconsistent . . ." KSZ, 1:84.—trans.]

43. Insofar as the horizon we are examining, we believe there is no harm done by considering iki to have the same meaning content as sui. In *Ukiyoburo* (The world at the bathhouse, sec. 2, vol. 1), Shikitei Sanba (1776–1822) wrote the following dialogue between a woman from Edo and a woman from Kansai about dye colors. Woman from Edo: "It is a little like blue purple; it is so iki." Woman from Kansai: "It is very sui. If it is indigo dyeing of Edo, I like it, I like it." This is to say, iki and sui, in this case,

are completely identical. After this discussion concerning dye colors, Shikitei Sanba continued the dialogue skillfully, each of the characters using the Edo and Kansai dialects, respectively. Further, Sanba also had them engage in an argument about the usage differences between *suppon* 'snapping turtle' (Edo dialect) and *maru* 'snapping turtle' (Kansai dialect), and *kara* 'so, therefore' (Edo dialect) and *sakai* 'so, therefore' (Kansai dialect). The difference between *iki* and *sui* appears to be dialectal between Edo and Kansai dialects, both referring to the same. It might be possible to define the development of these words chronologically (cf. *Genroku bungaku jiten* [Dictionary of Genroku literature] and *Chikamatsu goi* [Vocabulary of Chikamatsu]). There are cases, however, in which *sui* seems to be used more often for phenomena of consciousness, while *iki* for objective expressions. For instance, a popular song cited in vol. 7 of *Shunshoku umegoyomi* speaks of a person whose "temperament is **sui** and body movements and clothing, too, are **iki**." In vol. 9 of the same book, though, where there is a reference made to *iki no nasake no minamoto* "the source of **iki** compassion," there are frequent cases in which *iki* is used for characterizing phenomena of consciousness, and, further, in vol. 3 of *Shunshoku tatsumi no sono* is a description "Yonehachi, whose appearance is **iki**," so it is not rare that *iki* is used for objective expressions. In short, it is probably safe to regard *iki* and *sui* as having the same semantic content. Even if we hypothesize that one is used for phenomena of consciousness and the other principally for objective expressions, objective expressions are precisely an objectification of phenomena of consciousness. Therefore, they both, at the root, have the same semantic content. [(Kuki's note 2, chap. 2 in original.) The quotation from *Ukiyoburo* (The world at the bathhouse) can be found in NKBT, 63:131 et seq. In the NKBT version of *Shunshoku umegoyomi* (The love-tinted plum calendar, 64:178–179), one finds "*iki to nasake no minamoto*" (the source of iki and compassion), rather than Kuki's "*iki no nasake no minamoto*" (the source of iki compassion). In the last part of this note, Kuki attributes two meanings to "*sui*," a synonym of "*iki*" (*sui*) and "*sui*" as a word meaning "essence, core." —trans.]

44. [This passage is reminiscent of Husserl, who contended that one must strip off (or "bracket") all presuppositions and preconceived ideas, a process called phenomenological reduction, in order to understand the essence of different manifestations of consciousness. This passage also makes a reference to Kant, who spoke of the role of disinterested and purposeless play in aesthetic experience. See note 10 above. —trans.]

45. [*Kōtei nagautashū*, by Okamura Kiichirō and revised by Okayasu Nanpo, 185. This fragment is from a melody called "Sono omokage ninin wankyū" (Love story of Wankyū and Matsuyama). —trans.]

46. [Ibid. —trans.]

47. [This part is sung in a Kabuki dance routine called *Rokkasen sugata no irodori* (Dance of the six poets immortal). —trans.]

48. [The original text, perhaps an excerpt from a *dodoitsu* love verse, reads: "*Mata itoshisa ga iya mashite fukaku naruko no yabo-rashii*," which conceals several layers of hid-

den meanings. The words "*fukaku naru*" mean "deepen" but also are a play on Fukagawa and refer to it, as the "*fuka-*" part is written with the same kanji character. *Naruko* are noisemakers at the boat landing of Fukagawa, used to announce the arrival of customers by boat to the red-light district.—trans.]

49. [Kuki quotes from *Shunshoku umegoyomi*, sec. 2, vol. 5, scene 9 (NKBT, 64:115). Koume, the name of a girl here, was also the name of an area that produced roof tiles, thus the wordplay.—trans.]

50. Stendhal, *De l'amour (livre 1, chapitre 1).* [(Kuki's note 3, chap. 2 in original.) In Stendhal's own words, it appears as "*C'est un tableau où, jusqu'aux ombres, tout droit être couleur de rose.*" *De l'amour* (London: J. M. Dent and Sons, Ltd., 1912), 15. See section 5 of the translation for the reason pale brown stands in contrast to rose color in this context.—trans.]

51. [*Hakama* is the pleated and divided skirt of men's formal wear. The quotation comes from *Kōtei nagautashū*, by Okamura Kiichirō and revised by Okayasu Nanpo, 66. These phrases originate in a melody entitled "Tsui no amigasa" (A pair of braided hats).—trans.]

52. [The terminology comes from Aristotle, who contended that there are four senses of "cause," or explanations of causation: the formal cause, which is the form an object takes when complete; the material cause, which is the material from which objects come to be; the efficient cause, which is the process that brings about this completion; and the final cause, which is the ultimate purpose of such objects.—trans.]

53. [*Kōtei nagautashū*, by Okamura Kiichirō and revised by Okayasu Nanpo, 248. The quote is from a melody entitled "Nokiba no matsu" (A pine tree by the eaves).—trans.]

54. Kellermann, *Ein Spaziergang in Japan,* 1924, S. 256. [(Kuki's note 4, chap. 2 in original.) This work was originally published by Bernhard Kellermann as *Ein Spaziergang in Japan* (Berlin: Verlegt bei Paul Cassirer Berlin, 1910). The quoted passage reads: "*Sie kokettierte mit einer Anmut, die eine Europäerin nie erreicht.*"—trans.]

55. [Although these words signifying taste in Japanese are nouns and should therefore be glossed as corresponding English nouns (i.e., *shibumi* "understatement, astringency" rather than "understated, astringent"), these taste words are sometimes treated as adjectives to avoid awkward phrasing in the translation.—trans.]

56. ["Domain of the public" refers to an aggregation of modes in which people engage; in other words, the variety of human behavior in their daily lives. The two categories distinguish between general, sexually neutral social relationships and specifically sexual (or erotic) relationships between individuals.—trans.]

57. [*Shibucha* refers to tea that contains a large amount of tannin, a sign of strong or bitter-tasting tea. *Amacha*, hydrangea tea, which is somewhat sweet, is made from the leaves of a certain variety of hydrangea. Figuratively, treating someone to sweet tea refers to deceptive, sweet talk. *Shibukasu* is what is left after squeezing *shibu* "tannin compound" out of persimmon seeds. The extracted tannin juice was used for waterproofing and strengthening paper products. *Amakasu* refers to the liquid squeezed from rice used for making sake; *amakasu* was sweetened and used as an ingredient for a

beverage. *Shibukawa* is the very strong astringent tasting outer skin, epidermis, which envelops the meat of the chestnut, right below the hard outer shell. *"Amakawa"* refers also to epidermis but does not have this astringent taste. —trans.]

58. ["Jōhin" is written 上品, as a combination of 上 "superior" and 品 "quality." "Gehin" is written as 下品, as a combination of 下 "inferior" and 品 "quality." —trans.]

59. [The comparison makes sense only because *"jōhin"* and *"jōbon"* are written using the same characters (上品), as is the case with *"gehin"* and *"gebon"* (下品). The quotation comes from a Chinese history chronicle *Jin shu* (History of Jin) written during the reign of Emperor Taizong (598–649). —trans.]

60. [Kitagawa Utamaro (1753–1806) was an *ukiyoe* artist known for his images of women. He is one of the few among his contemporaries whose works influenced impressionists, including Toulouse-Lautrec, Mary Cassatt, and so forth. —trans.]

61. [The Wu dynasty pronunciation of the kanji 品 in Japanese is *hon* (var. -*bon*, -*ppon*). —trans.]

62. [A type of romance novel (*ninjōbon*) written by Tamenaga Shunsui (1790–1843). *Shunshoku umegoyomi* (The love-tinted plum calendar) was probably published beginning in 1832. It is a story of Tanjirō, who is involved in a love triangle with his fiancée Ochō and his lover Yonehachi, a geisha in Fukagawa. The source of this quote is found in sec. 4, vol. 11, scene 22; see NKBT, (64:217), the phrase is apparently meant to be read as *"samo ōyō naru sono idetachi,"* where 上品 is read *ōyō* "magnanimous," not *jōbon* "high class" as Kuki contended. —trans.]

63. [The quotation is from the introduction to sec. 3 of *Shunshoku umegoyomi*. See NKBT, 64:138. —trans.]

64. [Kuki equates 派手 *hade* "flashy" with another homophonic kanji compound 葉出 *hade* "leaves come out." Since they share the same readings, Kuki uses this evidence in support of the notion that *"hade"* is polysemic, having both "flashy" and "leaves come out" as meanings. —trans.]

65. [Kuki takes the kanji used to write *"jimi"* 地味 and analyzes its morphology as being a combination of two kanji 地 "earth" and 味 "taste," respectively, or "taste the earth." —trans.]

66. [Toyotomi Hideyoshi (1536–1598), who unified Japan in 1590, supported the arts during his rule. Momoyama period (a.k.a. Azuchi Momoyama period) refers roughly to the latter third of the sixteenth century until the death of Hideyoshi. —trans.]

67. [Tokugawa Ieyasu (1542–1616) was the first of the fifteen military rulers of the Tokugawa family who ruled Japan (1603–1868). —trans.]

68. [See vol. 8, scene 16 in *Shunshoku umegoyomi*, NKBT, 64:165. —trans.]

69. [This quotation comes from Saitō Ryūzō, *Kinsei nihon sesōshi*, Taishō 15 (1926), 812. —trans.]

70. [*Senryū* is a witty, often satirical, verse in the form of 5-7-5 syllables. "Edozuma kimono," popular beginning in the 1830s, refers to kimono on which designs were

placed diagonally along the front and back hemlines, in a manner similar to *tomesode*. Kamogawazome "lit. dyeing done near the Kamo River in Kyoto" is the present-day equivalent of Yūzenzome (Yūzen dyeing), a technique of rice-paste-resist cloth dyeing for which Kyoto is famous. — trans.]

71. [Yūki weave is produced in present-day Ibaraki prefecture and is known for its silk (or sometimes cotton) cloths, typically bearing stripe designs. The linings of kimono were sometimes purposely sewn around and over the edges so as to become visible, especially from the outside at the hem and the sleeve, a technique known as *fukikaeshi*. "Hanairo" or "*hanadairo*" refers to a light violet color. Kuki's quote is from sec. 4, vol. 11, article 10 of *Shunshoku tatsumi no sono* (NKBT, 64:416). — trans.]

72. [*Harutsugedori* (A bird heralding spring), written by Tamenaga Shunsui (1790–1843) was first published in Tenpō 7 (1836). The passage comes from vol. 11, chap. 21 (NKBZ, 47:453). — trans.]

73. [*Shunshoku eitaidango* was written in Tenpō 9 (1838) by Tamenaga Shunsui. The passage comes from episode 10. For a version of this story in contemporary Japanese, see *Nihon kokumin bungaku zenshū* (Tokyo: Kawade shobō shinsha, 1957), 18:161–235. — trans.]

74. [By saying this, Kuki wishes to point out that neither of these words has a negative morpheme attached to it, unlike the case of "*mushinkō*" (irreligious), in which "*mu-*" is the negative prefix. — trans.]

75. ["Buiki" (not iki) derives from the combination of "bu-," a negative prefix, and "*iki*." Similarly for "*busui*" (not *sui*). — trans.]

76. [This quote is from *Shunshoku tatsumi no sono* (Love-tinted garden of love), beginning of pt. 3, vol. 8, article 3 (NKBT, 64:358). — trans.]

77. [The liquid extracted from persimmon seeds was used for waterproofing various items, including paper. See also note 57. "Jūmen" (or more commonly "shibutsura" or "shibuttsura," "shibu" [tannin] plus "tsura" [face]) "sullen face, glum expression" refers to the expression one might see on a person biting into an unripe persimmon, thus denoting someone (or the face of such a person) wearing a glum expression all the time. — trans.]

78. [*Amaeru mono* and *amaerareru mono*. "Amaeru mono" means "a person who is spoiled, dependent, undisciplined." In contrast, someone who provides a person with such dependency, who spoils, or who permits a lack of discipline is *amaerareru mono* (perhaps more commonly now *amayakasu mono*) "the provider of dependency." Etymologically, both of these words are related to "*amai*" (sweet, undisciplined) and "*amami*" (sweetness), thus Kuki's reference to this pair. — trans.]

79. ["Sweet tea" refers to the deceptive "sweet talk" mentioned in note 57 above. — trans.]

80. [Literally, "*shibukawa*" means "astringent skin, tannin skin," but it also refers to unrefined manners of, for instance, servants from the countryside. "Edo no mizu" (water of the Edo River) probably refers to a brand of cosmetic lotion (used as a cleansing

lotion before white makeup is applied) that Shikitei Sanba marketed along with various types of cosmetics and medicine from a Kyoto concern owned by a certain Tanaka Sōetsu. Sanba advertised these products in many of his publications (see NKBT, 63:16, 189 for examples). The passage cited was probably written by Sanba himself, though its source is unclear on that point. Another possibility is that *"Edo no mizu"* simply refers to the water of the Edo river, emblematic of the spirit of that place. In that case the *senryū* could be translated: "Her complexion is so unrefined. To lave it with the water of the Edo river is preposterous!"—trans.]

81. [*Shibuuruka* is the salted intestines of a small, river fish called *ayu*, a species endemic to Japan. This delicacy is relished for its bitter taste.—trans.]

82. [According to Laotzu, a Chinese Daoist, *kanro* (sweets) are said to fall when the country is governed properly. *"Kanro"* has also been translated as "heavenly spirits," "divine medicine of eternal life," or "sweet dew."—trans.]

83. [*"Amatcho"* is an informal and slightly derogatory word for a "young woman," now fallen into desuetude. *"Amai bungaku"* (shallow literature) refers to simple literature dealing with romances (KSZ, 12:9).—trans.]

84. [Both of these quotations are from scene 10, vol. 5 of *Shunshoku umegoyomi*, NKBT, 64: 119, 118, respectively.—trans.]

85. [*Nēsan* can be a generic address form for young women, but in this context, it is probably closer to "the geisha (who is so famous that one needn't mention her name to refer to her)." Nagai Kafū (1879–1959) wrote this short story in Meiji 42 (1909). See "Kanraku," in *Nagai Kafū zenshū* (Tokyo: Iwanami shoten, 1992), 6:37—trans.]

86. In *Sendōbeya* there is a passage that reads: "This is Fukagawa in Edo, where we partake of Kisen morning tea with salted plum, where the corners of dumplings from the area of the Eitaibashi bridge are all rounded off, and where we have tasted both the sweet and sour of life." From this we learn that the taste of **sui** is **sour**. Regardless of its relation in the natural world, in the world of consciousness, the sour taste lies between sweetness and *shibumi* 'understated, astringent' taste. In the natural world, *shibumi* 'understated, astringent' is often associated with unripe fruit. In the spiritual realm, it is often understood in the taste of maturity. This difference explains why archaic usage, broadly speaking, favors age and a kind of crudeness found in a rustic style. *Shibumi* also lends itself to the dialectics of thesis, antithesis, and synthesis. We see this in a *tanka* like the following: *Uguisu no mada shibuku kikoyu nari, sudachi no Ono no haru no akebono* "I can still hear the faint singing of bush warblers, ready to leave their nests. At dawn in springtime, at Ono." *Shibumi* in this poem refers to an obstruction and corresponds to the "thesis" step. In contrast, *amami* 'sweetness' comprises the second step "antithesis." Finally, *shibumi* 'understated, astringent' in *muji omote ura moyō* "(fabric which is) solid in front but patterned on the lining," that is, *shibumi* 'understated, astringent' that refers to taste, is a sublation of *amami* and represents the third step "synthesis." [(Kuki's note 1, chap. 3 in original.) *Sendōbeya* is a *sharebon* (novelette dealing with Edo dandies) written by Shikitei Sanba (1776–1822) in

Bunka 4 (1807). *Tatsumifugen* (published in Kansei 10 [1798]), *Sendō shinwa* (published in Bunka 3 [1806]), and *Sendōbeya* constitute a series. For a modern reprint of *Sendōbeya* and *Sendō shinwa*, see *Shikitei Sanba shū* (reprint, Tokyo: Honpō shoseki, 1989), 2:39–129. The special tea and dumplings are things that are considered to possess iki, as are other things in Fukagawa. By saying that "from this we learn that the taste of **sui** is **sour**," Kuki plays with the word "*sui*" (a homonym for "*iki*") with the homophonic "*sui*" (sour). Kisen, named after one of the Six Poets of the Heian period, was a brand of tea popular in those days. *Dango* rice dumplings, whose corners were rounded, suggesting that their "rough edges" had worn off and that they were thus more urbane, were sold at stores (Sawaraya and Yawataya) located near the Eitaibashi bridge, in Edo. The earliest reference to these particular dumplings was made in Kansei 10 (1798), according to *Edogo no jiten* (The dictionary of the Edo language). The title *Shunshoku eitaidango*, mentioned earlier in the text and written in 1838 by Tamenaga Shunsui, is a parody on this *dango*, albeit a different kanji is used for the title. The tanka poem is among the collected poems of Fujiwara no Nagakata (1139–1191) compiled in the second half of the twelfth century. The obstruction Kuki speaks of here refers to the muffling of the birds' singing by the foliage of the trees or the birds' distance. Here the poet takes advantage of the double meaning of the word "*sudachi*"—"leaving the nest" and "grove." See *Kokka taikan* (Tokyo: Kadokawa shoten, 1986), 4:35, 686–687.—trans.]

87. [Kuki wrote the German "*freie Spiel*" in the marginalia of his manuscript, a term Kant uses in his discussion of taste in the *Critique of Judgment*, trans. J. H. Bernard (New York: Hafner, 1951)—trans.]

88. [Utazawa-bushi and Kiyomoto-bushi are types of singing popular in the late Edo period. The founder of the former was Utazawa Yamato no Daijō, a samurai, who founded this new school of singing in 1859. Kiyomoto-bushi is older, having gained popularity in the Bunka era (1804–1818). It was initiated by Kiyomoto Enjudayū (1777–1825).—trans.]

89. ["*Shibushi*" is an older form of "*shibui*," which in turn is an adjectival form of "*shibumi*" (understated, astringent).—trans.]

90. [Utagawa Kunisada (1786–1864), Torii Kiyonaga (1752–1815), and Kitagawa Utamaro (1753–1806) were all *ukiyoe* artists known for their woodblock-print designs.—trans.]

91. Concerning this problem, see [Emil] Utitz, *Grundlegung der allgemeinen Kunstwissenschaft* [Munich: W. Fink], 1914, 1:74 ct seq., and [Johannes] Volkelt, *System der Ästhetik* [Munich: C. H. Beck], 1925, 3:3 et seq. [Kuki's note 1, chap. 4 in original.]

92. [Both of these quotations come from *Harutsugedori* (A bird heralding spring), the first from sec. 3, vol. 7, chap. 14, and the second from sec. 3, vol. 9, chap. 17; cf. NKBZ, 47:493, 506, respectively.—trans.]

93. Iki pertaining to the sense of taste, smell, and touch has much relevance to the understanding of *iki*. We can say the following about iki, pertaining to the sense of taste. First, a taste that is iki is not simply a taste that is on its own and inde-

pendent from others. In *Shunshoku megumi no hana*, Yonehachi chastized someone for eating *tsukeyaki dango*, for consuming "something so vulgar," that is, something that offers the palate nothing beyond its taste. *Iki* taste is a spicy and complex one, as, for example, adding to the seasoning the aroma of *kinome* 'buds of Japanese pepper', *yuzu* 'yuzu citrus', *sansho* 'Japanese pepper', *wasabi* 'Japanese horseradish', and such. Secondly, *iki* seasoning is not heavy; it is light. To find *iki* in taste, one must look to *eitai no shirauo* 'whitebait from Eitai', *kemonodana no yamakujira* 'wildboar meat from the butcher's', and *Megawa no dengaku* 'dengaku of Megawa', rather than to *anago no tenpura* 'fried sea eel'. In short, *iki* taste is light and well modulated; it stimulates several bodily senses at once—smell and touch as well as palate. However, the sense of taste, of smell, and of touch does not become an *iki* expression as a physical manifestation; it is only that a kind of natural symbolism is manifested by means of "symbolic empathy." We can safely assume that natural forms of *iki* as physical manifestations express themselves concurrently with other sensations as well, notably sight and hearing. And, as for the visual sense, the words of Aristotle from the beginning of the *Metaphysics* apply here well, namely, ". . . [sight], most of all the senses, makes us know and brings to light many differences between things." (Aristotle, *Metaphysics* A, 1, 980a.) [Kuki's note 2, chap. 4 in original. It was said that Edokko's taste was so discriminating that, figuratively speaking, they would not eat the flesh close to the bone of *shirauo* "whitebait" harvested in the Sumida river. *Tsukeyaki dango* are rice dumplings grilled with a soy-sauce-based sauce. *Dengaku* is skewered squares of tofu that have been doused with spiced bean paste (*miso*) and grilled. This delicacy seems to have been marketed around Bunka 5 (1808) for the first time in Edo and thereafter gained popularity. The opening portion of Santō Kyōden's *Tsūgen sōmagaki* lists these and further attributes of Edokko. See NKBT, 59:357. The English translation of the passage from *Metaphysics* is from *The Complete Works of Aristotle*, ed. Jonathan Barnes (Princeton: Princeton University Press, 1984).—trans.]

94. [According to Homer's *Odyssey*, where the sirens were first mentioned, the women's singing was so magical that seamen passing by the island on which the women lived were unable to resist being possessed by it—and once the seamen were lured ashore, they were killed. In the sources that were consulted, there was no reference to the enchantresses' dancing. "Aspen" here could also be rendered as "poplar" or "abele" (Lat. *Populus alba*). The reference to any tree, however, is also uncertain as no known source makes reference to this in connection with the sirens; the island of the sirens is ordinarily described as one with a rocky shore or as having a grassy meadow.—trans.]

95. [Satyrs in Greek mythology are hairy, large-mouthed humanlike animals with horns, ears of a goat, hoofed feet, and large penises. Like Pan, they are good-natured, childlike, lovable wild animals who dance and play pipes and who often accompany Bacchus. Maenads are said to be some of the main participants of the cult ritual of Bacchus, a festival of orgiastic ceremonies and ecstatic rituals of communion. —trans.]

96. [Akashi in present-day Hyōgo prefecture was known for this fabric until mid-Meiji. The quote comes from Saitō Ryūzō, *Kinsei nihon sesōshi*, 817.—trans.]

97. [Ukiyoe are literally pictures of *ukiyo* "the floating world, this transient world." —trans.]

98. [The quote comes from the opening line of *Shunshoku tatsumi no sono* (Love-tinted garden of love), which was written by Tamenaga Shunsui and published during Tenpō 4–6 (1833–1835), sec. 1, vol. 3, episode 6. It can be found in NKBT, 64: 280.—trans.]

99. [*Benie* "red prints" are hand-colored woodblock prints typical of the early eighteenth century, especially in the Kyōhō era. They were printed in black contour lines only and were hand colored in *beni* "red pigment."—trans.]

100. [Suzuki Harunobu (1724–1770), Okumura Masanobu (1686–1764), and Torii Kiyomitsu (1735–1785) were *ukiyoe* print designers. Here Kuki is probably referring to a print in Utamaro's series "Fujin sōgaku juttai" (Ten examples of female physiognomy), as the series entitled "Fujo sōgaku juttai" is not known. For an example from this series, see *The Flirt* on the title page of this volume.—trans.]

101. [Bunka and Bunsei eras span the years between 1804 and 1830. Genroku era is from 1688–1704.—trans.]

102. [*Ukiyoburo*, published between 1809 and 1813, comically portrays the customers of the public bath in Edo. This quotation can be found in sec. 3, vol. 3 (NKBT, 63:228). Also see note 43.—trans.]

103. [Kant also discusses *Zweckmässigkeit ohne Zweck* "purposiveness without purpose" in taste, in the *Critique of Judgment.*—trans.]

104. [Yoshii Isamu (1886–1960) was a well-known poet and writer, most noted for his participation in the aestheticism movement in the late Meiji to Taishō eras. —trans.]

105. [The expression "playing jazz with both cheeks" refers to pouting quickly and provocatively as one sticks one's lips out with a sucking motion.—trans.]

106. [The cleaning powder used for bathing in the Edo period was normally rice bran, sometimes scented, placed in a cotton or silk bag, roughly the size of a hand. It was soaked in water and used like today's soapy sponge. The contents of the bag were discarded after each use. Soap was known to Japan as *shabon* (from Port. *jabon* or Sp. *xabon* "soap") beginning in the seventeenth century, but it was exceedingly rare and only a few were able to obtain it or knew how to use it (cf. Konno Nobuo, *Edo no furo* (Tokyo: Shinchōsha, 1989). Senjokō is a brand of *oshiroi* "white facial powder" makeup sold in the store Sakamoto-ya in Kyōbashi in Edo in the Bunsei era. (Maeda Isamu, *Edogo no jiten* [Tokyo: Kodansha, 1979]. Also see Maeda Ai's annotation in *Harutsugedori*, in NKBZ, 47:417.) This quote comes from *Shunshoku umegoyomi*, sec. 3, vol. 7, episode 14 (NKBT, 64:151). Kuki's comment regarding the application of light makeup in the preceding sentence can be corroborated by MM, 3:133.—trans.]

107. [Nishizawa Risō, active in the Kaei era (1848–1854), wrote a book called *Kōto gosui*, which contains a description of Edo women's makeup.—trans.]

108. [

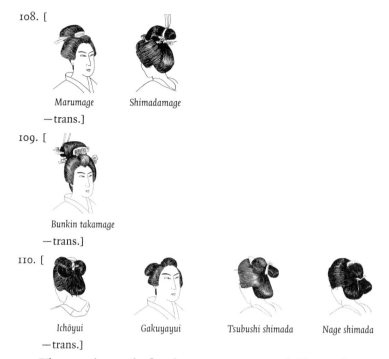

Marumage   Shimadamage

—trans.]

109. [

Bunkin takamage

—trans.]

110. [

Ichōyui   Gakuyayui   Tsubushi shimada   Nage shimada

—trans.]

111. [The quotation can be found on page 55, scene 1 of *Shikitei Sanba shū*, vol. 2 (reprint, Tokyo: Honpō shoseki, 1989), 39–102. See also Saitō Ryūzō, *Kinsei nihon sesōshi*, 807, where the same passage is cited. *Sendō shinwa*, the *sharebon* written by Shikitei Sanba, is the second in the series that began with *Tatsumifugen*. The third and last in the series is *Sendōbeya*. See note 86 above.—trans.]

112. [The reference is to Debussy's *Pelléas et Mélisande*, an opera based on Maurice Maeterlinck's 1892 play.—trans.]

113. [In contrast to the Western meaning of the word, décolletage here refers to baring the back of the neck by lowering the collar of the kimono. This practice gained popularity in the Kyoto-Osaka area beginning in Bunsei 8 (1825). See Maeda Ai's annotation in *Harutsugedori* (A bird heralding spring), NKBZ, 47:425.—trans.]

114. [According to Maeda Isamu (*Edogo no jiten*), ippon'ashi "one-legged" in the Edo area does not specifically refer to the application of makeup on the neck but to the hairline that drops low at the nape at two places, each on either side of the spine, and is left unpainted. One-leggedness comes from counting the unpainted space between the two downward hairlines. The method of deciding the "leggedness" was apparently different in the Kyoto-Osaka area, where the number of downward hairlines determined the leggedness. The quote can be found in Kitagawa Morisada's *Ruijū kinsei fūzokushi* (reprinted as *Morisada mankō*), 1927, 2:9 et seq. For more illustrations and an explanation, see MM, 2:116, 149.—trans.]

Ippon'ashi

115. [*Hidarizuma* refers to gathering up and lifting the front of the kimono with a left hand to facilitate easier movements of the feet. —trans.]

116. [It is not clear what *hatsuchi*, translated as "undergarment" here, refers to. It may be an orthographic variation of *patchi* "longjohns" (var. *hatchi*) worn by men, but a question remains if a woman with *iki* sensibility would wear these (cf. MM, 2:280 et seq.). It is possible, however, that Fukagawa courtesans, known also as *otoko geisha*, wore men's undergarments like *patchi*. Kuki cites the first quotation in the secondary source *Kinsei nihon sesōshi*, 668, where Saitō states that the quotation is from an Edo literary work called "Ikki yakō" (alt. "Ikki yagyō"). The second quote appears in *Harutsugedori*, sec. 1, vol. 3, chap. 6 (NKBZ, 47:426). —trans.]

117. [The passage is from sec. 4, vol. 11, chap. 21 (NKBZ, 47:540). The woman in the original is described as being a former courtesan with "no *iroke* but is a naturally beautiful and sophisticated woman, who has gone through many of life's trials." —trans.]

118. [The quote is from *Shunshoku umegoyomi*, sec. 3, vol. 7, scene 14 (NKBT, 64: 149) —trans.]

119. [Here Kuki probably had in mind burlesque revues he witnessed in Paris. —trans.]

120. The physical manifestation of *iki* can transfer itself naturally to dance. There is nothing artificial or unreasonable in that transition. Unreasonable artifice comes in when we call physical movements dance, name it an "art" form, and draw a line of demarcation between physical movements and dance. Albert Maybon, in *Le théâtre japonais*, says that "Japanese geisha are most ingenious when it comes to decorative and descriptive gesture." He goes on to describe dancing in these terms: "As to the interpretation of thought and emotion by means of physical movements, the Japanese school is inexhaustible. . . . Legs and calves mark and maintain the main rhythm. The upper body, shoulders, neck, head, arms, hands, and fingers are tools for expressing the psyche." (Albert Maybon, *Le théâtre japonais*, 1925, 75–76.) For the sake of convenience, we viewed physical manifestations of *iki* as a natural form and treated them separately from dance. An examination of the artistic forms of *iki* that are shown in dance will probably result in a repetition of the examination of natural forms, or in having to make only minor changes to such an analysis. [Kuki's note 3, chap. 4 in original. The comment by Maybon is as follows (Paris: Henri Laurens, 1925):

C'est ce que fait la *geisha*, «saltatrix» du Japon, qui représente les danses vulgaires. Gardons-nous cependant de mépriser cette officiante de maisons spéciales où l'on sert grands et petits repas: elle étale de la grâce aux yeux des convives, elle a une entente subtile du geste décoratif ou descriptif, du pas cadencé, elle sait tirer des cordes du *shamisen*, sa guitare, des sanglots et des rires et rendre son chant doucement expressif. . . . Sur ce chapitre de l'interprétation des pensées et des sentiments par la mimique, la science de l'école japonaise est intarissable. . . .

Les pieds, les jambes, servent à marquer, à garder la cadence dominante;

le torse, les épaules, le cou, la tête, les bras, les mains, les doigts, sont les intruments de l'expression psychique.

—trans.]

121. [Dodoitsu is a 7-7-7-5-syllable romantic verse that is sung in the colloquial language to the shamisen accompaniment, often composed impromptu. This form of entertainment was popular during the Tenpō and Kaei eras (1830–1854).—trans.]

122. [Here, kosode refers to a type of kimono with long full sleeves that was prevalent in late Tokugawa Japan. The nuihaku embroidery was designs stitched with silver and golden threads on fabric. According to Kuki's notation in the marginalia of a draft for this book, he obtained this information from Ruijū kinsei fūzokushi, currently known as Morisada mankō, 2:58. See also MM, 3:14–15, 120, 127.—trans.]

123. [Tenmei era lasted from 1781 to 1789.—trans.]

124. [Nanbujirimen (Nanbu [region] plus chirimen 'seersucker') is seersucker or crepe produced in the Nanbu province, presently an area of Aomori, Iwate, and Akita prefectures. Haori is a waist-length overcoat of light material tied in front, worn over a kimono. Tōzan is a woven cotton fabric, often with pale yellow, green, or dark red stripes woven into the indigo background. Santome is a fabric imported by Portuguese merchants (some say it was made in Holland) from São Thomé, then a Portuguese port on the Coromandel Coast of India (Jap. santome), or, according to another theory, the Japanese copy of the imported fabric (i.e., tōzan). The quoted passage comes from sec. 3, vol. 8, chap. 21 of Harutsugedori (NKBZ, 47:505).—trans.]

125. [Kujira obi is a kimono sash with different colors back and front. The obi that is described here is made of two pieces of fabric sewn together. One is black silk satin, the other blue purple seersucker with mountain silk interwoven. Mountain silk's resistance to dye would have created an effect of white stripes against blue purple background. (See, for instance, Maeda Ai's annotation for Harutsugedori, NKBZ, 47:406.) The Ueda weave is produced in Ueda in present-day Nagano prefecture. Kuki's quote comes from Shunshoku umegoyomi, sec. 1, vol. 1, scene 1 (NKBT, 64:47). Kuki's discussions of patterns of stripes seem heavily reliant on MM (see, for example, MM, 3:75 et seq.).—trans.]

126. ["Horizontal stripes" refers to stripes that run parallel to the weft of the weave, and vertical stripes are those that run along the warp. When making a kimono, the most common practice is to lay out the fabric with the warp running vertically. Thus, a kimono made from fabric with vertical stripes would have the stripes running vertically.—trans.]

127. [The Hōreki era spanned 1751–1764.—trans.]

128. [Noshime is a kimono made from silk primarily in a solid color excepting the waist area where stripes are woven in. In the Edo period, this was made into a kosode-style kimono and then worn under a formal skirt. Torizome is a dyeing technique (or the fabric dyed using this technique) where a small portion of fabric is dyed with fine stripes.—trans.]

Noshime

129. [Meiwa era spanned 1764–1772.—trans.]

130. [See Dessoir's statement "The effectiveness of horizontals is slighter, and so tends to be strengthened by repetition, by thickening, and by explicit involvement in the whole. Full-length horizontal lines evoke the feeling not only of breadth, but also of weight, of rest, indeed of sadness." Max Dessoir, *Ästhetik und allgemeine Kunstwissenschaft* (titled in English as *Aesthetics and Theory of Art*), translated by Stephen A. Emery (Detroit: Wayne State University Press, 1970), 363. The original German text reads as follows:

[D]ie Wirksamkeit der Wagerechten ist geringer und pflegt daher durch Wiederholung, der Verdickung und betonte Einbeziehung in das Ganze verstärkt zu werden. An durchgehende Horizontallinien knüpft sich nicht nur der Gefühlston der Breite, sondern auch derjenige des Lastens, der Ruhe, ja sogar der Traurigkeit.

Max Dessoir, *Ästhetik und allgemeine Kunstwissenschaft* (Stuttgart: Verlag von Ferdinand Enke, 1923), 357.—trans.]

131. [For a draft of *The Structure*, Kuki sketched his own conception of how horizontal stripes would work in a pleasing way on wooden sandals (seen from the top) (KSZ, 12:28).

Wooden sandals
(top view)

The other figure here illustrates the sandals from the side (prepared by the translator).—trans.]

Wooden sandals
(side view)

132. [*Sensuji* "thousand stripes, pinstripe" has broader stripes than *mansuji* "ten thousand stripes" within a given unit of width. *Komochijima* is a stripe pattern in which a stripe is flanked by a thin line, or is a pattern in which a thick line and thin one alternate.—trans.]

Sensuji   Mansuji   Komochijima

133. [

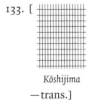

Kōshijima

—trans.]

134. [*Kasuri* is a dyeing and weaving technique in which the thread is laid out and dyed for a pattern before it is carefully woven into fabric. The pattern thus obtained is fuzzy around the edges, giving a look as if the pattern has been rubbed off. *Kasuri* designs are often representative but sometimes simply geometric.—trans.]

Kasuri

135. [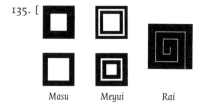

Masu   Meyui   Rai

Genjikōzu refers to a set of fifty-two patterns, used in incense games to signify a sequence of five scents of incense. First, five packets each of five different incense are prepared. Of these twenty-five packets, five are chosen for a game. Each player's task is to determine which of the five are same or different. After smelling incense in the first packet, the player draws a vertical line. If the scent of the second packet is judged to be the same as the first, another vertical line is drawn to the left of the first, and the tops of the lines are connected with a line. In this way, tops of lines are connected for the same incense; other lines are left unconnected. Each of the possible patterns is named for a book in the *Tale of Genji*, excepting the first and last books (*Kiritsubo* [The Paulownia court] and *Yume no ukibashi* [Floating bridge of dreams]).

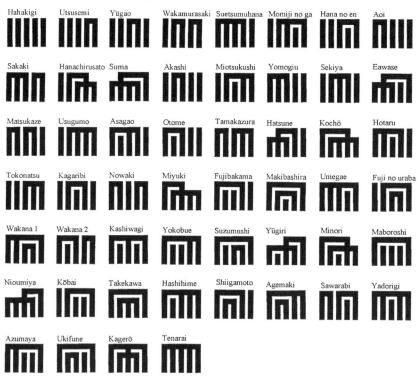

Genjikōzu

—trans.]

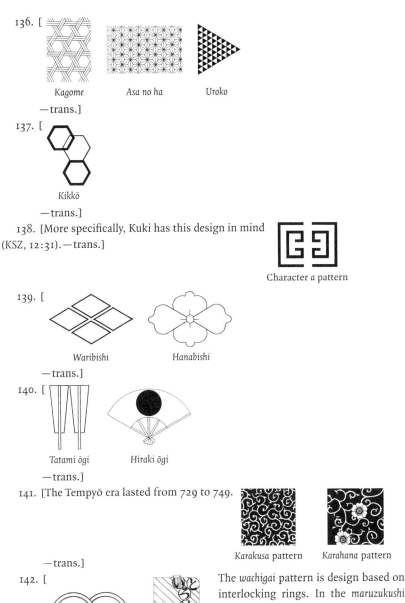

136. [

Kagome   Asa no ha   Uroko

—trans.]

137. [

Kikkō

—trans.]

138. [More specifically, Kuki has this design in mind (KSZ, 12:31).—trans.]

Character *a* pattern

139. [

Waribishi   Hanabishi

—trans.]

140. [

Tatami ōgi   Hiraki ōgi

—trans.]

141. [The Tempyō era lasted from 729 to 749.

Karakusa pattern   Karahana pattern

—trans.]

142. [

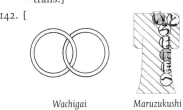

Wachigai   Maruzukushi

The *wachigai* pattern is design based on interlocking rings. In the *maruzukushi* pattern, each circle is often filled with a kana, numerals, and kanji for the names of the twelve zodiac animals. By "Fujiwara period," Kuki refers to a cultural period from approximately the end of the ninth century to the end of the twelfth. The Momoyama era is a cultural period, referring to the approximately twenty years during which Toyotomi Hideyoshi was in power, and sometimes the surrounding years (e.g., 1568–1615). The Genroku era is 1688–1704. — trans.]

143. See Dessoir, *Ästhetik und allgemeine Kunstwissenschaft*, 1923, S. 361. [Kuki's note 1, chap. 5 in original. Kuki translated the German corresponding to "immobile, worthless, and hateful" as *mukanshin na* "disinterested." The English quote is from Stephen A. Emery's translation of Dessoir's *Ästhetik und allgemeine Kunstwissenschaft* (titled *Aesthetics and Theory of Art*), 367. In the original German, we find the following text:

> Alle Wärme, alle Bewegung, alle Liebe ist rund oder wenigstens oval, geht in Spiralen oder anderen Bogenlinien! Nur das Kalte, Unbewegliche, Gleichgültige und Hassenswerte ist schnurgerade und kantig. Wenn man Soldaten in Rondellen anstatt in Gliedern aufstellte, würden sie tanzen, nicht sich schlagen.

Max Dessoir, *Ästhetik und allgemeine Kunstwissenschaft*, 361. — trans.]

144. For the concept of "Beautiful Objects Small," see Lipps, *Ästhetik*, 1914, I, S. 574. [(Kuki's note 2, chap. 5 in original.) Ger. *das ästhetisch Klein*. In short, this phrase means that beautiful things are small. See Theodor Lipps, *Ästhetik* (Leipzig and Hamburg: Verlag von Leopold Voss, 1914), 1:574–575. — trans.]

145. The passage comes from *Harutsugedori*, sec. 3, chap. 14 (NKBZ, 47:492). — trans.]

146. [*Shamisen* is a three-stringed instrument played with a pick (*bachi*), as shown in the illustration. The other is a design Kuki sketched incorporating a *shamisen* pick, which he believed to have had a quality that was *jōhin* (elegant, high class) but not *iki* (KSZ, 12:29).

A design
that is *jōhin*

Shamisen, with a pick

— trans.]

147. [Hon'ami Kōetsu (1558–1637), born to a merchant family in Kyoto whose business was to restore and appraise swords, was highly talented in all the arts, including calligraphy, painting, pottery, garden design, and lacquer work. He was particularly skilled in calligraphy. Kōetsu is generally regarded as the founder of the Rinpa school of art. Ogata Kōrin (1658–1716), a major figure in the Rinpa school, was a painter, potter, and lacquerer, who was very much influenced by Kōetsu. Themes favored by the Rinpa school were representative designs, sometimes stylized, such as bird and flower; nature scenes like clouds, rivers, and mountains; and people. Their artworks were executed in richly saturated colors, resulting in opulent and decorative appeal to the eye. — trans.]

148. [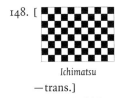

Ichimatsu

—trans.]

149. [A *tatami* obi is a type of obi that has no stiff lining and is worn folded over several times. The reference comes from *Kōshoku gonin onna*, vol. 3, by Ihara Saikaku (1642–1693), written in Jōkyō 3 (1686). *Dandara zome* is a stripes pattern in which each stripe is dyed with a different color. *Yūzen* is the technique of rice-paste-resist dyeing of cloth used in the Kyoto area beginning in the late seventeenth century. Also see note 70.—trans.]

150. There may be other reasons why the American Stars and Stripes and the sign for a barber shop are not *iki*. While both are unmistakably striped, they are not *iki* chiefly because the color is *hade*. Certain smoking pipes for women have a mouthpiece and bowl of silver and *shakudō* combined to create an effect of silvery white and dark bluish gray stripes. This design has formal characteristics in common with those of a barber pole, but the pipe is *iki* and the pole is not. Color makes the difference. [(Kuki's note 3, chap. 5 in original.) The *shakudō* metal is a copper alloy made from copper and small amounts of gold and silver, which is then treated in an acid bath. The metal takes on a very dark bluish color.—trans.]

151. [This quotation can be found in vol. 2, episode 3 of Tamenaga Sunshui, *Shunshoku koi no shiranami* (Love-tinted white waves of love), (Tokyo: Kotenbunko, 1967), 36–37. The iron club design *(tokko)* Kuki refers to is based on a *vadura*, an implement used in Buddhist ceremonies. The design was often woven into Hakata fabric.—trans.]

Tokko

152. [In other sources, *onando cha* is characterized as reddish navy (according to the annotation by Nakamura Yukihiko, NKBT, 64:47). It is also possible that *onando cha* is a base of navy to which other colors are added (see, for instance, Maeda Isamu, *Edogo no jiten*). MM suggests that *onando cha* refers to a group of browns, including *ainando* 'navy brown' and *tetsunando* 'reddish brown' (MM, 3:96).—trans.]

153. [*Tazunazome* is a dyed pattern of diagonal stripes, normally in red and white. A *bu* is one tenth of a *sun*, which is about 3 cm. Five *bu* will therefore be approximately 1.5 cm or three fifths of an inch. The quoted passage can be found in *Harutsugedori*, sec. 3, vol. 8, chap. 15 (NKBZ, 47:495). The apron referred to was worn by women, over a kimono, while doing housework. See MM, 2:127, 270.—trans.]

154. The reference comes from *Faust* by von Goethe, translated by Walter Arndt (New York: W. W. Norton & Co., Inc., 1976), lines 2038–2039: "Grey, dear young fellow, is all theorizing / And green, life's golden tree." The German original reads: "*Grau, teurer Freund, ist alle Theorie / und grün des Lebens goldner Baum.*" I thank Jon Mark Mikkelsen for bringing this reference to my attention.

155. [This phrase is a fused compound of "*omoizome*" (a newly found love; love in an early stage) and "*some cha no edozuma*" (*edozuma* in dyed brown). The word *some* (which becomes -*zome* in some compounds), meaning "beginning" and "dyeing," is the fused portion, with a playful, double meaning.—trans.]

156. [These browns are listed in Kitagawa Morisada's *Ruijū kinsei fūzokushi* (a.k.a. *Morisada mankō*) in precisely this order, suggesting that Kuki used this as a reference work (see MM, 3:96). As Kuki says, these colors from the Bunka to the Tenpō eras (1804–1844) were named after popular Kabuki actors in the Kyoto-Osaka and Edo areas. For instance, it is known that *shikan cha* was a particular brown favored by the actor Nakamura Utaemon III, also known as Shikan. It is recorded as becoming popular in the sixth month of Bunka 11 (1814). For a portrayal of this actor, as represented by the woodblock designer Kunisada, see the woodcut print on the title page for part 1 of this text. *Rokō cha* was named after a famed Kabuki actor Segawa Kikunojō II (a.k.a. Rokō, d. An'ei 2 [1773]). He was extremely popular for a few years beginning in Hōreki 8 (1758). See Suzuki Katsutada's annotation in NKBZ, 46:381. This particular shade of brown became popular again in the Bunka era. There is no known description of *shikō cha*, but the kanji characters for the color (市紅茶) suggest a reddish-brown persimmon color, the Ichikawa family's color for superheroes, favored probably by Ichikawa Danjūrō V (1741–1805), in his role in a Kabuki play *Shibaraku*. See K. Jinbō's annotation in *Ukiyodoko* (The world's barbershop) in NKBZ, 47:304.—trans.]

157. [According to Kuki's account, this phenomenon was named after Purkinje, a Bohemian biologist, who proposed a theory of color perception. Purkinje held that the perception of color varies according to the time of day. At dusk, reds and yellows appear darker, and blues and violets remain relatively bright. Thus reds and yellows diminish quickly in low light, while blues and violets linger. See "Bungaku gairon," KSZ, 11:34.—trans.]

158. [Kuki writes "*iki* **lives**," playing on the phonetic similarity between *iki* and *ikite iru* "lives."—trans.]

159. ["Teahouses" refers to eating establishments of various kinds patronized by customers of brothels, such as *ryōriya*, *machiai*, and *ochaya*, not to be confused with tearooms where tea ceremonies are held (*chashitsu*).—trans.]

160. [A four-and-a-half-tatami-mat room measures approximately nine feet square. The quoted phrase can be found in *Shunshoku umegoyomi*, sec. 4, vol. 11, scene 22 (NKBT, 64:216–217).—trans.]

161. [This Kafū quote can be found in *Nagai Kafū zenshū*, 10:240 (see note 17 above). Kafū is discussing here a woodblock print by Utagawa Kuninao (1793–1854) illustrating a scene for a *ninjōbon* called *Umemi no fune* (var. *Umemibune*), vol. 7.—trans.]

Shōji   Chōzu bachi

162. [Nagai Kafū, "Edo Geijutsuron," in *Nagai Kafū zenshū*, 10:241.—trans.]

163. [Both of these haiku are by Takarai Kikaku (1661–1707), a disciple of Bashō,

known for his flamboyant style. The legend alluded to in the first haiku is also mentioned in Yoshida Kenkō's *Tsurezuregusa* (Essays in idleness) chap. 18 and the third-century Chinese chronicle *Gao shi zhuan*. It concerns the ancient Chinese ascetic Kyoyū. When Emperor Gyō proposed to transfer his rank to Kyoyū, Kyoyū detested the idea so much that he went to the Eisen river to wash the vulgar proposal from his ears and secluded himself in the Kisan (var. Kizan) mountains. According to the legend, a man who saw Kyoyū drinking from his hands gave him a calabash to use for dipping water from the stream. Kyoyū did so until one day the sound it made hanging in a tree annoyed him. He lost no time throwing it away. See NKBT, vol. 30, for *Tsurezuregusa* or Donald Keene's translation *Essays in idleness: The Tsurezuregusa of Kenkō* (New York: Columbia University Press, 1967). For the Chinese chronicle, see Huangfu Mi, *Gao shi zhuan*, (reprint, Taipei: Taiwan zhonghua shu ju, 1965).—trans.]

164. [The quoted passage can be found in the very beginning prose of *Shunshoku tatsumi no sono*, sec. 1, vol. 1, installment 1. Cf. NKBT, 64:247.—trans.]

165. [Tatami, the traditional flooring used in Japanese homes, measures 3-by-6 feet and about 2 inches thick, with the core made of tightly bound rice straw. A matting woven from the rush plant (Jap. *igusa*) is sewn on top. Fresh tatami is pale yellowish green in color and slowly takes on a pale brown tinge as it ages.—trans.]

166. [In *saobuchi tenjō*, the ceiling boards are held up by wooden poles placed in regular intervals. In *ajiro tenjō*, the ceiling is made of woven mats, fashioned from very thinly cut wood or bamboo, and is held in place with poles placed at regular intervals.

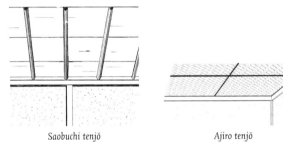

Saobuchi tenjō   Ajiro tenjō

—trans.]

167. [*Kakekomi tenjō* is the underside of a roof that is left visible, which in a sense serves the purpose of a "ceiling."

Kakekomi tenjō

—trans.]

168. [*Kekomidoko* is a floor raised above the tatami surface, with a piece of wood set

perpendicular to the tatami surface (called *tokogamachi*, var. *tokokamachi*), much like the riser of a stair, to mark off the raised *tokonoma* area. Shikikomidoko (a.k.a. *fumikomidoko*) is the wood flooring for *tokonoma* without *tokogamachi* and is therefore level with the tatami floor.

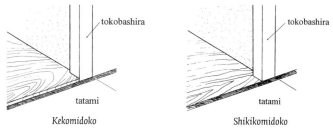

Kekomidoko   *Shikikomidoko*

—trans.]

169. [*Tokobashira* "tokonoma pillar" is a vertical piece that separates the *tokonoma* from the adjacent shelving. The most formal kind is made from a center cut of a Japanese cypress tree, but in *sukiya* architecture, it may sometimes be other types of wood with the bark left on, including *shi-tan* "red sandalwood," *kokutan* "ebony," bamboo, et cetera. *Otoshigake* is a piece of wood that is placed horizontally above the alcove that serves, as it were, the upper crossbeam of a frame that encloses the *tokonoma*, thus creating a lowered ceiling. Here a typical *tokonoma* is illustrated, with its principal parts identified.—trans.]

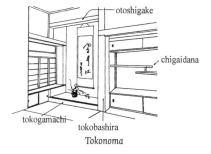

Tokonoma

170. [*Katō mado* is a more or less trapezoidal "flame-pattern" window that is often seen in Zen temples, fashioned to bring in outside light. *Mokkō mado* is an oval or circular window with four equidistant points on the oval or circle "pinched in."

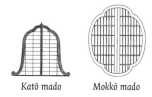

Katō mado   *Mokkō mado*

—trans.]

171. [*Ranma* is the decorative transom between rooms, above the sliding doors, most often fashioned out of wood. *Kushigata* "comb shape" refers to the slightly curved line of the spine of a wooden comb and signifies the overall shape of a *ranma*.—trans.]

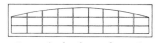

Ranma, in the shape of a comb

172. [*Shitajimado* windows are windows made as if stucco had not been applied completely, leaving an area in the wall that shows the inner reed mesh. It is used often in tearoom construction.

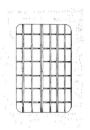

Shitajimado

—trans.]

173. [Kuki is most likely referring to neon light.—trans.]

174. [*Tasoya andon* (var. *andō*) "oil-lit paper lanterns" here refer to small streetlights that were placed in the streets of red-light districts. These were essentially similar to *tsuji andon*, which were employed in street corners elsewhere in Edo.

Tasoya andon

—trans.]

175. [Kuki uses "*tagasode*" in reference to an old custom of inserting a pair of small pouches made in the shape of kimono sleeves. They were, in effect, sachets tied with string. A pair of *tagasode* was placed in each of the sleeves of a kimono. The name *taga-sode* and the practice mentioned here appear to have originated from an anonymous *waka* in the *Kokin wakashū*: "*Iro yori mo ka koso aware to omō yure ta ga sode fureshi yado no ume zo mo*" (More than the color of the flower, the fragrance delights my senses—whose scented sleeve brushed against the plum blossoms near my house). *Kokinshū*, translated and annotated by Laural Rasplica Rodd with Mary Catherine Henkenius (Princeton: Princeton University Press, 1984), 58.—trans.]

176. *Tetsugaku zasshi*, vol. 24, number 264. [Kuki's note 4, chap. 5 in original. —trans.]

177. [The five-tone scale described here corresponding approximately to the tones in the Western musical scale are, in the ascending order, *hyōjō* E, *sōjō* (or *shōzetsu*) G (or F), *ōshiki* A, *banshiki* B, and *ichikotsu* (or *shinsen*) D (or C). The scale is presented in descending order in the text.—trans.]

Japanese miyakobushi scale

178. [*Nagauta* (or Edo nagauta) "long narrative songs" were popular *shamisen* music that developed out of accompaniments to Kabuki plays. *Nagauta* became a dominant form of popular music during the Kyōhō era. It was also used for dance as well as vocal solo. Kiyomoto is a school of *jōruri*, singing accompanying the Japanese puppet theater. It was founded by Kiyomoto Enjudayū in 1814 as an offshoot of the Tomimoto-bushi music style. Many consider it the flashiest, most *iki* of all *jōruri* singing styles.

Utazawa is a type of shamisen music that became popular at the end of the Edo period. Started by a group of aficionados and headed up by the high-ranking samurai Utagawa Sasatarō (later named Utagawa Yamatono daijō), it was hauta that was sung in a particularly shibui "understated, astringent" way. Hauta "miscellaneous songs" was also shamisen music popular in Edo at the end of the Edo period. It maintained popularity especially among those in the pleasure quarters and their patrons through the Meiji period, spreading through the general public by means of radio broadcasts and recordings.—trans.]

179. [Blue purple ([Edo] murasaki) was often synonymous with "yukari no iro" (color of yukari). The allusion is to an anonymous Kokinshū poem "Murasaki no hito moto yue ni Musashino no kusa wa minagara aware to zo miru" (Because of this one precious murasaki plant, I feel affection for all the grasses and shrubs growing on Musashi plain). Translated by Helen Craig McCullough, Kokin Wakashū: The First Imperial Anthology of Japanese Poetry (Stanford: Stanford University Press, 1985), 190.—trans.]

180. [Singing accompanying the first act of the Kabuki play Satomoyō azami no ironui (a.k.a. Izayoi Seishin). (See note 34 above.)—trans.]

181. Maine de Biran, "Essai sur les fondements de la psychologie" (Oeuvres inédites, Naville, I, p. 208). [(Kuki's note 1, chap. 6 in original.) A 1932 reprint of this essay by Maine de Biran reads as follows:

> S'il y avait, par exemple, quelque paralytique de naissance qui n'eût jamais agi volontairement pour remuer ses membres ou pour mouvoir les corps étrangers, en supposant que cet être pût avoir le moindre degré d'intelligence, ce qui me paraît impossible, il n'y aurait pas plus moyen de lui faire comprendre par des mots ce qu'est l'effort, qu'il n'y en a expliquer à un aveugle-né ce que sont les couleurs et le sens de la vue.

"Essai sur les fondements de la psychologie et sur ses rapports avec l'étude de la nature," in Oeuvres de Maine de Biran, ed. Pierre Tisserand (Paris: Librairie Félix Alcan, 1932), 8:180.—trans.]

182. Nietzsche, Also sprach Zarathustra, Teil IV, Vom höheren Menschen. [(Kuki's note 2, chap. 6 in original.) This translation can be found in chap. 13, "On the Higher Man," in Thus Spoke Zarathustra, trans. Walter A. Kaufmann (New York: The Viking Press, 1966), 293.—trans.]

183. Verlaine, Art poétique. [(Kuki's note 3, chap. 6 in original.) The relevant stanza in "The Art of Poetry" reads as follows (French, flanked by an English translation):

Car nous voulons la Nuance encor,	Never the Color, always the Shade,
Pas la Couleur, rien que la nuance!	always the nuance is supreme!
Oh! la nuance seule fiance	Only by shade is the trothal made
Le rêve au rêve et la flûte au cor!	between flute and horn, of dream with dream!

Paul Verlaine, "Art Poétique" in Oeuvres Poétiques Complètes, revised and completed by Jacques Borel (Paris: Gallimard, 1962), 326–327; Paul Verlaine Selected Poems, translated by C. F. MacIntyre (Berkeley and Los Angeles: University of California Press, 1948), 181.—trans.]

184. [Occasionalism sought to explain the causal connection (or occasional cause, *causa occasionalis*) between the Cartesian halves of the soul and the body, while strictly maintaining the separation. Kuki uses *causa occasionalism* to describe the bridging of the gap between a conceptual analysis of *iki* and the experiential meaning of *iki*.—trans.]

185. [This Latin interrogative pronoun *quis* means "who" when the referent is masculine or feminine, and *quid* "what" if neuter. By saying that we should first ask "who," then "what," Kuki espouses a Heideggerian approach to understanding *iki*, that is, we must first understand who does what (i.e., particular cases or *existentia*) before understanding what it is (i.e., *essentia*). For Kuki's own explanation of this, see KSZ, 9:404 et seq.—trans.]

186. Becker stated that "The study of Being of the beautiful must begin with the existential analysis that creates objects aesthetically (i.e., artistically) or enjoys them aesthetically." Oskar Becker, "Von der Hinfälligkeit des Schönen und der Abenteuerlichkeit des Künstlers," in *Jahrbuch für Philosophie und Phänomenologische Forschung, Ergänzungsband; Husserl-Festschrift*, 1929, S. 40.) [Kuki's note 4, chap. 6 in original.—trans.]

187. Paul Valéry, *Eupalinos ou l'architecte*, 15e éd., p. 104. [(Kuki's note 5, chap. 6 in original.) Paul Valéry states the following in *Eupalinos* (Paris: Gallimard, 1944), 34.

> Écoute, Phèdre (me disait-il encore), ce petit temple que j'ai bâti pour Hermès, à quelques pas d'ici, si tu savais ce qu'il est pour moi!—Où le passant ne voit qu'une élégante chapelle,— c'est peu de chose: quatre colonnes, un style très simple,—j'ai mis le souvenir d'un clair jour de ma vie. O douce métamorphose! Ce temple délicat, nul ne le sait, est l'image mathématique d'une fille de Corinthe, que j'ai heureusement aimée. Il en reproduit fidèlement les proportions particulières.

The translation that appears here is from Paul Valéry, *Dialogues*, translated by William McCausland Stewart (New York: Pantheon Books, 1956), 82.—trans.]

188. *Jahrbuch der Musikbibliothek Peters*, 1926, S. 67. [(Kuki's note 6, chap. 6 in original.) The quoted passage reads "toutes mes choses ont été faites de vostre sentement" and is found on page 67 of Heinrich Besseler, "Grundfragen der Musikästhetik," in *Jahrbuch der Musikbibliothek Peters*, ? 1926, 63–80. Besseler did not cite the source of this quotation.—trans.]

189. Lettre à Titus Woyciechowski, le 3 octobre 1829. [(Kuki's note 7, chap. 6 in original.) The letter in question makes only a fleeting reference to this concerto or to Konstancja Gladkowska, Chopin's love in his youth, who is referred to as his "ideal" in a letter to his best friend Tytus Woyciechowski: "[Panna Blahetka] is young and pretty, and a pianist; but I, perhaps unfortunately, already have my own ideal, which I have served faithfully, though silently, for half a year; of which I dream, to thoughts of which the *adagio* [sic] of my concerto belongs, and of which inspired the little waltz I am sending you." Henryk Opienski, *Chopin's Letters* (New York: Alfred A. Knopf, 1931), 69. The letter was probably written in Polish, a French translation of which Kuki must

have read. In Opienski's translation of this letter to English, however, "larghetto" appears as "adagio." — trans.]

190. Takahashi Yuzuru, *Shinrigaku* (Psychology), revised edition, cf. 327–328. [Kuki's note 8, chap. 6 in original. — trans.]

191. [Constantin Guys (1804–1892) was a French illustrator. Kees van Dongen (1877–?), a Dutch-born artist who later became a French citizen, exhibited with the Fauvists and later with the German Expressionists, the Brücke. For examples of Guys' work, see pp. 138, 140, and 141. — trans.]

192. [Charles Baudelaire, *Les fleurs du mal* (The flowers of evil), edited by Marthiel and Jackson Mathews (Norfolk, Conn.: New Directions, 1962), 94–95. The English translation by Barbara Gibbs reads as follows:

> Sad spirit who once loved the battle-ground,
> Hope whose bright spur used to arouse your flame
> No longer rides you! Sleep then without shame,
> Old horse whose stumbling feet furrow each mound.
>
> Resign yourself my heart, poor beast, sleep sound.
>
> Vanquished spirit with foundered feet, old jade,
> You find no joy in love nor in dispute;
> Farewell then songs of brass and sighs of flute!
> Pleasure, tempt not the heart in sullen shade!
>
> The spring is gone and all its odors fade.
>
> As the immense snows a stiffened body hide,
> So Time devours me momentarily;
> I contemplate the earth's rotundity,
> Seeking no hut's door where I may abide.
>
> Avalanche, take me with you in your slide!

— trans.]

193. [Charles Baudelaire, *Les fleurs du mal*, 72–73. C. F. MacIntyre provides the following translation:

> I
>
> Soon we shall plunge into the chilly fogs;
> Farewell, swift light! our summers are too short!
> I hear already the mournful fall of logs
> Re-echoing from the pavement of the court.
>
> All of winter will gather in my soul:
> Hate, anger, horror, chills, the hard forced work;
> And, like the sun in his hell by the north pole,
> My heart will be only a red and frozen block.

I shudder, hearing every log that falls;
No scaffold could be built with hollower sounds.
My spirit is like a tower whose crumbling walls
The tireless battering-ram brings to the ground.

It seems to me, lulled by monotonous shocks,
As if they were hastily nailing a coffin today.
For whom?—Yesterday was summer. Now autumn knocks.
That mysterious sound is like someone's going away.

II

I love your long eyes with their greenish light,
But, sweetheart, today everything seems bitter to me;
Nothing, neither your love nor your hearth at night,
Is worth as much as the sunshine on the sea.

But love me still, my dear! Be as a mother
To this ungrateful, even this wicked son;
Be the ephemeral sweetness, sister or lover,
Of a glorious autumn or a setting sun.

The tomb is hungry, and it waits! Short task!
But with my forehead resting on your knees,
Regretting this torrid summer, let me bask
Awhile in autumn's gentle yellow rays.

—trans.]

194. [Charles Baudelaire, Les fleurs du mal, 201. "Meditation," translation by Robert Lowell, reads as follows:

Calm down, my Sorrow, we must move with care.
You called for evening; it descends, it's here.
The town is coffined in its atmosphere,
bringing relief to some, to others care.

Now while the common multitude strips bare,
feels pleasure's cat o' nine tails on its back,
and fights off anguish at the great bazaar,
give me your hand, my Sorrow. Let's stand back;

back from these people! Look, the dead years dressed
in old clothes crowd the balconies of the sky.
Regret emerges smiling from the sea,

the sick sun slumbers underneath an arch,
and like a shroud strung out from east to west,
listen, my Dearest, hear the sweet night march!

—trans.]

195. Baudelaire, *Le peintre de la vie moderne*, IX, Le dandy. See the following for discussion of dandyism.

Hazlitt, "The dandy school," *Examiner*, 1828.
Sieveking, "Dandyism and Brummell," *The Contemporary Review*, 1912.
Otto Mann, *Der moderne Dandy*, 1925.

[Kuki's note 9, chap. 6 in original. — trans.]

196. [The full quote, in English translation, reads as follows:

Dandyism is the last spark of heroism and decadence; and the type of dandy discovered by our traveler in North America does nothing to validate this idea; for how can we be sure that those tribes which we call 'savage' may not in fact be the *disjecta membra* of great extinct civilizations? Dandyism is a sunset; like the declining daystar, it is glorious, without heat and full of melancholy.

Charles Baudelaire, *Le peintre de la vie moderne*, translated and edited by Jonathan Mayne (London: Phaidon Press, 1965), 28–29. — trans.]

197. [The English translation is as follows:

The strictest monastic rule, the inexorable order of the Assassins according to which the penalty for drunkenness was enforced suicide, were no more despotic, and no more obeyed, than this doctrine of elegance and originality, which also imposes upon its humble and ambitious disciples — men often full of fire, passion, courage and restrained energy — the terrible formula: *Perinde ac cadaver!*"

Charles Baudelaire, *Le peintre de la vie moderne*, 28. — trans.]

198. [Baudelaire puts it thus: "In truth I was not altogether wrong to consider dandyism as a kind of religion." Charles Baudelaire, *Le peintre de la vie moderne*, 28. — trans.]

199. [Charles Baudelaire, *Le peintre de la vie moderne*, 26. — trans.]

200. See Nietzsche, *Jenseits von Gut und Böse*, IX, "Was ist vornehm?" [(Kuki's note 10, chap. 6 in original.) This is available in English translation as *Beyond Good and Evil*, translated by Walter A. Kaufmann (New York: Vintage Books, 1966). See the opening paragraph of part 9, beginning on page 201. — trans.]

201. Nietzsche, *Also sprach Zarathustra*, Teil I, Von alten und jungen Weiblein. [(Kuki's note 11, chap. 6 in original.) The translation is by Walter A. Kaufmann and appears in "On little old and young women," in *Thus Spoke Zarathustra*, chap. 18, 67. — trans.]

202. [*Flatus vocis* "a breathing of a word" (also *nomina pos res* "name after a thing") is a phrase credited to Roscelin, the founder of early medieval nominalism, active in the second half of the eleventh century, who used this phrase to refer to universal concepts, which he believed did not exist. The phrase "ready-made" refers to Henri Bergson's admonition; in Kuki's own words: "M. Bergson nous conseille de ne jamais nous contenter de ces 'vêtements de confection que son nos concepts tout faits,' il nous montre 'la nécessité de travailler sur mesure'" (Bergson urged us never to be happy with "ready-made clothes

which are ready-made concepts for us" and showed us "the need to work to measure." "Bergson au Japon," KSZ, 1:260.—trans.]

203. ἅ ποτ᾽ εἶδεν ἡμῶν ἡ ψυχὴ (Plato, *Phaedrus*, 249c). A strong emphasis must be placed on ἡμῶν ('our'). But ἀνάμνησις ('recollection, reminiscence') has two meanings, both pertaining to self-realization. First, it means the realizing of the ethnic self, indicated by means of the emphasis of ἡμῶν ('our'). Secondly, it means that the idealism of the self realizes itself. This is based on the fact that there is a fundamental relationship between ψυχὴ ('soul, spirit') and iki ('pride and honor'). [(Kuki's note 12, chap. 6 in original.) The beginning part of Plato's *Phaedrus* (249c) from which this quote was taken reads as follows: "This process is a remembering of what our soul once saw as it made its journey with a god, looking down upon what we now assert to be real and gazing upwards at what is Reality itself." *Plato's Phaedrus*, translated by W. C. Helmbold and W. G. Rabinowitz (New York: Macmillan Publishing Co., 1956), 32.—trans.]

204. The etymology of the word iki must be elucidated ontologically along with its relationship to such words as **iki** 生 'life, living', **iki** 息 'breath, breathing', **iki** 行 'going', and **iki** 意気 'pride and honor'. There is no question that iki 'life, living' is the basic horizon of meaning for this word. There are two meanings that are associated with ikiru 'live'. One is to "live **physiologically.** Peculiarities based on the opposite sex are founded on this. Thus, "coquetry," the material cause of iki, arises from this meaning of iki 'live'. "Breathing" is a physiological necessity to sustain our lives. The relationship between iki and iki 'breathing' in *Haru no ume, aki no obana no motsurezake, sore o koiki ni nominaosu* "Umemoto in the spring and Obanaya in the fall. If a party gets knotted up there, have a drink and forget about it in style" is not simply that they happen to be phonologically identical. The word ikizashi 'breathing, appearance' proves this point. *Ikizashi* in *Sono ikizashi wa natsu no ike ni kurenai no hachisu, hajimete aketaru ni ya to miyu* "It looks as if it were the first scarlet lotus flower to open on a summer pond" must have come from ikizashi in *ikizashi mo sezu ukagaeba* "when I peered through it without even taking a breath . . ." Further iki 'going' has also an inseparable relationship to ikiru 'live'. Descartes argued whether or not *ambulo* could be the origin of understanding of *sum*. And, iki is clearly pronounced iki 'going' in such forms as *ikikata* "way of going, mode of transportation" and *kokoroiki* "disposition, temper." *Ikikata yoshi* 意気方よし is identical to ikikata yoshi 行きかた善し. As seen in such phrases as *suita tonogo e kokoroiki* "my sentiment to a man I love" and *Oshichi-san e no kokoroiki* "my feeling toward Oshichi," kokoroiki 'disposition, temper, spirit' speaks of "going to (someone)" in the structure ". . . e no kokoroiki." Both iki 'breathing, breath', in the form of ikizashi 'taking a breath, appearance' and iki 'going', in the forms of ikikata 'way of going, mode of transportation' and kokoroiki 'disposition, temper, sentiment toward someone', and akirame 'resignation', both formal causes of iki, have the roots in this meaning "living." When iki 'breath, breathing' and iki 'going' are heightened to the horizon of iki 'pride and honor', they both return to the original being of iki 'life, living'. In other words, iki 'pride and honor' means for iki to "live" in its fundamen-

tal sense. [(Kuki's note 13, chap. 6 in original.) Kuki's quotation "*Haru no ume, aki no obana no motsurezake, sore o koiki ni nominaosu*" can be found in *Shunshoku tatsumi no sono*, sec. 2, vol. 6, episode 10 (NKBT, 64:322). Umemoto and Obanaya were well-known restaurants in Fukagawa. The allusion to spring comes from the fact that Umemoto contains a kanji for the plum tree, which is symbolic of the season. Similarly *obana* 'flowers of an eulalia' is conventionally associated with the autumn. The phrases "*suita tonogo e kokoroiki*" (my sentiment to a man I love) and "*Oshichi-san e no kokoroiki*" (my feeling toward Oshichi) appear, according to Kuki's marginalia, in *Kokyoku zenshū*, 410 and 423, respectively. — trans.]

PART II

Essays

Outing at Mimeguri Shrine, 1788, woodcut on paper, 10 ¾ ×
10 in. (37.47 × 25.40 cm), by Torii Kiyonaga (1752–1815).
Carnegie Museum of Art, Pittsburgh. Bequest of
Dr. James B. Austin.

Capturing the Shudders and Palpitations
Kuki's Quest for a Philosophy of Life

HIROSHI NARA

The Structure of Iki is an intriguing book. Its subject might lead one to expect the worst—a treatise couched in the densely complex language of many a weighty philosophical tome. But Kuki Shūzō engages his reader directly, informally, conversationally. He makes use of everyday language and refers to aspects of Japanese culture and tradition familiar even to many Westerners today. The reader he had in mind is clearly the average educated Japanese of his time. Casual readers then and now catch the drift quite easily.[1]

Yet a reader inclined to linger will find Kuki's take on *iki* intriguing in another sense as well. His easy conversational style involves such a reader in the writer's quest for certainty on several levels, each quite challenging in its own way. As Thomas Rimer shows in his essay here, *The Structure of Iki* can be construed as a work of literature to be read in the spirit of philosophers Kuki admired, notably Alain (1869–1951) and Bergson (1859–1941). At the same time, on another level, Kuki is addressing what he had felt was desperately needed in the Japan of his time: a revitalized cultural identity. In this he appears to have been following the lead of works by his contemporaries, philosophers such as Nishida Kitarō (1870–1945) and Watsuji Tetsurō (1889–1960). A reader versed in philosophy will detect Western influences like Kant (1724–1804), Husserl (1859–1938), Bergson, and Heidegger (1889–1976) on what amounts to a hermeneutic analysis of the phenomenon of *iki*. Some readers will recognize Kuki's debt to Heidegger's analysis of authenticity. That connection gives *The Structure of Iki* pride of place as the first use of Western analytical methods to open up discussion of a quintessential aspect of Japanese aesthetics—one stubbornly resistant to straightforward analysis.

For all its promise of studious complexity and subtle coloration of cultural references, however, *The Structure of Iki* remains remarkably readable, a welcome change even for readers accustomed to the arcane writing in this field. This ease of access owes something to Kuki's smooth shifts between concrete details and abstract thought. He may offer an inside view of the exquisite life lead by courtesans in the Edo pleasure quarters in one sentence, and in the next discuss some aspect of Platonic realism or a twist Heidegger brought to the meaning of a word. The result is a mix that refreshes and delights the mind and senses all at once—in a book that warrants rereading.

Needless to say, the author of such a book piques our curiosity. We want to place him as a writer, know him as a man. Scanning his chronology at the back of this book, we yearn to get past its dry list of facts and dates. To flesh out this man, in the absence of a reliable biography, the best we can do is to sketch his life in this book, exploring such matters as formative influences, professional development, and the broader context of Japanese life at the time. Doing that will allow us to place the subject of his book in Kuki's life and time.

Since Kuki was born in 1888, he grew to maturity during a period of radical change in Japan. Pride from having become Asia's most powerful nation fed an upswelling of nationalist feeling. Kuki's youth was spent near the epicenter of these moments of transformation. His father, Kuki Ryūichi, was a high-level official in the Education Ministry's division in charge of the preservation of Japanese traditional art, and the man's devotion to Japanese culture was a powerful influence on his son. Another early influence was also an official in the ministry, Okakura Tenshin (1862–1913). This highly intellectual man was more than a colleague; he was also Kuki's mentor and family friend.[2]

As a young man Kuki was in many respects typical of the fin de siècle aesthete in the West. He was an accomplished amateur, a budding man of letters attracted to romantic, self-consciously decadent poetry and to study of the exquisitely demanding Edo sensibilities typified by iki.[3] He immersed himself in the works of Nagai Kafū (1879–1959). Books like *Kanraku* (Pleasure), *Reishō* (Smile of contempt) and *Sumidagawa* (Sumida river) appear to have sparked Kuki's interest in iki. His interest in poetry led to verse of his own being published in the literary magazine *Myōjō* (Morning star). His poems appeared in 1925–1926, while he was studying abroad. The author was identified only as S. K.[4]

First Higher School, which he attended, was known for its highly charged student culture. No doubt that effervescent atmosphere helped form the idealistic individualist Kuki became.[5] Another likely source of that outcome was the progressive social stance adopted by Christians in late Meiji Japan.

Christianity had its imaginative appeal as well, so it is hardly surprising that Kuki became a convert to Catholicism at the age of twenty-three.[6] He also studied hard in the humanities, on the advice of his professor of philosophy at Tokyo Imperial University, Raphael von Koeber (1848–1923).[7] From von Koeber Kuki learned that studying philosophy is itself a way of life. Convinced—for life—Kuki became a philosopher on a quest, and *The Structure of Iki* documents a unique part of that quest.

So how are we to understand such a book, and how does it lead to understanding iki? Both questions point to the difficulties posed by a cultural phenomenon as complex as iki. Take, for example, the problem of historical context. We must also consider Kuki's Japanese upbringing and education, and the social context in which Kuki lived and studied as he wrote his book. Add to that context yet another: the one he was writing about—the rather specific slice of Japanese life he was trying to view through the eyes of Edo Fukagawa connoisseurs, the exquisite gentlemen and ladies who cultivated the iki sensibility. And finally, in the interest of scholarly accountability, we must add this caveat: Kuki's understanding, like ours, will necessarily exhibit all the obvious limitations of individual human experience.

That complex interplay of contexts argues for the nuanced reading of the text attempted here—an interpretation sensitive to the text's author, his time and place. Such an interpretation, however, is certainly not absolute in any sense; it leaves room for other points of view. The meaning of a text or a cultural phenomenon like iki is not immutable, because interpretations, like personal and cultural frames of reference, change over time and are limited by the horizons of our experience. And, of course, the same is true of the objects of our study. Heraclitus might have said that no scholar can dip twice into quite the same work! In fact, the logical extension of that parable of the old philosopher's view of flux would have Heraclitus feeling obliged to add that the scholar himself would not be quite the same the second time around.

Let me now sketch the business of this chapter. Since Kuki's quest owes much to certain influences from the West, I will first trace Kuki's keen interest in the philosophies of Husserl, Heidegger, and Bergson, which developed initially from exposure to the traditional phenomenology of Husserl, then took a turn to embrace Heidegger. By the end of Kuki's stay in Europe, however, his ideas were distanced from Heidegger's and had become more aligned with Bergson's. I will say a few things about Heidegger's influence on Kuki here, reserving a fuller discussion of this topic for Mikkelson's essay. In the remainder of the chapter, I will focus on two aspects of *The Structure of Iki*. The first has to do with the rather unconventional technique Kuki used to argue his core conviction, that iki is an abstract idea seated squarely in the center of the Japanese psyche and that this idea defines Japanese ethnic identity. I will show that Kuki's analytical techniques overlook, quite systematically, certain scholastic rules of engagement—a lacuna that would have been immediately apparent to fellow philosophers. The second aspect I explore is the influence of Heidegger, using Kuki's work in general, and some circumstantial evidence, to show that the link between the two philosophers is not nearly as important as some have thought and may in fact be quite tenuous. My conclusion then summarizes these findings.

Kuki's Philosophical Orientation

That Kuki's work and worldview alike were indebted to strains of thought associated with the three prominent philosophers of his time, Husserl, Bergson, and Heidegger, can be deduced from the lecture notes and published works he wrote with his own students in mind. A more interesting, because more personally revealing, account of his philosophical debts and perspectives emerges from private sources such as journal musings, informal lectures, and poems. There we find Kuki pondering his intellectual forebears and feeling profoundly disillusioned with "desiccated" German idealism that dealt with ideas but not with life.[8]

That same disillusionment appears to have been the cause of Kuki's move from Germany to Paris in 1924, to study in the literature faculty of the University of Paris. In 1927, however, he returned to Germany, this time to seek out Heidegger in Marburg. Heidegger, young and upcoming and Kuki's junior by one year, was a well-known luminary on the intellectual horizon of the late 1920s. Certainly Heidegger's ways of thinking struck a sympathetic chord with this visiting scholar from Japan.

After his return home in 1929, Kuki lectured primarily on French philosophy, getting to be known as a Japanese specialist in that field. Amano Teiyū (1884–1980), a philosopher and close friend of Kuki at that time, attested to Kuki's affinity for the French, and for aspects of Heidegger's hermeneutic phenomenology as well.[9] Kuki's professional reputation appears to corroborate his friend's observations, as does the fact that Kuki was invited to contribute to a dictionary of philosophy the publisher Iwanami shoten was planning in the 1930s: All seven entries assigned to Kuki were related to French philosophy, on topics ranging from "Bergson," "life," "philosophy of life," and "creative evolution."[10]

Kuki studied phenomenology with Husserl, whose thinking clearly had a profound effect on his own. The influence of Husserl's phenomenology is manifest in Kuki's work on iki, notably in his choice of phrasing, such as "free variation" and "bracketing," and a notion of eidetic reduction. The work of Husserl's student Becker as well as neo-Kantians like Rickert and Herrigel also influenced Kuki.

Where Kuki parted company with neo-Kantians was on the issue of real-life focus. He refused to be confined, as many neo-Kantians were, to the purely intellectual realm. Neo-Kantians envisaged a method of finding objective truth from a subjective mode of representation (e.g., experience), hoping to provide a possibility for empirical sciences to be founded on philosophical "theory of knowledge." But Kuki wanted to go beyond conceptual analysis and yearned for meaningful, "wet" connection with the material world. Husserl and Bergson, but not neo-Kantians, helped him connect the two, as his study of iki shows. It was the notion of intuition that helped him make that connection. He found it first in Husserl. Then he found a useful analytical echo in Bergson's view of intuition as a method of grasping the essence of an object. Even though Husserl and Bergson viewed intuition somewhat differently, Kuki saw a kinship admirably suited to his own existential yearnings. What then, is, intuition?

Intuition in general refers to the awareness of basic notions whose truths are self-evident, transparent, immediately comprehended. Bergson's use of the word intuition was different. He was diametrically opposed to analysis that had become the core of the then-prevailing scientific approach to understanding an object. Bergson offered an alternative approach, one of intuition, to reach a Platonic reality. To understand an object completely and absolutely, Bergson would suggest placing oneself in the object itself, becoming intellectually sympathetic with it. This is the way one intuits the full signification of the object. Analysis, in Bergson's view, offered a description of the object from only one perspective and therefore it was in principle incapable of giving us the complete picture of it.

For Husserl, intuition (eidetic intuition) was one process through which one may perceive directly the absolute nature of an object ("essence"). For example, by examining instances of threeness that abound in the world—three apples, three children, three parasols, and so forth—one obtains a direct, immediate, and unequivocal understanding of the concept "three." When all objects are reduced via phenomenological reduction to their essences, we are able to reach the transcendental ego, or pure consciousness. Though Bergson's and Husserl's conceptualization of intuition were different, they shared important common ground—so much so that when Husserl learned of Bergson's construal of duration, Husserl is said to have proclaimed phenomenologists consistent Bergsonians. We also find Bergson's admiration for Husserl ran equally deep.[11] The affinity between the two is expressed succinctly in Husserl's motto: *"Zu den Sachen selbst"* (To the things themselves). Bergson's exhortation spoke more specifically: *"Plaçons-nous face à face avec la réalité immédiate"* (Let us face reality directly).

Evidence from Kuki's private life, as opposed to his public, professorial one, suggests a ready-made disciple, especially where Bergson was concerned. Kuki was particularly drawn to the Frenchman's conviction that life, to be fully known, must be encountered fully, in the here and now of concrete sense experience, not just in the abstract, idealized realm of experience beloved by the German idealists.[12]

Reacting to Darwin's view, where human evolution could be accounted for by the mathematics and mechanics of mutation, Bergson offered that all human activity had creative process inherent in it; life was therefore a continual creation, powered by a vital life force (*élan vital*). In his *Essai sur les données immédiates de la conscience* (An essay on the immediate data of consciousness), Bergson deals with two diverging approaches to understanding the essence of movement and continuity of time, which, taken together, define life. One approach is scientific; its tool is analysis. The other approach is philosophical; its tool is intuition.[13]

Time, change, and life, according to Bergson, were defined in qualitatively different ways by science and philosophy. Kuki wholeheartedly accepted that view. The scientific explanation of movement in terms of an object's spatial coordinates at two different points in time did nothing for one's grasp of the essence of life. The scientist's approach made Zeno's paradox a paradox, confusing two qualitatively divergent cardinal concepts of movement and the space traversed by an object in motion. Bergson contended that movement could only be understood intuitively, or, as he put it, by immersing oneself in moving (*le mouvant*).

Kuki used the same paradox to illustrate his conception of the coquetry of iki: "But [Achilles] should not forget to make valid the paradox of Zeno." He was of course aware of the scientific explanation of that paradox but agreed with Bergson that movement, and, by extension, life, could be properly understood only with the aid of intuition.[14] Bergson also argued that the only means of establishing continuity between two instances of pure perception is by way of memory. Memory makes continuity over time, or historical being, possible. Memory brings the past to the present, makes it meaningful to man, binds discrete experiences of perception into one organic whole. It would be good to keep these perspectives in mind while reviewing the conclusion of Kuki's book. There he admonishes his reader to understand *iki* by living it, since not doing so is tantamount to consigning *iki* to oblivion.

Kuki's commitment to *iki* runs deep, and yet, the note of personal, passionate engagement in his parting admonition is all but a surprise. His choice of words here makes sense only in light of his philosophical orientation at the time. By the late 1920s, Kuki had turned away from any idea that the philosophy must commit itself to dogged pursuit of abstract thought. He had turned toward the immediate and concrete, toward philosophy that embraces "the shudders and palpitations" of life itself. He had accepted Bergson's conviction that philosophy should reflect on life itself.[15]

Ultimately, Kuki's thinking about *iki* aligned itself with Bergson's thinking. Like his mentor, he thought that conceptual analysis—that mainstay of neo-Kantians—failed to connect its findings. Neo-Kantians may have gotten their conceptual moments right but fell short of the validation in connecting those moments into organic wholes. The issue of connectedness explains Kuki's insistent emphasis on the unitary nature of *iki*. *Iki* could not be grasped piecemeal. No single detail could speak for it, as might be the case with fashion's passing whims. *Iki*, he insists, must be seen whole to be seen at all. That is to say, *iki* must be understood existentially, through detailed, experienced awareness of *le mouvant*, the flow of life itself. This is not to say that Kuki followed Bergson in dismissing conceptual analysis as useless. On the contrary, he considered it a necessary part of any systematic philosophical investigation.[16]

Another of Bergson's convictions is relevant here too—his belief that education should emphasize the value of hands-on experience. He advocated teaching arts and crafts in school, convinced as he was that developmental intelligence moved, as it were, from hand to head.[17] Words alone cannot educate, Bergson declared. Education should develop not merely Homo *loquax*, the talkative human, but Homo *faber*, the maker, working hand and mind with Homo sapiens, the thinking, knowing human. Bergson acknowledged intelligence as essential for science and technology but insisted that metaphysics was ruled by intuition.

Later on in life, Kuki followed Bergson almost word for word in a lecture he gave to high school students in 1937. He entitled his talk "The Japanese national character" ("Nihonteki seikaku ni tsuite"), but his focus was on daily life. He argued that the best way to preserve Japanese culture was by nurturing love of the Japanese way of life itself. His was not a call to high-flown admiration in the abstract but to concrete, direct daily action. He urged youngsters to cultivate a love for things as purely and variously Japanese as martial arts, music, kimono, or even details of everyday life, such as tofu or *udon*. Like Bergson, he argued that intelligence (*chisei*) moved from hand to head and that the practical arts made abstract ideas more concrete.[18]

In general, one might say that Kuki's debt to Bergson was real and warm and human. The same cannot be said about his debt to Heidegger. This is not to say that his debt to Germany was any less important to his work on *iki*. One critic has in fact argued that Kuki's book uses the phenomenology of Husserl to analyze *iki*, framing that philosophical exercise in introductory and concluding chapters clearly indebted to Heidegger.[19]

What then does Kuki's interpretation of *iki* owe to Heidegger? To answer this question, we need to first answer another: "What did he think of Heidegger's view of aesthetics?" Kuki's notes for both classroom and public lectures include a great many references to Heidegger, as do his published works. Yet, none of this evidence points to anything definite in the way of help in formulating ideas connecting art and politics, or the role art should play in the national discourse. For that matter, Kuki's stance on totalizing aesthetics, an ideal of a political state that gives a nod to certain aesthetic consciousness and activity and oppresses other alternatives, is far from convincing. The general consensus today appears to be that Kuki's work owes something to Heidegger's influence;[20] and it can definitely be argued that *The Structure of Iki* must be evaluated in that light.

Still the Kuki-Heidegger connection remains problematic. In 1933 Kuki contributed a lengthy explication of Heidegger's philosophy to a textbook in a series on philosophy, published by Iwanami. In it, Kuki confines himself to discussing the material contained in three of Heidegger's works, *Being and Time* (1927), *What is Metaphysics?* (first published as an article then as a book in 1929), and *Kant and the Problem of Metaphysics*, also published in 1929. Perhaps more telling is Kuki's tone when he writes about Heidegger—the man and his ideas. One sees there no sign of kindred-spirit warmth but rather a tendency toward analysis that is notably cool. For example, writing about Heidegger's notion of *Angst* (and the similarly anguished view of life found in Kierkegaard's philosophy), Kuki draws a comparison between the man's tormented worldview and the gloomy climate and darkening political situation in which he lives.[21] In this and other instances, Kuki's descriptions of Heidegger's philosophy convey not a passionate admiration for Heidegger but rather a distant and somewhat unsympathetic critique.

It cannot be said, however, that Kuki turned his back on Heidegger or Germany. He clearly kept abreast of political developments there, noting in one place that philosophers Karl Barth and Eduard Thurneysen opposed the Nazis while Friedrich Gogarten and Emile Brunner supported them.[22] Kuki's library included two Heidegger items from later in the 1930s, one, a typescript of the speech he delivered in May of 1933, his inaugural lecture as rector of the University of Freiburg entitled "The Self-Assertion of the German University." The other item was a book published in 1936, *Hölderlin and the Essence of Poetry*.[23] Kuki's papers contain no direct evidence of his attitude toward Heidegger's contribution to National Socialism. His own position vis-à-vis the ideological climate in Germany is hard to assess with any certainty. I return to this issue later.

Both of my collaborators in this book bring rather different perspectives to the question of Kuki's philosophical orientation and its effect on *The Structure of Iki*. Kuki's book clearly lends itself to the piecemeal approach of teasing apart and identifying various philosophical tendencies and debts. But no one philosopher or school of thought accounts for the whole of it. In fact, neither extreme of analysis can speak for the spirit in which the book was written. That spirit might be thought of as analogous to the complex weaving of stripes designs discussed by Kuki as he pondered evidence of *iki* in the everyday lives of those seeking to engage in its paradoxical balance of cool detachment and passionate embrace of life.

Use of Evidence in *The Structure of Iki*

Kuki's style in *The Structure* may be described as light and, at times, notably casual. One is struck by a manner of discourse so earnest, yet so skillfully free and easy in handling the evidence it marshals. The effect is one of serious argument lightened by a certain playful exposition. Much of Kuki's style is inevitably lost in translation, but his manner persists and poses a kind of puzzle that even readers of the original may feel a need to solve. This puzzle is resolved if one thinks of Kuki's discursive technique as it relates to his goal of explaining *iki* in terms of ethnic identity vital to the spiritual renewal of Japanese society and culture. I present evidence that a number of anomalies in Kuki's approach served this overall objective quite well. His ingenious combinations of linguistic and literary instances do sometimes verge on the eccentric. His schematic representation may in fact strike some readers as eccentric beyond any reasonable doubt. Yet even that deviation from conventional scholarly practice in this area relates to the goal of Kuki's inquiry in *The Structure*. A closer look at those anomalies will show how vital they are to interpreting Kuki's writing.

Kuki's approach to language offers many clues to his agenda in *The Structure*. He plays with a number of pivotal words, discovering kinship clues in etymologies that tend to lean on special pleading. For example, he uses the aspect of homophony to justify connecting two very different understandings of the word "*sui*." Speakers of English could understand this example as tantamount to arguing that a word describing a religious ceremony ("rite") borrows strength from its homophonous "other" denoting a just or legal claim or title ("right"). In this case, Kuki finds that kinship between *sui*, a definable aesthetic preference identical in meaning to *iki* for Kuki, and the *sui* "sour" of salted plums. Readers of his chapter 3 will see how he uses an etymology to support a highly unlikely confluence of meaning and intent (see note 86 of the translation). Someone unsympathetic to Kuki's quest might find only cause and effect of purely verbal accident in this case. Certainly historical linguists will not support this instance. And there are others. Kuki declares that *hade* "flashy" derives from "leaves come out," presumably because it may be written in kanji as 葉出 (a combination of characters for "leaf" and "emerge"). Unfortunately, that rendering of the word would be considered nonstandard. *Jimi* "quiet" is often written as 地味, a combination of characters for "earth" and "taste." And while it is true that the elements of those two characters can be construed to mean "root tastes earth," the ordinary Japanese would consider that outcome farfetched, to say the least. Maybe the thing to say is that Kuki's thesis sometimes leads him to see happy verbal marriage where dour, correct linguists find only *mésalliance*.

A telling example of this tendency occurs at the outset, where Kuki in his foreword (in this volume) seeks to enlist the reader in the larger, life-enhancing goal of his analysis.

> A living philosophy must be able to understand reality. We know there is a phenomenon called *iki*. What is the structure of this phenomenon? Is it not, after all, a way of "life" that is particular to our people?

The ploy is transparent enough here. Kuki is taking advantage of a homophonous relationship available between *iki* "life" and the aesthetic sensibility of *iki*. Farther on, he links *iki* with the verb *ikiru* "live" (see note 158 of the translation). "*Iki* **lives** in the future, holding the past in its arms," he writes. That same connection reappears in a note (translation note 204), where he links *iki* with *iki* "living, life," *iki* "breathing, breath," *iki* "going," and *iki* "pride," stretching etymological likelihood a bit too far.[24]

What are we to do, faced with linguistic adventurism of this sort? We could, of course, dismiss it as absurd, self-indulgent etymological fantasy.

Doing that, however, would deprive us of important clues to Kuki's method and meaning in his book. We would do better to accept the invited inferences offered by his plays on words.

Heidegger's influence would surely be the operative (and instructive) one here. Kuki must have been well acquainted with his German mentor's use of creative etymologies. Heidegger used this technique to explore the potential interpretations and significance in common words to demonstrate the intimate connection between language and truth. For him, this sort of wordplay worked a kind of magic; it was a tool or conduit for direct access to truth.

Kuki's version of that technique was intended to help his reader see a vital connection between iki and what people — here understood as the Japanese — do to exist as humans. In this sense everyday life could be linked in a wordplay chain based on iki. Kuki seeks to persuade us that the Japanese live (iki "living, life"), breathe (iki "breathing, breath"), and move (iki "going"), all in the context of an ethos whose distinguishing spiritual characteristic is, in a word, iki understood as "pride."

The goal of his book was nothing less than reviving and reinvigorating a nation — the Japan whose iki aesthetic sensibility is peculiarly its own, the iki that makes Japan unique among nations, the iki of everyday Japanese life seen as a single self-creating whole. This is not to say that Kuki saw iki in danger of vanishing. On the contrary, he saw signs of iki everywhere. What he argued for in his book was more conscious cultivation of its promise of more authentic existence. That is the consciousness he sought to enlist through wordplay that we should see as creative and purposeful, not special-pleading whimsy.

In *Being and Time* Heidegger analyzed everyday human existence, which he called Dasein, literally "there-being." The constituent features of Dasein are three-fold: One is the fact that we find ourselves thrown into this world without prior knowledge or consultation and that we must remain there as long as we live. Its outlook is past and historical. Second, as revealed in the moods that concern us in some way, is that we live our lives transcending the limitations of the present and moving toward tomorrow's as-yet-unrealized possibilities. Its outlook is both present and future oriented. The third feature refers to our tendency to become preoccupied with immediate concerns and go offtrack, eventually becoming unable to progress toward future possibilities. When we examine the first two features, it makes sense to say that our existence in this world embodies past, present, and future all at once.

It is hardly surprising to find a Japanese student of German Dasein telling his countrymen that "iki **lives** in the future, holding the past in its arms."

Wordplay or no wordplay, that statement lies at the heart of Kuki's method and argument in *The Structure*. Bergson would have agreed with Kuki, for he, too, believed that it was memory of the past that would allow us to make sense of the present and push us into the future. By saying this, Kuki locates *iki* at the heart of Japanese life, past and present. The purpose of his book is to give that heart new life by showing the Japanese how *iki* can help define a better future, one uniquely theirs. That is the message of his opening and closing chapters. One might say that Kuki's wordplay is borrowed from his German mentor: evidence of philosophical method and serious purpose, not linguistic ignorance.

This is not to say that Kuki's way with words can't seem fanciful to a fault at times. The treatment of aesthetic sensibilities in his chapter 3, "The Extensional Structure of *Iki*," may qualify as his most challenging in that way. His interest in a highly systematized approach is evident from the start. He introduces the oft-discussed rectangular prism he uses to chart relationships among four pairs of words that account for the aesthetic sensibilities basic to *iki*. Here the researcher has the advantage over the general reader. Kuki's preference for visual representation is abundantly evident. His personal notes and drafts for articles and books teem with graphs and diagrams. A few found their way into published work: "Fūryū ni kan-suru ichi-kōsatsu" (A Study of Fūryū) features an octahedron; "Jōcho no keifu" (A System of Lyricism) charts emotions with arrows and lines on a diagram. Surviving sketches in manuscripts show Kuki's trying out of triangular prisms, squares, and hexahedrons before making his final choice for *The Structure of Iki*.[25]

Trouble is, no amount of conscientious conviction on Kuki's part dispels one's feeling that his rectangular prism hangs more questions in the air than it can anchor. The placement of these pairs of aesthetic sensibilities ought to signify, but does it really? Why should *iki* be equidistant from *shibumi* and *amami* while *jōhin* lies somewhat farther off? Why is the pairing *yabo-gehin* not placed next to *iki-jōhin*? Yes, the words themselves relate, but their meaningful relations are too fluent to be held by any such scheme. Words, unlike the elements on chemistry's periodic table, are not quantifiable. Their meanings can't really be fixed, much less be easily affixed to a scheme implying immutable relationship. Numbers of critics have taken issue with Kuki here.[26]

His own claim for this visual mode of representation, in the closing paragraph of his chapter 3, ends on this note:

> In summary, the value of a graphic representation of this rectangular prism lies in the fact that a functional relation exists between the names

of various tastes like *iki* and in the fact that we can place these names on the surface or in the interior of this rectangular prism.

Kuki doesn't say just how he arrived at the arrangement proposed. One is forced to assume that he thought his prism clarified a set of complex relationships by making it instantly obvious, say, that *iki* lies somewhere between *amami* "sweetness" and *shibumi* "astringency." He can scarcely have thought that terms so general could aspire to the precision of a mathematical model.

Even assuming that pairs of words can be usefully cross-referenced in such a scheme, there remains the problem of terms that don't pair up so easily. *Kiza* "affected" would be one such semantic singleton. It doesn't figure here. Neither do *sabi*, *miyabi*, *aji*, *otsu*, and *irroposa*. It may well be that Kuki omits them as aesthetic sensibilities not arising from the three moments he posits at the outset of his chapter 2. Yet doing that would relegate them to merely tangential status. *Chic* is situated between *jōhin* and *iki*, and *raffiné* between *iki* and *shibumi*; this is after Kuki himself pointed out that meaning is culturally defined and no simple equation of this sort is possible. One can't help feeling that Kuki's argument for a core Japanese aesthetic sensibility is impoverished, not enriched, by this selective ploy. It would appear to make *iki* the touchstone for deciding the worth of every distinctive Japanese aesthetic concept.

Kuki strays into other peculiar byways, as when he assembles evidence to substantiate his claim that the locus classicus for *iki* is to be found in the Bunka and Bunsei eras (1804–1830). His claims for effects of *iki* specific to this time and place are exceedingly hard to substantiate. For example, he makes much of certain striped designs embodying *iki* in Bunka-Bunsei Edo. There is simply no hard evidence that fashion issued, much less followed, dictates so clear-cut and prescriptive with respect to *iki*, at that or at any time in the city of Edo or elsewhere.[27] On the contrary, historical evidence suggests that pattern styles were rich and various all through the Edo period. It was hardly a time for the highly restrictive dress code Kuki describes as separating those who were *iki* from those who were not.

Correcting authors long since dead is at best a mournful pleasure, though in this case the evidence itself is lovely to look at, as anyone can see who researches fashion in the Edo period generally. There one meets an astonishing array of patterns with names like *komon* "finely patterned," *kasuri* "spatter and daub," *asa no ha* "hemp leaf," *hanagatsumi* "small flowering plant pattern," and *manjitsunagi* "connected reverse swastika pattern."[28] One of Kuki's own sources, the *Morisada mankō*, mentions that the *asa no ha* and *hanagatsumi* patterns were both exceedingly popular in the Bunka and Bunsei eras. Neither would match his criteria for patterns possessing *iki*.[29] Worse yet, it would be very hard to say just which patterns were in style at any part of a thirty-year period notable for its quick-to-change attitude to fashion.[30]

The historical record for the Edo period in general, late Edo in particular, is complicated by the fact that each of many regions of Japan produced its own rich variety of textiles. All manner of silk and cotton fabrics were woven, dyed, embroidered, and textured (as with crepe) in highly localized designs and techniques. Add to all that a similar embarrassment of riches imported from China toward the end of the period and there you have it: an astonishing, seemingly inexhaustible range of choices. Even a compendium like the *Morisada mankō* could not encompass all of it. Small wonder, then, that Kuki's vision of Bunka-Bunsei Edo exquisites led him, on principle, to imagine them confining their choices to pattern in stripes arrayed just so, in accord with the *iki* sensibility he was seeking to reclaim as his country's own.

Kuki's approach to the history of costume invites similar reservations. He uses the following passage from the *Harutsugedori* (A bird heralding spring) as evidence of *iki* sensibility in a customer of a courtesan:

> the overcoat is dark brown . . . made from **striped** crepe from Nanbu . . . the *haori* coat is of *tōzan* in black and white **stripes** . . . and other accessories, too, are just as *iki* as these garments, as you should know. (p. 42)

Kuki fails to mention that this man is wearing an "indigo-colored belt from Hakata in a single iron club pattern." The pattern referred to alternated stripes with a chain of delicately rendered iron clubs, a design complexity that would not have met Kuki's criteria for *iki*.[31]

A lengthy quotation from the *Shunshoku koi no shiranami* (Love-tinted white waves of love) is also problematic:

> [The weave of the overcoat] incorporated a small and delicate checkerboard pattern with **deep orange** thread against **gray** in a formal crepe material. The *obi* was sewn from two pieces, one is an old-fashioned domestic weave, the other in a **navy** weave from Hakata without the iron club design of two **dark brown** lines woven in. (pp. 46–47)

Kuki adds that both over- and undergarments were "perfectly tailored, both with satin cuffs in **grayish navy** reminiscent of **green pine needles**" (p. 47). Here the mention of checkerboard pattern is inconsistent with Kuki's declaration early on that wide intersecting patterns, but not small or delicate ones, embody *iki* sensibility.

> The checkerboard pattern created by the widest of all intersecting stripes can be an expression of *iki*. For this to occur, however, the eye must pursue the duality in vertical parallel lines without interruption, unhindered by the horizontal parallels. (p. 44)

This inconsistency might pass for a trifle were it not for the fact that the *Shunshoku* passage he cites piecemeal contains, in its entirety, more evidence that Kuki read his sources—to put it charitably—selectively. For example, the courtesan's customer wears an undergarment bearing a *sumie* "ink painting" design created by four famous artists in collaboration—as well as a stamped red flower design. Add to that a design on the reverse of the fabric, a tie-dyed flower motif.[32] *Sumie* can render a scene on any theme using birds, flowers, figures, or landscape—in any case, a richness of complication scarcely compatible with Kuki's understanding of *iki*.

On a different note, sorting through historical evidence sifted so selectively by Kuki, it is pleasantly surprising to discover a richly layered aesthetic vocabulary Kuki saw fit to leave out of his discussion of *iki*. Alongside *iki* and its supposed synonym *sui*, we find a number of words that speak for a range of related sensibilities in *kibyōshi* "yellow-covered storybooks" and *ninjōbon* "romance novels" at around the same time.[33] The list of such words is far too long to consider here, though a sampling shows what is—and isn't—lost in Kuki's treatment of this evidence. As might be expected in a context of *iki* refinement and discriminating restraint, the concept of "connoisseur" is subject to any number of qualifications. So it is that we range from *tsū* "connoisseur" to *daitsū* "great connoisseur," and *tsūshi* "gentleman connoisseur" all the way to the derogatory *hankatsū* "demi-connoisseur." We also find terms clearly belonging to a highly self-conscious fashionable elite: *hasuha* "stylish," *otsu* "smart," *koiki* "a tiny bit *iki*," *share* "witty and refined," *kinkin* "fashionable," *hade* "flashy," *ada* "charming," *adappoi* "exuding charm," *isami* "dashing," and *nigamibashitta* "handsome."

Of all the above, only *hade* and *otsu*, and tangentially *koiki*, find a place in *Iki no kōzō*. Here, at least, Kuki's selective approach makes sense. Even a casual perusal of the many *ninjōbon* and *kibyōshi* books of the time indicates that *iki* was indeed the dominant sensibility in the late eighteenth and early nineteenth centuries. Though the word itself was first applied to connoisseurs of the pleasure quarters, *iki* took on a wide range of meanings capable of expressing subtle refinements of taste and attitude in every department of life. Matters as material as food and clothing could embody *iki;* so could matters as ineffable as choice of color or pattern or musical tone or harmony.

In fairness to Kuki it must be said that most of the words he chose not to discuss were not essential to his thesis. A good many were confined to rather narrow semantic domains. Examples would be *tsū, hankatsū, daitsū, otsu,* and *kinkin.* Some, like *kinkin,* appear to have passed out of use rather quickly.

Nakano Mitsutoshi sheds light on a related phenomenon. He found instances in which the kanji 雅 and 通, normally read as *miyabi* and *tsū,* meaning "elegance" and "connoisseur" respectively, had the pronunciation "*iki*" written alongside. He also found that the character for *sui* in *kibyōshi* and *ninjōbon* texts was routinely read as "*iki,*" suggesting that they are co-referential. Nakano claims that *sui, tsū,* and *iki* diverged from a shared etymology. First *sui,* prevalent in the early Edo period, gave way to *tsū* in mid Edo. *Iki* came into its own in late Edo, widening its range of connotations even as *sui* and *otsu* retained their narrower focus.[34]

Clearly it will never do to underestimate the difficulty posed by words given multiple, mutable meanings by persons of fashion long since dead and largely forgotten. *Share* and *kinkin,* for example, meant "fashionably dressed." Someone "dressed fit to kill," most often a man, could be either *share* or *kinkin.* Like many words at any time, especially words in contexts as evanescent as judgments on beauty and fashion, these late eighteenth- and early nineteenth-century terms lived in a state of flux. The changeable subtle differences they conveyed to speakers at that time just don't speak that reliably in the written evidence. No wonder Kuki opted for rigorous selectivity, faced with such a shadow-play of words. Still, it does appear that he made too much of *iki* at the expense of other words. True, *iki* was a dominant word in Bunka-Bunsei Edo; and it may have outlasted the other aesthetic keynote terms of those eras. But still it seems too much to claim that *iki* alone could speak for the spirit of the age.[35]

Another mystery of Kuki's historical method has to do with the *ukiyoe* prints of Bunka-Bunsei courtesans. Why would he ignore this obvious source of cultural and visual information?[36] Here again, we find a puzzling balance of pros and cons.

Kuki was well acquainted with Kitagawa Morisada's cautionary notes in *Morisada mankō* on *ukiyoe* prints. Morisada warns his readers that prints were highly idealized costume portraits of fashionable clothing worn by leading actors of the day. He considers them extremely unreliable as depictions of real-life manners and modes of dress.[37] Kuki had access to an edition of *Mori-*

sada mankō, which bore the earlier title *Kinsei fūzokushi* (History of modern popular culture). We know from his papers that Kuki studied *Morisada* carefully. Surviving manuscript drafts of *Iki no kōzō* have citations from *Kinsei fūzokushi* written in the margins. Kuki could have seen quite clearly in these prints that stripes were worn as early as the second half of the eighteenth century and were quite popular thereafter, for nearly a century, in fact. Moreover, what did it matter that these resplendent costumes belonged to actors? Actors set the fashion then. They led where others followed. Kuki himself cites a number of instances in which a famous actor popularized his favorite color.[38] Even so, Kuki took note of this well-known source of evidence and, for reasons unknown, ignored it.

Another seeming contradiction has to do with his use of two works by Tamenaga Shunsui (1790–1843), *Shunshoku umegoyomi* (The love-tinted plum calendar) and *Shunshoku tatsumi no sono* (Love-tinted garden of love). Shunsui's nineteenth-century historical recreations of Japanese life seem perfect for Kuki's purposes. Both books combine contemporary literary references beautifully illustrated in 156 plates all told. We learn from Kuki that three characters in particular—Yonehachi, Tanjirō, and Adakichi—possess the quintessential characteristics of *iki*. Their costume portraits, however, most often show them dressed in ways that do *not* embody *iki*.[39] There are significant exceptions. One illustration shows a woman dressed in accordance with Kuki's definition of *iki*. Shunsui, however, identifies her as the epitome of everything feminine and *ada* "charming," not *iki*.[40] This may not be a perfect match, but it does lend a suitable echo to Kuki's argument, since *ada* figures in his constellation of terms describing the aesthetic sensibility of *iki*.

Here, too, Kuki borrowed selectively from the text and ignored the prints entirely. His reason for that preference could be the same: Shunsui's illustrators, like the *ukiyoe* printmakers, presented dress for visual effect, not historical accuracy. That argument in this case is compromised by the fact that Shunsui's text is a construct, too, a novelistic re-creation of the past, with all that implies in the way of creative liberty. Yet Kuki used Shunsui as a source of evidence without the scholarly caveat that surely his readings warrant.

Kuki does fall back on visual evidence for one aspect of his argument, namely, the claim that women just after bathing embody *iki*. Here he ranges widely, discussing prints by Suzuki Harunobu (1724–1770), Okumura Masanobu (1686–1764), Torii Kiyomitsu (1735–1785), and Kitagawa Utamaro (1753–1806). The dates of their lives show clearly that, of all these artists, only Utamaro created images likely to bear witness to life in the Bunka and Bunsei eras. Yet Utamaro's prints, like those issued by the others, suggest nothing beyond the possibility that a woman fresh out of the bath might be seen to embody iki, no matter how she dresses. None of these printmakers dressed their women in a style that would answer to Kuki's description of iki.[41]

Leaving aside the question of a scholar's right to let the thesis direct his research, the absence of clear evidence in the work of these printmakers is puzzling. Surely if iki was so important to the connoisseurs of Bunka-Bunsei Edo, one or two images of women after bathing would confirm the iki value put on that exquisite moment. True, many of the women (and some men) in these prints do wear stripes; but the uncommitted viewer would be hard put to see iki dictating terms for those stripes as Kuki does. The disparity is all the more noticeable for the fact that iki stripes in these prints, as often as not, are worn with designs that do not embody iki.

What, then, are we to think of Kuki's research and conclusions? He seems to have viewed research as a matter of finding what he was looking for, even if it meant looking away from evidence that ran counter to his purpose. We have seen how much of that evidence suggests that his notion of iki was too rigid, too exacting to consort with the actual facts of human behavior, especially the behavior of a privileged, self-conscious, aesthete elite. But say we agree that he succeeds in establishing the sensibility of iki as central to the life of Fukagawa in the early nineteenth century. Does that prove that iki prevailed elsewhere in Edo, or in Japan as a whole? Surely not. In fact, the number of patrons who could afford the pleasures of Fukagawa would have been small to begin with; and the number of those who aspired to iki would have been much smaller still. We can thank Kuki for making that quite clear. Iki was for those folks whose notion of a life of pleasure required self-discipline to the utmost degree. He might have added that, even so, no discipline is proof against our human tendency to change over time. Even if iki ruled its elite in early nineteenth-century Edo, it seems highly unlikely to have survived un-changed into his own early twentieth century.

Kuki knew all that and that his reader likely knew it, too. He was, after all, an educated man addressing educated colleagues and students engaged in the process of learning. And so he pressed on to his sweeping bold con-clusion: that iki is the core value of Japanese ethnic being.[42] That conclusion itself demanded a commonsense freedom from his own selective research. Having caught the essence of iki in Bunka-Bunsei Fukagawa, he left the spe-cifics where they belong, in that definitive time and place in history. His con-cluding statement makes that clear. The iki he urges his countrymen to revive represents a cultural ideal. As such, he saw it as transcending many contemporary specifics as well—much, in fact, of the messy business of everyday real life. Kuki had, in effect, made *iki* into a rarified ideal.

One might expect such a construct to be built on solid foundations of scrupulous research and systematic argument—both notably shaky where Kuki is concerned. Or so it might appear. My colleagues in this volume have interesting things to say on that score.

Thomas Rimer makes a case for viewing *The Structure* as a literary work in a genre perfected by the French as a vehicle for light and lively argument, worlds apart from the plodding gloom of many a philosophical tome. Mikkelsen argues that Kuki's audience would not have mistaken his work for a systematic philosophical treatise on Japanese aesthetics. He shows how *The Structure* would have elicited respect of a different sort. The layman might not have seen it as such, but to Kuki's colleagues in Kyoto, his sources were too eclectic and his approach to them too elastic to submit to the strictures of any one philosophical discipline.

Rimer and Mikkelsen would agree, in sum, that *The Structure* should be seen as deliberately unsystematic, or Rimer might say "even playful."[43] To be sure, the Japanese, like the French, have a tradition of arguing serious matters with verve and wit. Kuki's contemporaries would have relished the *zuihitsu*-like informality of his book. Too literal a reading robs *The Structure* of its witty liveliness. Lose sight of that quintessence of style and we risk the really damning distortion it would be to bracket Kuki's work with Heidegger's view on art with all its troubled connections to German National Socialism.

Kuki and Nationalism During the Interwar Years

Kuki's claims for *iki* at such a troubled time in world and Japanese history were bound to involve him in a national debate whose social and political outcomes still resonate in discussions of him and his work. Leslie Pincus aptly describes this conundrum in her 1996 study of Kuki. Reduced to its essence, the question is: Did Kuki promote a brand of aesthetic vision, claimed to be ethnically unique, for a political purpose? If so, did his ideas serve the cause of Japanese imperialist expansion in the 1930s?

First, did Kuki promote this uniquely Japanese vision—a purified ideal, detached from its time and place? Kuki's proposed aesthetic was not to be the property of the contemporary equivalent of a privileged Fukagawa few. *Iki* would inform every aspect of national as well as personal life. So the answer to our question would be "yes," but with an important qualification, that we do not yet know whether he did this with a political purpose. Did his writing contribute to the prevailing militarism? Did Kuki intend it to be so? If we follow this line of thinking, we might hear Kuki say that iki was not just about color and kimono; it was all things Japanese to all Japanese; it was a force for ethnic good, for living every day in possession of identity and destiny uniquely Japanese. If we follow along this trajectory a little further, we would hear Kuki say that to understand this totality of iki is to understand why the prewar German model was relevant. Then it's only a theoretical stone's throw away from claiming that the word *totalitarian* helps us understand how what seems a well-intentioned ivory-tower treatise involved Kuki in troubling questions then—questions still troubling now.

Kuki did not take this second step. The German model is relevant, for a different reason, since Kuki's mentor Heidegger played a role in National Socialism's drive to refine and purify its totalitarian master race. But should Heidegger's influence on Kuki be seen as casting so dark a shadow? Mikkelsen discusses in his essay the specifically philosophical aspects of that question. For its personal and literary aspects, let us turn to Kuki himself, to evidence contained in *Kuki Shūzō zenshū* (The complete works of Kuki Shūzō) and examine what Kuki himself has to say about where he stands on this issue.

Beginning in 1936, a series of newspaper and magazine articles (e.g., *Bungei shunjū* and *Tōkyō Asahi Shinbun*) as well as some unpublished articles show Kuki speaking out on questions related to the war in China. They suggest that Kuki felt called upon to defend both his devotion to time-honored Japanese traditions and his independence from foreign influences, those from the West in particular. "Tradition and Progress" ("Dentō to shinshu") angrily dismisses the charge that he is the kind of traditionalist who wallows in complacent illusions of a hallowed outdated past. He presents himself as a discriminating, open-minded critic who knows quite well how to pick and choose among influences domestic and foreign.[44] "Thoughts on Foreign Loan Words" ("Gairaigo shokan") heaps scorn on trendy borrowings, even intimating that the government ought to have a policy aimed at defending the Japanese language against linguistic invasion.[45] This essay ends on a note of shrill affirmation, suggesting that the nation's leaders should inspire the public with more heartfelt devotion to the Japanese spirit, at the same time cutting off at the root any tendency to worship Western innovation.[46]

Kuki in these years appears to have been slanted toward nationalism. In 1938 a newspaper invited him to contribute a brief inspirational slogan for Japanese women, which appeared under the title "Protect the Beautiful Japanese Kimono" ("Utsukushiki nihon no kimono o mamore"). In it, he expresses dislike for Western clothing and advocates for the kimono as more becoming in every way for Japanese women.[47] "On the Eve of the Imperial Year 2000" ("Nisen roppyaku-nen no zen'ya") is a brief, unpublished encomium extolling the virtues of Japanese women and advising them to "remain feminine, considerate women of bygone years."[48]

If evidence casting Kuki in a bad light is among these occasional pieces, it would be in one from 1937, "Thoughts on the Current State of Affairs" ("Jikyoku no kansō"). Some scholars think this essay proves that Kuki was an agent of imperialism. In it, "after due reflection as a philosopher," he supports the Japanese campaign to "reeducate" the Chinese through military conquest, bestowing on them a gift they lacked, namely a brand of Japanese spiritualism, *seishinshugi*.[49] These do seem rather like the "due reflections" of a man whose philosophy is anything but skeptical where the imperialist dogma of the day was concerned. Still, it is hard to know quite how much weight to give this piece in the whole of Kuki's work. We don't know what occasion prompted it. And I myself know of no other place where Kuki couples "philosophy" and political persuasion in the same context. Certainly he isn't on record as a proponent of political action taking Japan in any specific direction in the future.

One might say that Kuki's agenda for the future of Japan was cultural, not political, driven by the vision of ethnic authenticity laid out in *The Structure*. His public lectures in the 1930s speak for this. "About the Japanese Character" ("Nihonteki seikaku ni tsuite"), delivered in 1937, is typical of Kuki's approach in this genre. He invites his audience to view the future of Japan in terms of three aspects of national character that he sees as definitive: *shizen* "reverence and affinity to nature," *iki* "pride and honor," and *akirame* "resignation to fate."[50]

Kuki envisioned two quite specific outcomes of greater awareness here. First, Japanese more keenly aware of ethnic authenticity would cherish and cultivate Japanese culture and values (*nihonshugi* "Japanism") more faithfully in daily life now and in the future. Secondly, Japanese endowed with this deeper, truer sense of themselves would have no fear of foreign influences. They would pick and choose with perfect confidence, enriched by cultural exchange that brings them much that is good, even as it defines them and their contribution to the world at large more clearly. Kuki, in effect, dares his audience *not* to accept this paradoxical enrichment from abroad:

> If we as citizens of Japan fail to recognize this uniquely national character in ourselves, we will lose more than our drive to live as Japanese. . . .

We will be powerless to keep our place in creating world culture. Moreover, if we don't muster the courage to reject certain influences of the
Western culture, as we have done since Meiji, we will in turn stunt the
growth and development of the Japanese character.[51]

Kuki concludes this lecture with the following call to the Japanese people:

> I believe the principle that guides Japanese culture may simply be some-
> thing seemingly paradoxical—*Japanese internationalism* or *international
> Japanism* as the case may be. *On one hand*, the future of the Japanese char-
> acter or path that Japanism takes must be rooted in the guiding prin-
> ciple of world history. We must, *on the other*, recognize clearly that the
> citizens of Japan cannot hope to contribute to world history without
> the people's realization of their own national character.[52]

Is this a call to arms? Is Kuki urging his countrymen to rise up in defense
of fascist military rule? Pincus has argued that elements of *The Structure* foreshadow what appears to be a vein of jingoism in these essays and lectures.
Two elements in particular appear to support that argument, the essence of
which is contained in the question I set forth above. The first is Kuki's definition of *iki* as a sensibility so uniquely Japanese it could only be learned by
living in Japan. The second is Kuki's claim that *iki* is the definitive, formative essence of being truly Japanese. It is easy to see how that definition and
that claim could lead to the kind of thinking that justifies the formation and
enforcement of a nationalized aesthetics whose totalitarian drive would consort quite happily with an ideology of militaristic imperialism.[53] That string
of historically fearsome words itself explains how Kuki is cast in a very bad
light by comparisons of his writings with Heidegger's writings and politics in
Nazi Germany. We have no way of knowing if Kuki and Heidegger discussed
the subject of art, poetry especially, as privileged because it is truth-revealing.
We do know that Kuki connected art and truth in *The Structure*, where his commitment to art *as* truth could be construed as favorable to totalitarian aesthetics. But did he in actual fact become that kind of ideologue in the 1930s?
Should that 1937 lecture on Japanese national character ("Nihonteki seikaku
ni tsuite") be read as a manifest attempt to link art and politics in a way that
links him with an historical outcome we judge so harshly now?

The answer to this question may come from a closer, more contextualized
reading of the lecture. As Graham Parkes, who has published extensively on
German and Japanese philosophy, points out quite aptly, there is no mention
of an essential element of totalitarianism, a type of chauvinism that states

that Japanese culture is superior to all others and that its precepts should be upheld in other cultures.[54] In fact, Kuki argues the opposite, that Japanese character is defined in relation to others. Another bit of evidence to support this nuanced interpretation of Kuki's position comes from his lecture notes for a literary theory class at Kyoto. There he argues that art is a reflection of historical being—a reflection, not a shaping instrument, of history. Indulging his love of visual representation, he diagrams the relationship. History is a directional line intersected by a circle representing art. Art is circular. But Kuki sees it as a mirror, too, whose surface faces the past, reflecting history. Art is history—history mirrored to perfection.[55]

Since history is perfected in art, he argues, its being must be intuited to be understood. Once it is intuited, its true meaning can be appreciated. That appreciation makes it possible for the spirit of a time to be reflected meaningfully in art. The answer to Kuki's perspective on art and truth may lie in other essays Kuki wrote, notably one that appeared in the June 1933 issue of the philosophical journal Risō (Ideal). In "A Personal View of Philosophy" ("Tetsugaku shiken"), Kuki's argument insists on the autonomy of art:

> Because one man's mode of existence includes the modes of existence of others as moments, boundaries between them tend to blur. Thus we have those who believe that art is a means of understanding being through intuition and that, therefore, the value of art lies in its truth. Yet as long as individuality is asserted by art, this individuality must always be derived from appreciation of art for pleasure. The saying "In art man savors himself as perfection" is true; if there is no taste to be savored, it is not art. The fact that art can serve as a means of comprehending being is no more than its secondary side-effect.[56]

Cleary, Kuki is not in full agreement with Heidegger's view that the primary function of art (i.e., poetry) is revealing truth. One might say that for Kuki, art appreciation comes first. Art gives us pleasure we learn to treasure. Any comprimario role it plays would have to do with understanding ethnic identity. Art, for him, does not play politics. Iki would not be the tool of some cultural commissar entrusted with enforcing some form or function of national aesthetics. The whiff of agenda one gets from his essay on Japanese national character is more like a wish list drawn up by an ardent nationalist eager to recover values lost in the recent past. Like The Structure, Kuki's essays offer guidelines or advice for a general future direction. No marching orders are given. This stands to reason since for him art mirrors the past; it doesn't shape the future.

Kuki writes elsewhere that man is free to make choices at any given point in time. What happens next is up to him in many important respects. Choice is what makes man free. History is made by a succession of free choices.[57] Kuki is no believer in historical inevitability looking for reasons why individuals or nations *must* choose a certain path in preference to all others. He is more like the proponent for informed free choice—the one who believes that the best choices made are those that keep the past clearly in view.

This emphasis on freedom also explains why Kuki was comparatively unbothered by truth-of-art concerns. Again, he is no enforcer. The general picture that emerges from the conclusion of *The Structure* is one of iki as a choice of identity, which he urges his countrymen to make in daily life. True, his plea includes some notion of a price to be paid for ignoring his advice—call it loss of vital ethnic energy. At times, his tone in the essays may seem a bit strident, but even then he is exhorting and imploring, not inciting, 1930s-style. Dig deeper into Kuki and you find Kuki—any resemblance to Heidegger is only superficial.

Even so, some critics force us to ask: Does Kuki's 1930s thinking reflect his association with Heidegger in the 1920s, or his present-day awareness of Heidegger's 1930s writings?

The answer, such as it is, depends on circumstantial evidence. To begin with, we have no evidence that Heidegger communicated his belief in the political role of art when Kuki was in Europe. There is, in fact, no reason to believe that Heidegger had reached that conclusion by the late 1920s. Some Heidegger scholars date that aspect of his thought to the mid-1930s, when he delivered the lectures later published as "The Origin of the Work of Art."[58] Copies of the lectures did circulate beforehand, but they were not made public and we have no reason to believe that Kuki in faraway Japan was privileged to have one.

It seems far more likely that the intellectual resemblance here, such as it is, can be laid at the door of a philosopher-to-philosopher influence in the past leading to a later coincidence of thought. We must also not forget that Kuki probably viewed Heidegger as a colleague with similar interests but a curiosity of sorts, and it is doubtful that Kuki took to Heidegger readily. They came from opposite ends of the world, literally and figuratively—Kuki was cosmopolitan, aristocratic, affluent, and highly refined and educated; Heidegger was a pious student of spiritual questions, so much so that he knew little of modern amenities and temptations. The southern German's mannerisms and attire were reminiscent of his peasant roots in Messkirch, a town on the border with Switzerland.[59] But Heidegger's philosophy lay closer to Kuki's heart than his other German contemporaries. We know that Kuki moved to Freiburg in the spring of 1927 to seek out Heidegger. We have "Iki no honshitsu" (Essence of *iki*), a 1926 draft for *The Structure*, and *The Structure* itself to compare; and evidence of Kuki's expanding confidence and skill as a philosopher alive to momentous change taking place in the Japan of the 1930s.[60] Surely Kuki's view of the relation between art and truth makes perfect sense as the maturing thought process of a gifted student of Heideggerian hermeneutic phenomenology.[61] Better yet, this student paid Heidegger's philosophy the compliment of using some of its tenets to describe a uniquely Japanese sensibility.

It is sadly easy to look back and see no comparison whatever between the stir being made in Germany by Heidegger and the Japanese reception of Kuki's little book. Kuki's surviving papers show friends and colleagues responding cordially, praising his effort to establish *iki* as a sensibility uniquely Japanese.[62] Of course, we have no way of knowing whose praise was sincere and whose was merely diplomatic. A number of correspondents focus on Kuki's insight into the role *iki* might play in matters erotic. Some say they had no idea he took such an interest in secular culture as a whole. That vein of comment shows how little Kuki's colleagues knew of his wide-ranging intellectual life and his secluded nightlife in Kyoto. One gets the impression that he paid a price personally, as well as professionally, for keeping to himself.

Conspicuously absent in all this faded correspondence is any suggestion that *The Structure* was seen as a work with political aspirations of any kind. It seems safe to say that it was seen as a highly personal, even eccentric, work of philosophy. As such, it appears to have surprised a good many and wounded no one—with the possible exception of Kuki himself. There are several reasons why Kuki's colleagues at Kyoto University might have given *The Structure* a politely evasive welcome. The philosophy department there was considered the finest in the country, the work of its scholars most significant. The chairmanship had passed from Nishida Kitarō to Tanabe Hajime (1885–1962), who had abandoned Husserl and Heidegger for Hegel's dialectic. Kuki's emulation of Heidegger may have seemed like a rearguard action. Another possibility is that Tanabe, perhaps Nishida, too, considered Kuki's pleasure-quarters frame of reference unsuitable to serious philosophical enquiry. Why study the worldly aesthetic sensibility of a chosen few Edo exquisites in such meticulous detail? And in a style so lighthearted and accessible, too? And so unsystematic! One imagines copy after copy of *The Structure* snapped shut with a grunt of dissatisfaction or sigh of polite exasperation. A researcher leafing through Kuki's papers, however, does encounter welcome evidence of warmer response. For example, Watsuji Tetsurō was a friend who would join the faculty at Kyoto in 1931. On a postcard dated November 13, 1930, he gratefully acknowledges Kuki's gift of a copy of The Structure and invites him to his home.[63]

Kuki's work was certainly marginal to the trend of Japanese philosophy in the 1920s and 1930s, when publishers issued a spate of books and articles on pragmatism, historical materialism, Marxism, Hegelian dialectics, and capitalism. In 1936 Kuki himself complained of feeling surrounded by "the enemy" when The Structure came out and Marxism was all the rage.[64] The Structure was an oddity, a work out of touch with the academic zeitgeist.

Kuki's colleagues at Kyoto thought of him as a Francophile. That can't have done his standing much good in a department committed to German idealism, a school of thought he had turned away from in the late 1920s. His chronology (at the back of this volume) shows how often he lectured on French philosophy. Though he divided his time fairly equally between German and French schools of thought, Kuki's lecture schedule attests to special interests in, for example, Bergsonian vitalism. In fact, his contemporary Amano Teiyū characterizes Kuki as a scholar working in French philosophy.[65]

This scattering of facts and inferences might be used to argue that Kuki and his work were sidelined by a 1930s Japanese variation on a theme as timeless as faculty politics as usual. It seems more likely that Kuki did much to distance himself, reclusive as he was, and to dedicate his time to interests and research out of the mainstream.[66] Surely that would explain why we find so little evidence that The Structure had any noticeable effect on his peers, much less the nation as a whole. Books dealing with the history of Japanese philosophy tend to slight it, too. Some don't even mention Kuki's book in their chronologies.

If we were to assume a more major role for Kuki in the national debate on aesthetics, the apparent lack of interest on the part of ideologues in charge of promoting Japan's imperialist expansion in the 1930s would be puzzling. Other works advancing interest in Japanese cultural values and successes had achieved some renown. Among them were early works by scholars Kuki knew quite well. One was A Study of Goodness (Zen no kenkyū, 1911, Meiji 44) by his department chairman Nishida Kitarō. Two others were by his good friend Watsuji Tetsurō: A Pilgrimage to Old Temples (Koji junrei, 1918, Taishō 8) and Ancient Culture of Japan (Nihon kodai bunka, 1919, Taishō 9). The titles themselves suggest opportunities for nationalist propaganda, far less easy to imagine springing to life from the pages of a book like The Structure.

The clearest sign we have that Kuki and/or his writings found favor with the ruling military is the fact that he was granted permission to travel to Manchuria and northern China in 1939. Even then, as far as we know, he traveled as a scholar, a man of no importance beyond his own eccentric vision of national renewal. Kuki's means to that end would not be military conquest. Taken together, *The Structure* and Kuki's occasional writings in the 1930s suggest what he had in mind: something more like a thoughtful response to an artful reflection caught in history's backward-looking mirror. The more one studies that reflection, the more its author seems an unlikely tool, willing or unwilling, of imperialist expansion.

Conclusion

We sift through Kuki's books and papers, thinking about his life and times. The basic facts of a life come easily to hand: A privileged young man studies abroad and comes back home to live out a privileged life as a tenured professor of philosophy at a prestigious university. It's easy to see how this quiet professor was in some sense compromised by history, living and writing as he did in Japan in the 1930s—a decade looked back at, and looked down upon, as "the dirty '30s" East and West. Kuki isn't dead and forgotten but alive— alive and open to question. Every afterlife bears a price. Case dismissed? Not quite. Because Kuki himself remains an enigma.

Among the letters in Kuki's files is a heartrending plea for help from one Karl Löwith (1897–1973) in Germany. The year is 1936. Löwith is a philosopher, a Jew in urgent need of a job that will give him an exit visa. Kuki and Löwith had met in Germany as fellow philosophers who shared a common interest in Heidegger's philosophy. Kuki's files make it clear that he got right to work and had much to do with getting Löwith a position at Tohoku University.[67] What's missing is any evidence of Kuki's motives, personal or political. As so often is the case with him, the afterlife evidence fails to bring the man himself to life. This is why it is impossible to say for certain that he did or didn't aspire to social or political activism. We can only make conscientious, educated guesses.

My own guess begins and ends with thinking that Kuki means what he says at the end of *The Structure*. There he makes it clear that *iki* is a personal choice, a commitment to everyday living defined by a certain aesthetic sensibility, *iki*. He has written this book to make it clear that *iki* is complex, even contrary— precise in so many ways, yet hard to define precisely. No wonder he ends on a note part elegy part manifesto. No wonder he leans on the "shudders and pal-pitations," the contrariness of life as it is known by those exquisitely attuned to it—through *iki*.

Aesthetes in the West had thrilled to similar messages decades before. But that resemblance fans out in significant Eastern differences. Chief among them, I would say, is the question of ethnic authenticity. *Iki* would make every Japanese more Japanese. He defines *iki* in terms of a specific time and place in the past that he sees as desirable for more than its aesthetic discipline; he saw it as ethnically definitive, a source of personal and national identity in danger of being lost.

Why shouldn't a reclusive professor write books and articles and give talks in service of his vision, to do his countrymen some good? We have given that question our best-guess answer already. The question returns here because the enigmatic Kuki leaves open a nagging question, namely, could this man have wanted to cooperate with those who sought to enlist Japanese ethnicity in a program of imperial conquest?

Here we are helped by some facts of Kuki's life, sketchy as they are. We know that Kuki's fascination with Japanese art originated with his father, that his mother had been a geisha in Kyoto, and that he felt spiritually close to Okakura Tenshin.[68] Even though Kuki sampled the novel Western pleasures then available in Tokyo, we know that cafés and jazz halls didn't take hold in his passionate young imagination. From there, led by a love of his coun-try's past, and with help from Nagai Kafū (1879–1959), he traveled back in time to the Bunka and Bunsei eras (1804–1830), where he found the aesthetic sensibility that responded to his needs.

We can't of course know exactly what those needs were. Guesswork in that direction could lead us badly astray. We can, however, generalize on the basis of Kuki's upbringing and education. His father, no doubt like many men of his class, lived a life ruled by strong contrast. He had to accommodate very different public and private selves: one severely formal, serenely respectable; the other highly individual, passionately experimental. Kuki's mother, Hatsu, was a delicate woman in the classic mode, a devoted wife dedicated to the cultivation of the traditional Japanese arts.[69] Not a bad parental recipe for birthing an aesthete.

Long before *The Structure* concludes on what might be called an aesthete's high note, we find every reason *not* to be surprised by an outcome that modu-lates from theoretical exposition to highly personal exhortation. We should be equally unsurprised to learn that Kuki exhibited the classic symptoms of divided self so common among aesthetes. Analysis of *The Structure* has shown us how contradictory, selective, and eclectic its author's research methods were. Reflection on his life and work together suggest that any Kuki we are likely to know will not be found easily on the page, and never just so. He has been described as "both stoic and epicurean, serene and passionate, theoretical and emotional."[70] He himself gives evidence of being modern and traditional, Japanese and Western, Christian and pagan, idealistic and pragmatic.

All that, and by all accounts, personally inaccessible, too. Kuki led a resolutely private life, wary and chary of social and intellectual contact with colleagues and students. Just the sort of reclusive, highly focused visionary one might expect to sublimate so much that was personal in a work like *The Structure*, where, sure enough, the ending translates that reticence into an unmistakably personal credo.

Still, a work as complex as *The Structure* could afford its author a measure of privacy. All the evidence suggests that Kuki had no desire to be famous in person or in print. In fact, judging from his complaints about a professor's meager salary, he would have preferred a quiet subvention for studies conducted after dark in a certain quarter of the city.[71] In any case, he clearly felt obliged to publish *The Structure*. His researches had deepened his romantic and nostalgic love of this traditional Japanese aesthetic; and that love could not bear to stand by and see it vanish, and with it (he thought) the true core of Japanese life and culture. And so he committed, quite literally, this highly personal part of himself to print.

So why not enlist a few years later in a public campaign analogous to the German rage for ethnic purity? Because Kuki had none of his father's political ambitions or social acumen. Like many aesthetes, Kuki was politically inert. As we have seen, he was socially unwilling, too. His divided self was conflicted and contradictory but always self-critical, always self-aware—subject first and last to the highest standards of taste. Could there be a more unlikely conscript for any kind of government-issue campaign?

Trouble was, Kuki lived at a time of cultural crisis, of East-West imbalance. It made sense for the Japanese to turn inward and look backward, to self-assess and self-critique, to revive the ethnic authenticity Kuki labored to define. Obviously, he couldn't hold back entirely. And so in the 1930s, somewhat in print, and, we think, somewhat more enthusiastically in real life, he followed up on the advice he gave to readers at the end of *The Structure*.

There's the place to look for him, and for the truth of his story. This Kuki set out to discover and preserve the raison d'être of Japanese culture; its definitive historical moment; its authentic ethnic sustenance (he would have called it being); its wonderful seamless way of connecting past and present;

its disciplined fusion of high art and daily life; its heightened awareness of sensual appeal, with special emphasis on sights and sounds and smells and all unique to life in Japan. And so on. Kuki's notion of *iki*, exclusive as it is, is wonderfully inclusive, too. It is also wisely permissive, taking into account life's mix of pleasurable rewards and messy complications. What political ideologue would go so far in that direction? Kuki was otherwise engaged. Maybe the last best thing to say is that he was a student of life, one committed to making sense of its "shudders and palpitations."

Notes

1. Such accessibility represents stark contrast to the style of writing in *The Structure* and some of Kuki's other academic writing, including *Gūzensei no mondai* (The problem of contingency) (Tokyo: Iwanami shoten, 1935) and *Seiyō tetsugakushikō* (A history of western philosophy) (Tokyo: Iwanami shoten, 1944).

2. Kuki's mother had a storied romance with Okakura Tenshin, which resulted in her being separated from Kuki's father. Kuki's mother remained sickly for many years, apparently went mad, and was committed to an insane asylum. For an account of this and other aspects of Kuki's relationship with Tenshin, see, for instance, Matsumoto Seichō, *Okakura Tenshin, sono uchinaru teki* (Okakura Tenshin, the enemy within) (Tokyo: Shinchōsha, 1984).

3. In the 1910s and 1920s, Kuki was a follower of a trend initiated by a group of writers who subscribed to the notion that the only function of literature is to pursue the creation of beauty. The group, loosely centered around the group Pan no kai (Association of the Greek god of Pan), included a large number of now well-known writers, such as Mori Ōgai, Takamura Kōtarō, Kinoshita Mokutarō, Kitahara Hakushū, Ishii Hakutei, Tanizaki Jun'ichirō, Satō Haruo, Nagai Kafū, to name a few. They preferred to write creative (as opposed to true-to-life) stories appealing to the senses, exhibiting human sensuality and decadent aestheticism, set in historical times and exotic places. See, for further details of this literary movement, Noda Utarō, *Nihon tanbiha bungaku no tanjō* (Birth of literary aestheticism in Japan) (Tokyo: Kawade shobō shinsha, 1975).

4. This literary magazine was published in two series—the original series edited by Yosano Akiko and the second edited by Yosano Tekkan from Taishō 10 (1921) to Showa 2 (1926). The second series, to which Kuki contributed, had a diminished literary impact in comparison to the first, but it still showed the preference for opulent, romantic poetry inherited from the original series.

5. Donald Roden's *Schooldays in Imperial Japan* (Berkeley: University of California Press, 1980) captures the spirit and the complexities of life at the First Higher School. See also Sugai Yoshinobu, *Meiji kōki ni okeru Daiichi Kōtōgakkō gakusei no shichō* (The trend in the thought of the First Higher School during late Meiji), in *Nihon kin gendaishi* (History of modern and contemporary Japan), ed. Banno Junji, et al. (Tokyo: Iwanami shoten, 1993), 145–183.

6. His philosophy teacher at the higher school, Iwamoto Tei (1869–1941), was a Christian, as were many of his friends. The idealistic, progressive stance taken by Christianity appears to have affected Kuki's spiritual direction at this time—he even contemplated joining a Trappist monastery in Hokkaidō. See KSZ, 5:111.

7. Von Koeber came to Japan in 1893 by invitation of the Meiji government for Tokyo Imperial University's opening of its philosophy department, and held there the position of professor of philosophy until 1914. Trained as a concert pianist and philosopher, von Koeber was a knowledgeable, conscientious, caring teacher and a practitioner of *humanistische Bildung* "wide humanistic learning," with an obvious connection to the *kyōyō shugi* (culturalism) that captured the intellectual moment of the Taishō era. Von Koeber was said to have been warm, quiet, and deferential, and encouraged his students to not limit their learning to a narrow field of philosophy but to expand to classical studies. Kuki's love for classical literature and poetry (Japanese, Chinese, French, and German), his knowledge of the classics (Greek and Latin), his intense interest in life's manifestations, not to mention his language facility in all major European languages, appear to have been forged under Iwamoto's and von Koeber's guidance. Perhaps it is not at all an exaggeration to say that Kuki's orientation in scholarship, his breadth and depth of knowledge, and his critical thinking are owed to these two very influential teachers during his formative years.

8. This orientation in philosophy is consistent with his experiences and inclinations during his youth. See also his poem entitled "A day in autumn," in KSZ, 1:129.

9. KSZ, 8:iii–iv. Amano was the closest friend whose advice Kuki trusted most (KSZ, 5:246). He began his tenure as Kuki's colleague in the Kyoto University's philosophy department in 1931.

10. KSZ, 3:445–446.

11. We find this among Kuki's statements as well: see "A Recollection of Henri Bergson," KSZ, 5:141, in which Kuki writes that Bergson is the greatest philosopher of the first half of the twentieth century.

12. KSZ, 9:380–381; KSZ, 5:49–51.

13. Henri Bergson, *Essai sur les données immédiates de la conscience*, translated by F. L. Pogson as *Time and Free Will: An Essay on the Immediate Data of Consciousness* (London: George Allen and Unwin, 1920).

14. KSZ, 9:381–382; KSZ, 8:316–318; KSZ, 3:101.

15. KSZ, 3:412–414.

16. KSZ, 3:112. In fact, Bergson himself, often labeled as antiscientific, did not consider science useless but merely that it offered one type of, and incomplete, knowledge about an object.

17. KSZ, 10:492–493.

18. KSZ, 3:397.

19. Leslie Pincus, *Authenticating Culture in Imperial Japan: Kuki Shūzō and the Rise of National Aesthetics* (Berkeley: University of California Press, 1996).

20. Pincus, *Authenticating Culture*. See also Mikkelsen's chapter in this volume.

21. KSZ, 9:410; KSZ, 5:193–194. In his essay "Tōkyō to Kyōto," Kuki again draws

a parallel between Heidegger's dark philosophy and the darkness of the Black Forest. Also see Kuki's discussion of Sehnsucht in the opening paragraphs of *The Structure of Iki*, in which he makes a similar point about Germans' dreary outlook on life.

22. KSZ, 9:403.

23. *Kuki Shūzō bunko mokuroku* (Catalog of the Kuki Shūzō Memorial Library) Kobe: Kōnan Daigaku tetsugaku kenkyūshitsu, 1976), 94, 109. Kuki's library held several books of Hölderlin's poetry.

24. A variety of kanji were used to write the word "iki," some of which are nonstandard or have fallen into disuse today. Kuki's renditions here have not been historically documented and are probably innovated for *The Structure* as published originally.

25. KSZ, 12:47.

26. *Iki no kōzō o yomu* (Reading *The Structure of iki*) by Yasuda Takeshi and Tada Michitarō (Tokyo: Asahi shinbunsha, 1979).

27. Kitagawa Morisada, *Morisada mankō*, comp. Asakura Haruhiko and Kashikawa Shūichi (Tokyo: Tōkyōdō shuppan, 1992), 3:75 et seq. *Morisada mankō* is abbreviated MM hereafter. MM was originally published as *Kinsei fūzokushi*, 1852.

28. For some representative fabric designs during Edo, see Nagai Michiko and Ihara Aki, *Ukiyo e ni miru iro to moyō* (Tokyo: Kawade shobō, 1995). Also MM is a good source.

29. MM, 3:83–84.

30. MM, 3:38, 78.

31. MM, 2:249.

32. Tamenaga Shunsui, *Shunshoku koi no shiranami* (Tokyo: Koten bunko, 1967), vol. 2, installation 3, 36–37.

33. *Ninjōbon* (popular romance novels) and *kibyōshi* (lit. "yellow covers") were books dealing with human feeling and popular stories with many adult themes, respectively; both popular in the late Edo period.

34. Nakano Mitsutoshi, "Sui, tsū, iki," in *Nihon shisō*, vol. 5, ed. by Sagara Tōru, Bitō Masahide, and Akiyama Ken (Tokyo: University of Tokyo Press, 1985), 109–141.

35. Nishiyama Matsunosuke, *Edo Culture: Daily Life and Diversions in Urban Japan, 1600–1868*, translated and edited by Gerald Groemer (Honolulu: University of Hawai'i Press, 1997).

36. In earlier drafts of *Iki no kōzō*, Kuki refers to the later eighteenth-century print designer Suzuki Harunobu's prints frequently, many of which were dropped in the final version of the text. Note also that Harunobu lived 1724–1770, many years earlier than the Bunka and Bunsei eras.

37. MM, 2:48, 3:54.

38. See note 156 in the translation herein, and Laurence Kominz, "Ichikawa Danjūrō V and Kabuki's Golden Age," in *The Floating World Revisited*, ed. Donald Jenkins (Portland: Portland Art Museum, 1993), 63–83.

39. Also apparent is the fact that the name Adakichi is a combination of *ada* "charming" and *kichi*, which is a suffix for male names. In contrast to the women in

Yoshiwara, those in Fukagawa were said to be more manly (as Kuki indicates in *The Structure*), thus it was not unusual to have a name of this sort. What is perhaps ironic is that the name of the epitome of a woman embodying the sensibility of *iki* turns out to contain another word of aesthetic sensibility, *ada* "charming."

40. Tamenaga Shunsui, *Shunshoku tatsumi no sono*, NKBT, 64:277.

41. This is true as far as we can ascertain from publications of extant prints of these artists. See Asano Shūgō and Timothy Clark, *The Passionate Art of Kitagawa Utamaro* (Tokyo: Asahi shinbun, 1995), and Richard Lane, *Images from the Floating World* (New York: Dorset Press, 1978).

42. Kuki could have argued that the prevailing aesthetic sensibility in any given historical period after the Bunka and Bunsei eras is a permutation of the original *iki*. That is, Kuki could have presented the argument that the three intensional moments he identifies for *iki* remain constant through time, but different sociocultural conditions at various times in history sanction different manifestations of this sensibility. Demonstrating this would have made stronger Kuki's point that *iki* is in the ethnic core of Japan.

43. A book entitled *Iki no kōzō o yomu* (Reading *The Structure of iki*), by Yasuda Takeshi and Tada Michitarō (Tokyo: Asahi shinbunsha, 1979), is a transcript of a discussion between the two prominent authors about each chapter of *The Structure*. The tone of their discussion is chatty, too, and does not at all resemble what one might expect from commentaries on a book on philosophical aesthetics.

44. KSZ, 5:207–208. It is worthwhile to note that, given the political climate of the day, the charge that Kuki was out of step with the times or too traditional would not have been made against Kuki if he had been perceived to be a leading proponent of national aesthetics or of the Japanese war efforts. This undated essay was never published.

45. KSZ, 5:95. Words such as *nyūsu* "news," *sābisu* "service," and *depāto* "department store" are a few he cited as being offensive, but are ironically in common use today.

46. KSZ, 5:91–99.

47. KSZ, 5:244.

48. KSZ, 5:250–251.

49. This appeared in the influential monthly magazine *Bungei shunjū* (KSZ, 5:36–39). In the same article, Kuki acknowledges extraordinary Japanese debt to the Chinese culture and tradition.

50. The talk, delivered to students at the Third Higher School, was preceded by an article with a similar title, "Nihonteki seikaku" (Japanese character), which appeared in the February 1937 issue of the journal *Shisō*. See KSZ, 3:378–387 for the script of this talk. This *iki* should not to be confused with the aesthetic sensibility of *iki*.

51. KSZ, 3:398.

52. KSZ, 3:399. Emphasis is Kuki's.

53. One can argue that Kuki's writing during the interwar years does embody many

elements that suggest an inclination toward fascism. The symptoms include an emphasis of spiritualism over materialism, interest in a national rather than individual cause, mass mobilization for a national cause, reverence of nature, resistance to foreign influences, use of art, myths, and idealized aesthetic constructs to serve a cause, to name a few.

54. Graham Parkes, "The Putative Fascism of the Kyoto School and the Political Correctness of the Modern Academy," *Philosophy East and West* 47 (3): 322 (1997).

55. KSZ, 11:138. See also Kuki's essay "Bungaku no keijijōgaku" (The metaphysics of literature) in KSZ, 4, spec. 8–9.

56. KSZ, 3:107.

57. KSZ, 3:100.

58. Michael Inwood, *Heidegger* (Oxford and New York: Oxford University Press, 1997), 107.

59. In an essay entitled "Tōkyō to Kyōto" (Tokyo and Kyoto), Kuki relates a story about Heidegger's business trip that took him to Berlin, wherein Kuki describes how he was surprised by the fact that Heidegger had been there only once before, during World War One, and that Heidegger was apparently astonished by modern lifestyle there. "I could not help but smile secretly about the idea of being astounded by as little as Berlin" (KSZ, 5:194).

60. "The Essense of Iki," which served as a draft of *The Structure*, was completed in Paris in December of 1926. This draft is completely free from the many technical elements that are associated with Heidegger's hermeneutic phenomenology, which found their places in the 1930 publication *The Structure of Iki*.

61. Kuki met Heidegger at the home of Edmund Husserl in the spring of 1927, but he was well aware of Heidegger's philosophy by the time he'd met Sartre four months earlier, partially through Tanabe's article published in 1924; see Tanabe Hajime, "Genshōgaku ni okeru atarashiki tenkō" (A new turn in phenomenology), *Shisō* 36:1–23. Sartre is said to have taken a letter of introduction from Kuki when he met Heidegger. (For the details of the Kuki-Sartre connection, see Stephen Light's *Shūzō Kuki and Jean-Paul Sartre* (Carbondale: Southern Illinois University Press, 1987). For an account of Kuki from Heidegger's point of view, see "A Dialogue on Language," in Heidegger's *On the Way to Language* (New York: Harper and Row, 1971), in which Heidegger states that he and Kuki met and discussed *iki*.

62. The letters and cards reside in the Kuki Memorial Library.

63. It is perhaps significant that, although Kuki and Watsuji belonged to the same department, they were only loosely associated with the so-called Kyoto school insofar as their intellectual endeavors were concerned. Given this, it would make sense that it was Watsuji who warmly welcomed Kuki's publication venture into aesthetics. By the time *The Structure* was published, Nishida Kitarō had handed over the chairmanship of the department to Tanabe Hajime.

64. Kuki himself mentioned that Marxism was in full swing when his book came out. See "Dentō to shinshu" (Tradition and progress), KSZ, 5:208.

65. KSZ, 8:iii–vi.

66. Kuki seems to have distanced himself deliberately from engaging intellectually with his students and colleagues. See Nakano Hajimu, "Kuki Shūzō and the Structure of Iki," in Culture and Identity: Japanese Intellectuals during the Interwar Years, ed. J. Thomas Rimer (Princeton: Princeton University Press, 1990), 271.

67. According to Löwith's account, a Japanese student had come to study under him in Marburg in 1935, not knowing Löwith was no longer teaching in Germany. This student suggested he write to Kuki to obtain a position in Japan (the letter is in the Kuki Memorial Library). At this point he knew Kuki only slightly from Kuki's Marburg days, but desperate to secure a position abroad, Löwith acted on this suggestion. He wrote a letter to Kuki in Kyoto in January of 1936. After he was appointed at Tohoku University, he learned that the German embassy and the German Cultural Institute had both attempted unsuccessfully to stop this appointment. The academic landscape in Japan in the 1930s resists a broad-brush characterization that it acted in unison to support the national political agenda. For Löwith's observations about National Socialists posted in Japan, émigré from Germany and other parts of Europe, and Japanese academics during this time, see Karl Löwith, My Life in Germany before and after 1933, translated by Elizabeth King (Urbana and Chicago: University of Illinois Press, 1994).

68. There is a speculation that Hatsu might have been a servant at Kuki's home prior to her marriage to Kuki Ryūichi (Kuki's father); see Matsumoto Seichō, Okakura Tenshin, sono uchinaru teki (Okakura Tenshin: the enemy within) (Tokyo: Shinchōsha, 1984), 104.

69. Kuki's memoir also gives support to this, e.g., "Negishi," KSZ, 5:227; also "Okakura Kakuzō-shi no omoide" (Memories of Mr. Okakura Kakuzō), KSZ, 5:233.

70. Nakano Hajimu, "Kuki Shūzō and the Structure of Iki," in Culture and Identity: Japanese Intellectuals during the Interwar Years, ed. by J. Thomas Rimer, 261–272.

71. KSZ, 12:180.

Literary Stances
The Structure of Iki

J. THOMAS RIMER

The Structure of Iki is a most unusual text. Atypical among the works composed by Kuki Shūzō, this brief and sometimes provocative study, although most often read and commented upon as a work of philosophy, actually opens itself up for examination from several directions at once. Read as philosophy, it has been subjected to analysis in terms of the formal ideas its author presents, as well as in the context of the book's philosophical, cultural, even political implications. This is as it should be; still, it seems to me that there are other ways to examine this text. *The Structure of Iki* could be read as a kind of elegant example of cultural anthropology, or, in my view, as an example of a work of literature, composed in the spirit of the heritage of the European manner.

Literary texts, as opposed to many other kinds of writing, are by their inherent nature many-sided and ambiguous. They exist both inside and outside their time, one generation after another drawing from them the insights that best match their own concerns. Some texts fade from view because they apparently do not manage to transcend their period sufficiently to interest readers at a later time. Some reemerge and find new relevance.

The Structure of Iki may not, to a reader raised in the traditions of American or British literature, appear on the surface to qualify as a work of literature, setting out as it does to explicate a series of ideas within what appears to be a Western philosophical framework. Continental European and East Asian assumptions about the nature and scope of literature and of literary texts, however, are generally more inclusive. While the essay form is relegated to a marginal position in the British and American literary canon, there is a long tradition, particularly in France, of regarding such writers as Montaigne, Pascal, and many others as central to the literary traditions of that civilization.

The same is certainly true in the Japanese literary heritage, where such highly regarded medieval classical texts as Kamo no Chōmei's *An Account of My Hut* and the *Essays in Idleness* of Yoshida Kenkō have for many centuries been read as literature, both for the power of the style in which they are written and for the ideas and emotions they express. Taken in this light, Kuki's *Structure of Iki* may justifiably also be considered and so examined as a work of literature. Indeed, I would make a case for the fact that this text is in many ways a literary *performance*, in which Kuki articulates with considerable fairness and more than occasional irony his personal responses to his own education, the human experience, and personal temperament. It is true, by the same token, that there lies within his exposition a certain sense of urgency, for the author betrays implicitly a conviction that many of the elegant and sophisticated attitudes found in early nineteenth-century Japan with which he felt such sympathy were disappearing from his contemporary culture and, indeed, from even the consciousness among his contemporaries of their prior existence. Insofar as Kuki addresses or comments on these matters, it seems to me, *The Structure of Iki* can absolutely be read and examined as a work of literature, at least in the European sense.

Hiroshi Nara, in his essay in this volume, has provided some striking and informative details on Kuki's upbringing and education. These need not be repeated here, other than to note that Kuki's exposure to the kind of broad and inclusive categories of thought propounded by his teacher Raphael von Koeber, stand revealed in the attitudes toward culture and the nature of the aesthetic experience adopted by a number of that European teacher's gifted Japanese intellectual progeny (here the writer Abe Jirō and the philosopher Watsuji Tetsurō come to mind). If von Koeber was to create in Kuki his initial enthusiasm for German culture, Kuki's first period of residence in Paris, from 1924 to 1927, brought him under the kind of French influences that confirmed other aspects of his tastes and inclinations, just as they had for the writer Nagai Kafū during his visit to France some twenty years before.

It is undoubtedly true that Kuki devoted a good deal of attention throughout his career to what might be termed professional philosophy. Even the essays he wrote while in France in order to explicate Japanese values, at a time when he felt that his country was ill understood in Europe, are relatively sober and analytical. But France and French literature helped him to develop a sense of the playful, an attitude that is certainly apparent in *The Structure of Iki*. It is this French connection that I attempt to sketch out here, for I believe that a case can be made for the fact that Kuki's immersion in French philosophy, literature, and culture gave him — perhaps for the first time in his

European experience—a model of how to compose a work that might combine the realm of ideas with a certain degree of self-revelation. In some ways, then, *The Structure of Iki* may be seen as Kuki's homage to France. Writers who mix personal observation with formal ideas go back in the French tradition to Petrarch (in exile from Italy) and Montaigne. Kuki himself opens *The Structure of Iki* with a citation from Maine de Biran (1766–1824), another philosopher who used a similar personal style to set forth his ideas, often related to an examination of the shifting relationships between outward sensation and interior self-perception, which combined, for Biran, lead to knowledge. It is not surprising then that Kuki cites on his opening page a quotation from the French philosopher's *Journal intime*, which for Kuki, reading Biran's work some hundred years later, suggests the primacy of his thought.

Closer to Kuki's time and perhaps more directly influential to his own thought, however, is the twentieth-century French essayist and philosopher Alain (Émile-Auguste Chartier; 1868–1951), a reigning figure in his own time and a writer still vastly admired in France today, although relatively little of his important work has been translated into English. As a teacher, he had many distinguished pupils, including Simone Weil, the philosopher and mystic so much read and admired these days.

Alain made use of the personal essay in a form he referred to as "*propos.*" In these brief essays, in the words of his English translator, Alain creates "propositions which the reader is invited, and indeed urged, to examine." Most often short essays, "aphoristic pieces of fifty or sixty lines, they move along easily and wittily."[1] Alain's work is deceptively simple to read, and many of his essays are relatively brief, as they were written for publication in newspapers. He remains a figure of such importance in France precisely because, like so many of his distinguished predecessors, he was able to approach the realm of ideas without abandoning the elegance, and in his case, I am tempted to add, the refreshing modesty of his personal and literary stance. His work is not rigorous (or occasionally portentous) in the fashion of Heidegger, but his observations remain penetrating.

An invaluable volume devoted to listing the contents of Kuki's library,[2] including the volumes he brought back with him from France, lists quite a number of books by Alain, some twelve in all, including his influential *Système des beaux-arts*, first published by Gallimard in 1926, several years before Kuki published *The Structure of Iki*. Kuki does not mention Alain directly in the text of *The Structure of Iki*, but it is likely that, as well read as Kuki was in contemporary French and European thought, he had become acquainted with the work of the French master while in Paris. In any case, a certain resemblance can be noted in their stylistic strategies. Alain, like Kuki, often uses art and litera-ture as trenchant examples for his various philosophical attitudes. Indeed, in his later years, the French master produced studies on such writers as Balzac, Stendhal, and Valéry.

Alain's basic convictions on the connections between art and philoso-phy are stated with elegance and clarity in the "Avant-Propos" to his *Sys-tème des beaux-arts*, which proceeds through essays on topics ranging from the nature of the imagination to dance, poetry, music, theater, architecture, poetry, prose, painting, and other manifestations of the artistic spirit. In his brief opening, Alain stresses the importance of Kant's writings on aesthetics, reminding his readers that the full extent of the German philosopher's genius can only be seen in his trenchant use of detail. Still, Alain's first caution is typical of his strategies of thought: "one can prove anything that one wants to; the real difficulty lies in knowing what one *wants* to prove."[3] Beauty is not part of a system, Alain goes on to insist, and our reactions to the beautiful are instinctual; the work of philosophy is therefore to *explain* those feelings, but it cannot take primacy over them. It is the work of art, he concludes, that ultimately judges the form. Alain is concerned about those aspects of human consciousness that set out "with a mania to *prove*," rather than to merely and more modestly suggest. As successful works of art are unique, they can be re-lated only indirectly to universal principles, since each work of art, each type of art, "speaks" in its own language. The example must, therefore, reign over the principle.

Looking at Kuki's method of constructing *The Structure of Iki* in this light, his dense interweaving of linguistic, literary, and artistic examples seems in consonance with Alain's dictums; like the French philosopher, Kuki often seems to develop his ideas from his examples, rather than choosing them to illustrate his more general points. Kuki also seems to be of like mind with Alain that one must indeed "listen" to works of art and draw observations and conclusions from that act of initial volition. "Individual thought can only take form in terms of communal expression," Alain writes, and so "one under-stands better the virtue of signs, from which no thought can be separated." For both these writers, art can convince without exact proof. In this context, it is of some interest that Alain entitles the first chapter of *Système* "The Folly of Logic."

Kuki also possessed what is perhaps the best known and loved of Alain's many works, *Propos sur le bonheur*, a series of short essays published over a num-ber of years and collected for publication together in 1928 and, to my knowl-edge, the only one of his works to be translated into English. Here, too, a reading of Alain's essays reveals certain similarities in strategy with Kuki's work. Robert Cottrell remarks in his introduction to the translation that "although Alain's *propos* are firmly rooted in physical reality, they often bear, lightly and even gaily, a rich cargo of legend, myth, philosophy, and literature." In terms of structure, Alain's remarks cluster "around the single idea contained in the opening sentences. They spiral around the basic theme, illuminating it from unexpected angles. The tone is alert, relaxed, and friendly."[4]

An example from Alain's essay "Politeness," number 82 in the collection, will show this amiable strategy at its best. The opening paragraph reads as follows.

> Politeness is learned, like dancing. He who does not know how to dance thinks that the difficult part is learning the rules of dancing and making his movements conform to them; this is only a superficial view of the matter; one must be able to dance without stiffness or awkwardness, and therefore without fear. In just the same way, learning the rules of politeness is only a small part of it; and even if you obey them, you are still only on the edge of politeness. Your movements must be precise and supple, without stiffness and uneasiness; for the least uneasiness can be passed on to others. What kind of politeness is it if it makes other people uneasy?[5]

Alain's tone is precise, informal (virtually chatty) and through his questions and speculations quickly engages the reader in a dialogue.

Kuki sometimes adopts, within the contours of his own style, something of the same strategy in the course of his own text. On the subject of coquetry in chapter 2 of *The Structure*, for example, Kuki combines principle, example, and wry observation in an effective fashion, his slightly ironic tone adding to the effectiveness of the whole.

> The hypothetical goal of coquetry is conquest, destined to disappear when this goal is fulfilled. As Nagai Kafū says in his novel *Kanraku*, "there is nothing more pathetic than having a woman after trying to have the woman." He must surely have in mind the "boredom, despair, and aversion" arising from the disappearance of coquetry that once played such an active role in both sexes. For that reason, the main concern of coquetry—and the essence of pleasure—is maintaining a dualistic relationship, that is to say, protecting the possibility as a possibility.[6]

Kuki may have drawn inspiration in terms of style and literary demeanor, as it were, from a contemporary French writer such as Alain. He drew more explicitly from the work of two of the seminal and most forward-looking figures in nineteenth-century French literature, Stendhal and Baudelaire, both of whom Kuki mentions directly in the course of his text.

Stendhal's *De l'amour* (On love) is itself an important classic in the history of French literature, one which the author himself considered the most important of his works, despite the eventual greater fame in our century of two of his novels, *The Red and the Black* and *The Charterhouse of Parma*. *On Love* was first published in 1822, and then reissued with various revisions and additions over the course of two decades or so. Kuki certainly must have found Stendhal's ironic account of great interest, as his library contains three separate editions of the book in French as well as a translation into German. It may be worthwhile, then, to outline in brief some of the concerns that Stendhal takes up in his study of love, "the only passion which pays itself in a coin which it mints itself."[7] In many ways, Kuki's strategies resemble those of Stendhal's; indeed, one sometimes gets the feeling that Kuki, after reading *On Love*, said to himself, "Ah, so that's how these things were managed in France; now, let me tell you about how it was in Japan."

In Stendhal's first preface, printed in 1826 in the second edition of the book, he begins to define his topic in an ironic vein; for him, the coming of a mercantile spirit and bourgeois values to France has limited severely the emotional life of his contemporaries.

> This little book . . . is simply an accurate and scientific treatise on a type of madness which is very rare in France. The power of conventionality, which is growing daily, has, more because of the effects of the fear of ridicule than from any purity in our morals, made the word which serves this book as its title one which people avoid using by itself, and which may even seem a little indelicate.[8]

Both Kuki and Stendhal use their material to create a critique, often implicit, of their respective contemporary societies. Each sets up a contrasting model. Stendhal uses geography, and his examples are largely taken from his experiences while living in Italy. Kuki uses time rather than space, and chooses the Tokugawa period as a moment when a wider range of feeling was, he believed, possible in his culture. Kuki feels it necessary to explicate the meanings of *iki* because he finds that the meaning of that quality is no longer apparent to his generation. Stendhal is even more outspoken on the shifts he finds in French society.

> The laborious, active, eminently worthy and practical life of a privy councillor, of a manufacturer of cotton goods, or of a banker with a

shrewd eye to loans, is rewarded by wealth and not by tender emotions. Little by little the hearts of these gentlemen become ossified; facts and utilitarianism are everything to them, and their minds are closed to that one of all emotions which has the greatest need of leisure and which makes those who labour under it incapable of any rational or coherent occupation.[9]

Stendhal wants his treatise to explain his topic "simply, rationally, mathematically," he explains humorously in his first introduction, but he finds difficulties in bringing this plan into being.

Imagine a moderately complicated geometrical figure traced with white chalk on a blackboard: well! I am going to explain this geometrical figure; but in order for me to do so, it is essential that the figure itself should already exist on the slate; I cannot trace it myself. It is this inability which makes it so very difficult to write a book about Love which is not a novel. In order to follow a philosophical examination of this sentiment with interest, the reader must have something else besides intelligence; it is absolutely essential that he should have seen Love. Now, how can one see a passion? That is a cause of perplexity which I shall never be able to remove.[10]

Stendhal does provide a sketch or two to illustrate his ideas during the course of his account. Kuki, of course, does him one better in chapter 3 of *The Structure of Iki* with his famous diagram created to show the relationships connecting the emotional attitudes he is attempting to delineate, a task that Stendhal, in his remarks above, felt impossible to achieve in visual form.

In his first chapter, Stendhal lays out four kinds of possible love: passion (*l'amour-passion*), sympathy (*l'amour-goût*), the sensual (*l'amour-physique*), and vanity (*l'amour de vanité*). He then proceeds to take the reader through the permutations possible with this multiple model. He, like Kuki, uses many artistic and literary examples (primary for Stendhal are Goethe's Werther and Byron's Don Juan in his many literary and musical guises). The kinds of love and passion described by Stendhal are, not surprisingly, quite different from those explicated by Kuki, since the role of emotion, self-definition, and pleasure were grasped quite differently in the two societies. Kuki, of course, was very aware of these differences. Both writers, in any case, seem on the whole to adhere to the principle succinctly set forth by Stendhal: "I neither blame nor do I approve. I merely observe."[11] Yet while the particular contours of each emotion may differ in the cultures of nineteenth-century Japan and nineteenth-century France—for the books deal with virtually the same time period in their respective societies—certain topics taken up by their authors show considerable resemblances: modesty, feminine pride, jealousy, anticipation, the nature and dangers of uncontrolled infatuation. The striking, sometimes delicious, comparisons between the observations of these two writers are many, so many, in fact, that *On Love* must certainly be seen as one putative model for Kuki's own work.

Kuki's fascination with Baudelaire is even more explicit, and his sympathies for the attitudes of this celebrated figure of nineteenth-century French artistic and literary life are altogether apparent. In her important study, *Authenticating Culture in Imperial Japan*, Leslie Pincus makes a number of trenchant comments on the correspondences between Baudelaire and his Japanese admirer, to which the reader should be referred.[12] In some ways, Kuki's choice of Baudelaire is an obvious one, since, like his predecessor Stendhal, Baudelaire rails at modern life and the coming of a homogenized society, which reveals the "vulgarity of the explicitly optimistic." Paul Valéry said of Stendhal that "for him life was a private stage upon which he presented without interruption the performance of himself."[13] Baudelaire, while altering the locale and the scenery, chooses to play an equally central role.

Baudelaire is particularly remembered for his creation of the figure of the dandy, that figure who, with his rigorously artificial code of behavior, manages to keep himself aloof from the tiresomeness of the ordinary. Attitude, and a well-developed self-consciousness of that attitude, are all. Here is one description provided by the poet.

> A great man and a saint, for his own sake.
> Lives and sleeps in front of a mirror
> Is a man of leisure and general education
> Is rich and loves work
> Works in a disinterested manner
> Does nothing useful
> Is either a poet, a priest, or a soldier
> Is solitary
> Is unhappy
> Never speaks to the masses except to insult them
> Never touches a newspaper.[14]

In such a stance, the dandy is able, in the words of César Graña, to "defy society with the perfection of the individual." And while it is true that Kuki, in his description of Edo life (so circumscribed politically), does not describe

Salon, pen and brown ink with gray wash, watercolor, and black chalk
over graphite, 25.2 × 32.5 cm., by Constantin Guys (1802–1892).
The British Museum, London.

any such appositional qualities that might be found in the characteristics of
iki, he nevertheless seems to have felt in Baudelaire's conception a great sympathy for one who subjects himself or herself to a rigorous, implicit code of
behavior and being.

Some of Baudelaire's most explicit pronouncements concerning the way
in which such a special caste can function in the life of his time can be found
in his trenchant essay of 1863, "The Painter of Modern Life," which, needless to say, is another of his texts found in Kuki's personal library. In this
essay, Baudelaire, doubtless the finest art critic of his time, pays homage
to the artist Constantin Guys (1802–1892), who was of such a retiring temperament that he would only permit the use of his initials in that celebrated
essay. Guys specialized in sketches of society life, usually captured in wash
drawings of startling immediacy. His work was admired by Manet and influenced such later artists as Toulouse-Lautrec and even Picasso. Guys set
out to capture the essence of his society through recording habits of dress,
physical carriage, and social situations. A comparative study of his depiction

of nineteenth-century French society with the similar work of the Japanese woodblock printmakers cited by Kuki would surely yield striking results.

Many of Baudelaire's comments on the artistry of Guys center on the fact that art, which can capture the immediate, may through it suggest the eternal. "Modernity is the transient, the fleeting, the contingent," he remarks, "it is one half of art, the other being the eternal and the immovable."[15] What is more, each epoch has its own peculiar manifestations.

> I have said that every age has its own carriage, its expression, its gestures. This proposition may be easily verified in a large portrait gallery (the one at Versailles, for example). But it can be yet further extended. In a unity we call a nation, the professions, the social classes, the successive centuries, introduce variety not only in gestures and manners, but also in the general outlines of faces. Such and such nose, mouth, forehead, will be standard for a given interval of time, the length of which I shall not claim to determine here, but which may certainly be a matter of calculation.[16]

In his remarks, Baudelaire has no hesitancy in establishing national parameters for the visual aspects of culture that artists record, and it might therefore be permitted to grant Kuki the same indulgence; or at least if he is to be considered a nationalist, then so must his French mentors, a charge seldom, if ever, leveled against them. Thus, when Kuki remarks in the last lines of the final page of his study that "[w]e comprehend and understand completely the core meaning of iki only when we grasp its structure as a self-revelation of **the being of our people,**" his stance in defining a national culture would not have been found exceptionable by such a writer as Baudelaire, who felt he had every reason to define the essence of the French character by means of physique, behavior, and clothing. For French conservatives, Baudelaire's definition of his culture in these terms, rather than by singling out the paragons of official virtue to be found in the military, the church, and the bureaucracy, may well have seemed scandalous. As a further observation, I might suggest that there may well be a similarly subversive element in Kuki's observations as well, since, in the view of the Meiji and Taishō elite, the nation should be defined in terms of the kind of hardworking, spartan virtues associated with traditional samurai values. In that regard, the famous study of Nitobe Inazō, Bushidō: The Soul of Japan, first published in 1905 and widely circulated for many years in the West, which praised such a vision of high-level self-sacrifice, appears somewhat hollow and self-serving when compared to Kuki's often openly erotic vision, in which he locates the essence of the national charac-

At Mabille's, brush drawing with brown ink, with brown wash and watercolor over graphite, 28.0 × 22.5 cm., by Constantin Guys (1802–1892). The British Museum, London.

Cuirassiers, pen and black ink with gray wash over graphite, 32.1 × 50.0 cm., by Constantin Guys (1802–1892). The British Museum, London.

ter in a spirit of play and conscious self-regard. In this regard, Kuki may owe much to Baudelaire's concept of the dandy.

For Baudelaire, dandyism, which he defines with considerable elegance in the course of the essay, has its proscribed ways of behavior.

> Dandyism, which is an institution outside the law, has a rigorous code of laws that all its subjects are strictly bound by, however ardent and independent their individual characters may be.[17]

Such a code can be found in Japan, and it is revealed in many ways, among them, as Kuki was later to insist as well, in the use of clothing and the body, as outlined in chapter 2 of *The Structure of Iki*, in Kuki's description of the use of thin fabrics, types of hairstyles, and the way in which clothing was manipulated for sexual effect.

In the section of the essay entitled "Woman," Baudelaire writes that:

> Woman is doubtless a light, a glance, an invitation to happiness, sometimes a spoken word; but above all, she is a harmonious whole, not only in her carriage and in the movement of her limbs, but also in the mus-

lins and the gauzes, in the vast and iridescent clouds of draperies in which she envelops herself and which are, so to speak, the attributes and pedestal of her divinity; in the metal and precious stones that serpentine around her arms and neck, that add their sparkle to the fire of her eyes, or whisper softly at her ears. When he describes the pleasure caused by the sight of a beautiful woman, what poet would dare to distinguish between her and her apparel? Show me the man who, in the street, at the theatre, or in the Bois, has not enjoyed, in a wholly detached way, the sight of a beautifully composed attire, and has not carried away with him an image inseparable from the beauty of the woman wearing it, thus making of the two, the woman and the dress, an indivisible whole.[18]

Kuki, of course, is describing a very different culture; but in his own examination of clothing, posture, and attitude, he is certainly making use of the French master's strategies; and indeed, Baudelaire's sense of the visual image that stimulates the male gaze is mirrored in Kuki's remark that "colors expressive of *iki* offer inactive afterimages that accompany a luscious experience."[19] Kuki, trained as he was in philosophy, uses a more neutral and analytical language in his descriptions of fashion, a strategy less successful in articulating the kind of ironic, sometimes bantering tone that his French mentors create with the freedom of their often whimsical literary flair. Nevertheless, insofar as Kuki's text can be envisioned as a series of imaginary dialogues with one after another of his French mentors whom he admires, Kuki does, in my view at least, manage to hold up his end of the conversation. Indeed, Kuki's way of framing his arguments—in which he puts forth a proposition, then provides evidence to affirm it—is occasionally reminiscent of the strategy of the imagined dialogue employed by Paul Valéry in his *Eupalinos, or the Architect,* a work that Kuki himself cites. (In that instance, Valéry creates a conversation between Socrates and Phaedrus in order to discuss certain problems of art and aesthetics.)

Whatever the unique qualities of Kuki's personal thought and experience, however, it also seems pertinent to read his work in juxtaposition to other Japanese writers active in both Kuki's formative period and in his more mature years, in order to see how others took up each in their own way some of the same concerns that suggest themselves when we read *The Structure of Iki* now, at the beginning of the twenty-first century. For, in a very real sense, Kuki was a child of his time, and subject to the same trajectories of experience and response encountered by others.

The first of these is doubtless Mori Ōgai (1862–1922), a doctor (and eventually the surgeon general of the Japanese army) and a great writer of the Meiji period whom Kuki's generation in particular respected enormously. Ōgai, like Kuki, spent formative years in Europe, years that changed both his vision of himself and of his world. In Germany from 1884 to 1888, he returned to Japan with both a great respect for the accomplishments of European civilization and a heightened awareness of the complex and contradictory nature of contemporary Japanese culture, caught up as it was in a whirlwind of change. Ōgai's often ironic treatment of that society is revealed in a number of trenchant works he composed in the early years of this century. After the death of Emperor Meiji, Ōgai, reflecting on those changes, began to write a series of striking and highly admired stories and accounts of life in the Tokugawa period, so as to cast in terms understandable to his contemporaries those attitudes and a sense of life that were rapidly vanishing.

For me personally, the most poignant of Ōgai's historical accounts, composed in 1916, involves the life of a doctor named Shibue Chūsai (1805–1858), who lived at the end of the Tokugawa period. Although Chūsai died only some sixty years before Ōgai wrote his biography, Chūsai inhabited a mental and physical world already virtually unrecognizable to Ōgai's younger contemporaries. In a celebrated passage, Ōgai describes his character, juxtaposing his own character with that of his predecessor.

> Chūsai was a physician and a bureaucrat. He studied books of philosophy on various aspects of Confucianism, he read history, and he studied in the field of the arts as well, literature and poetry. In this regard we resemble each other very closely indeed. Still, one noticeable difference, putting aside the fact that we have lived at different times, our lives have not had precisely the same value. No, in fact, I must admit there is one enormous difference. Although Chūsai was able to establish himself as a real student of philosophy and art, I have not been able to escape from my own vague world of the dilettante. Looking at Chūsai, I can only feel a sense of shame.
>
> Chūsai was indeed a man who walked the same road that I have. Yet his stride was something I could never hope to imitate. He was vastly superior to me in every way. I owe him all my respect. Indeed, the extraordinary thing is that he walked not only all the great roads but came and went by the byways as well. Not only did he study neo-Confucianism, but he amused himself with books of heraldry and old maps of Edo. If Chūsai had been my contemporary, our sleeves would surely have

rubbed as we walked through those muddy lanes. An intimacy would have developed between us. And I would have come to love him.[20]

Ōgai sees the past without sentimentality, and his exhaustive treatment of Chūsai's life, as well as many of his other stories about life in the Tokugawa period, were composed in a sophisticated effort to create a link to a powerful traditional culture that was in the process of being swept away and forgotten. Kuki, too, I believe, possessed in his own way that same sense of urgency.

In reading Ōgai's work, it seems clear that his heightened sense of real spiritual tensions within his own culture came about precisely because he was taken out of it at a crucial juncture in his life. Many of the great writers of this period underwent the same process, in which their own self-consciousness, both as Japanese and as artists, was to be immeasurably heightened through their experiences abroad. The great novelist Natsume Sōseki (1867–1916), for example, went to England (which he came to detest) in the early years of the century and returned to write a series of celebrated novels in which, he indicated, he wanted to discover what it meant to be a Japanese in his generation. Nagai Kafū (1879–1959), after his sojourns in America and France, came back to Japan and wrote with great eloquence concerning his new sense of the power of traditional Japanese architecture, learned through his exposure to the monumental buildings of France. Shimazaki Tōson (1872–1943), in France at the time of the First World War, came to realize the significance of the enormous changes already coming to Japan and, like Ōgai, decided to write his monumental *Before the Dawn* (*Yoakemae*) in order to conjure up his vision, based on his family's own history, of how traditional life and values were reshaped, in some ways tragically, by the coming of the West. And there are many similar examples. Seen in this perspective, *The Structure of Iki* can be seen as a work, although written by a philosopher and a poet rather than by a novelist, that attempts in a more immediately focused way to seek an understanding of qualities, already being forgotten by the author's contemporaries, that helped define the authentic life of his culture a mere hundred years before.

Most readers would agree, I feel sure, that as they read the works of the Japanese writers cited above, *The Structure of Iki* included, they will find little that is sentimental in them. None of these great writers and intellectuals— and I would include Kuki among them—reveals any desire to return to the past. Nor do they wish to prettify it. But all of them, explicitly or implicitly, see the yawning gulf between the old culture and the new. And the dangers of that gulf, for all of them, suggest a kind of nihilism that each, in his own way, acknowledges but abhors.

Then too, unfashionable as the exercise may be in these post-Foucault days, it may be worth ruminating on the nature of Kuki's own intentions in writing his study. If one juxtaposes *The Structure of Iki* with the writings of such other Japanese artists and intellectuals mentioned above, certain elements in Kuki's motivation suggest themselves.

Many Japanese writers traveling to Europe during this period felt that the Europeans with whom they came in contact were, at best, indifferent to Japan and, at worst, filled with misapprehensions and misunderstandings about the nature and significance of the Japanese tradition.

Again, the earliest of these writers to go abroad, Mori Ōgai, set the pattern. While in Munich in 1878, he heard a lecture by Edmund Naumann—a geologist who was one of the earliest of the "foreign experts" to teach in Japan, for a decade beginning in 1875—some six years after the Meiji restoration of 1868. Ōgai felt that, in this lecture, the German scientist had belittled both Japan's culture and the efforts his countrymen were making toward what Ōgai felt to be the absolutely necessary importation of Western technology. Ōgai eventually wrote an article in German to rebut such arguments, which was published in a leading newspaper. Caught up, as Richard Bowring points out, in his own sense of mission, Ōgai wrote in part:

> Naumann goes on to say that "the undiluted adoption of European culture might weaken instead of strengthen the Japanese, and bring about the collapse of the race." What kind of "European culture" is it which, if adopted, brings with it the danger of destruction? Does not true European culture lie in the recognition of freedom and beauty in the purest sense of those words? Is this recognition capable of bringing about destruction?[21]

Ōgai's own views were to be refined and altered after his return to Japan, when he would witness for himself the strains and dislocations produced by rapid shifts in technology and so in the culture that was inevitably to be deeply altered by such extreme changes. In that sense, then, one might argue that Ōgai was the first to establish a double-edged literary process, first explaining Japan to the West, and then, after returning to Japan, explaining what he had come to see as fundamental aspects of Japanese civilization to his contemporary Japanese, who were losing touch with their own past. This latter stage seemed necessary in an intellectual and social climate in which, as Richard Bowring succinctly puts it, "the problem was to be, to what extent could the importation of Western culture and thought continue before it caused a fatal break with the past."[22]

Kuki, some forty years later, was to follow the same trajectory. Back in Paris in 1928, he was asked to join a distinguished group of French philosophers and academicians as a participant in a series of meetings held in Pontigny, ostensibly on the subjects man and time, repetition in time, and immortality or eternity. None of the other participants evidently had any experience with Japan, so Kuki prepared two lectures in French to explain what were for him central elements in Asian and, specifically, Japanese culture. He entitled them "The Notion of Time and Repetition in Oriental Art" and "The Expression of the Infinite in Japanese Art." Subsequently published in France, they represent Kuki's first attempts to sum up certain basic values he located in his civilization. These lectures, now available in English translation, make useful reading for their intellectual proximity to ideas expressed in *The Structure of Iki*.[23] Although the specific topics he chose for this occasion bear little direct resemblance to those featured in his later study, Kuki follows the same path taken by Ōgai, who, after addressing his European counterparts, developed following his return to Japan the kind of self-consciousness that virtually propelled him to address his own compatriots concerning the nature of their culture.

The same trajectory can be found in Sōseki's writing, when, after his return to Japan, he wrote that his work would henceforth be dedicated, as already mentioned, to finding out what it meant to be a Japanese at the beginning of this century. It remains a striking fact that, in virtually every case, these writers turned to the past in order to articulate contrasts with the contemporary values they felt to be crucial. Sōseki himself came closest to this when he wrote *Kusamakura* (translated and published in English as *Three-Cornered World*), a final elegy to the traditional arts of Tokugawa Japan. The others, too, also wrote extensively on the Tokugawa period. Salvation lay in the past for none of them. Yet the past could provide possibly the only useful perspective and vantage point from which to examine an indifferent and shifting present.

In many ways, Kuki remains the most playful and ironic of those who addressed these concerns. By constructing his analyses of *iki* through his adopted modern and Western philosophical structural models of those aspects of Edo life and culture to which his temperament most strongly responded, his work reveals both a certain implicit resignation concerning the inevitable changes that contemporary life had brought his generation, as well as a half-articulated need to justify his own artistic, social, and deeply personal stance. The author's personality, for all the "objectivity" of his remarks, lurks here behind virtually every page. In that special sense, Kuki is also a writer in the great tradition of Japanese letters. He uses his writings, as did Kamo no Chōmei or Yoshida Kenkō many centuries before him, as a means to both reveal and conceal his deepest and most personal concerns.

Notes

1. For an enlightening discussion in English on Alain, see the introduction by Robert D. Cottrell in Alain, *Alain on Happiness* (New York: Frederick Ungar Publishing Company, 1973), xi–xix.

2. *Kuki Shūzō bunko mokuroku* (Kobe: Kōnan Daigaku tetsugaku kyōshitsu, 1976).

3. Alain, *Système des beaux-arts* (Paris: Gallimard, 1926), 8 [my translation].

4. Alain, *Alain on Happiness*, xvi–xvii.

5. Ibid., 221.

6. See Nara translation, 19.

7. Stendahl, *On Love* (New York: Liveright Publishing Corporation, 1947), 332.

8. Ibid., xi.

9. Ibid., xviii.

10. Ibid., xv–xvi.

11. Ibid., 172.

12. Leslie Pincus, *Authenticating Culture in Imperial Japan: Kuki Shūzō and the Rise of National Aesthetics* (Berkeley: University of California Press, 1996), see especially 137–138.

13. Cited in César Graña, *Bohemian Versus Bourgeois: French Society and the French Man of Letters in the Nineteenth Century* (New York: Basic Books, 1964), 142.

14. Cited in Graña, *Bohemian*, 149.

15. Baudelaire, *Selected Writings on Art and Artists* (Harmondsworth: Penguin Books, 1972), 403.

16. Ibid., 404.

17. Ibid., 419.

18. Ibid., 424.

19. Nara translation, 48.

20. Mori Ōgai, *Mori Ōgai zenshū* (Tokyo: Chikuma shobō, 1971), 4:52–53.

21. See Richard Bowring, *Mori Ōgai and the Modernization of Japanese Culture* (Cambridge: Cambridge University Press, 1979), 18–20.

22. Ibid., 19.

23. See Stephen Light, *Shūzō Kuki and Jean-Paul Sartre* (Carbondale: Southern Illinois University Press, 1987) for translations of the texts of these lectures and other short essays originally written in French.

Reading Kuki Shūzō's *The Structure of Iki* in the Shadow of *L'affaire Heidegger*

JON MARK MIKKELSEN

The names of Kuki Shūzō (1888–1941) and Martin Heidegger (1889–1976) have long been linked in discussion of Kuki's work. Consequently, it is hardly surprising that this linkage should be taken for granted in Leslie Pincus' recent, ambitious study, *Authenticating Culture in Imperial Japan: Kuki Shūzō and the Rise of National Aesthetics* (Berkeley: University of California Press, 1996).[1] But should it be taken for granted, or, more to the point, does highlighting Kuki's relationship to Heidegger even serve Kuki well? Could, in other words, the common practice of linking the name of Kuki with that of Heidegger have actually led to the misinterpretation of Kuki's work and distorted views of its significance?

The purpose of these remarks is to examine these questions. I suggest that this linkage should not be taken for granted, that highlighting Kuki's relationship to Heidegger does not necessarily serve him well, and that the usual way in which the names of Kuki and Heidegger are linked has likely led to misinterpretations of Kuki's work and distorted accounts of its significance. To suggest that the names of Kuki and Heidegger should, in effect, be "de-linked" is not, however, the same as claiming that there are no grounds for linking them; nor is it to suggest that nothing of value is to be gained from comparative studies of their works, including, in particular, their respective views of art. To be sure, the reasons typically given for linking these names are clear and well founded. They merit, therefore, some discussion before considering how this practice might also have contributed to the misinterpretation of Kuki's work and distorted views of its significance.

For example, we know that Kuki spent the years 1922–1929 in Europe, primarily in Germany and France, that he met Heidegger at the home of Heidegger's mentor, the phenomenologist Edmund Husserl (1859–1938), in Freiburg, Germany, during the summer of 1927, and that he subsequently returned to Marburg with Heidegger to attend his lectures and seminars the following academic year.[2] We also know that after Kuki returned to Japan, he published, in 1930, a work, reproduced in a new English translation in this volume, which is typically described as having been written largely under the influence of Heidegger's hermeneutic phenomenology, *The Structure of Iki*.[3]

No one who knows anything about Heidegger's hermeneutic phenomenology need doubt then, when reading *The Structure*, that Heidegger's philosophy must have had a significant impact upon Kuki. Nor can there be any doubt that Kuki played an important role in promoting the study of Heidegger's philosophy in Japan during the 1930s.[4] To understand more fully why the name of Kuki is typically linked with that of Heidegger, we must, however, recognize that Kuki's connection to Heidegger did not end with the publication of *The Structure*, or even with Kuki's premature death, in 1941. For nearly three decades after the publication of *The Structure*, Heidegger memorialized his earlier encounter with Kuki by publishing a brief text that has been translated into English under the title "A Dialogue on Language."[5] Further, Heidegger is said to have claimed in the years following the composition of this "dialogue" that he had once hoped to write a preface to a German translation of Kuki's *Structure*, or possibly another work, that was to have appeared during his lifetime.[6] So, the names of Kuki and Heidegger are also linked because of Heidegger's apparent interest in Kuki's work, that is, because Heidegger himself gives the impression in his "dialogue" that Kuki's use of the term *iki* faithfully conveys — or anticipates — the leading motifs of his own way of thinking.

There is, however, yet another, very significant reason why the names of Kuki and Heidegger are often linked together. This reason is, bluntly stated, that neither Kuki nor Heidegger seem to have been much disturbed by the fact that fascist regimes came to power in their respective nations during the 1930s. This reason for linking the names of these two philosophers has, however, naturally played a far different role in Kuki scholarship than those previously noted. For, viewed in the light of this connection, it should be obvious that linking the name of Kuki to that of Heidegger has tended to serve Kuki well in circles receptive to Heidegger's philosophy, but it has not served him well in circles where credence is given instead to Theodor Adorno's (1903–1969) criticism that Heidegger's philosophy is "fascist down to its most intimate components," Karl Jaspers' (1883–1969) judgment of it as "unfree, dictatorial and incapable of communication," or Karl Löwith's (1897–1973) report that Heidegger had once agreed with him, "without reservation," that "his partisanship for National Socialism lay in the essence of his philoso-phy."[7] Consequently, as criticism of Heidegger for his involvement with the Nazis has intensified in recent years, the desirability of linking the name of Kuki with that of Heidegger has surely diminished.

The impetus for de-linking the names of Kuki and Heidegger does not, however, stem only from a desire to free discussion of Kuki's work from that of Heidegger because of Heidegger's involvement with the Nazis. The impe-tus also stems from the fact that a number of scholars have begun to question the accuracy of Heidegger's account of his relationship to Kuki on indepen-dent scholarly grounds that have nothing to do with the political views of either figure. Perhaps foremost among such scholars is Reinhard May, who points out that *iki* is, in Heidegger's "dialogue," never defined in language at all comparable to that which Kuki uses in offering his own, tentative defi-nition at the end of the second chapter of *The Structure* ("**sophisticated** [aris-ing from *akirame* 'resignation'] **coquetry** [*bitai*] with **pluck** [arising from *ikiji* 'pride and honor']").[8] Heidegger instead describes *iki* as "the breath of still-ness of luminous delight" (ADL, 44) and "the pure delight of the beckoning stillness" (ADL, 45). Indeed, even when Heidegger claims in this text to be recalling Kuki's own description of *iki*, he uses terminology that is foreign to *The Structure*, saying that Kuki had described *iki* as that "sensuous radiance through whose lively delight there breaks the radiance of something super-sensuous" (ADL, 14). *Iki* is, in other words, stripped in Heidegger's "dia-logue" of its peculiarly Japanese character and seems instead to point only to an experience, or, as Heidegger would prefer to say, an "event" (*Ereignis*), that "opens" us to the self-disclosure of "Being," or, alternatively, a "clear-ing" (*Lichtung*). As Heidegger describes it, in other words, Kuki's account of *iki* should be of interest to us primarily because it anticipates the subse-quent direction of his own philosophical development. Consequently, May ultimately concludes that Heidegger's "dialogue" is probably not even based on an actual conversation between Heidegger and Kuki.[9]

The need for a reexamination of Kuki's relationship to Heidegger is thus surely in order, although I naturally cannot promise, within the brief space of an introductory essay, to address fully all of the issues that such a reexamina-tion might require. I can, however, introduce two theses into the discussion for the purpose of stimulating new work on Kuki's relationship to Heideg-ger. The first thesis is that we should not expect to find in Kuki's *Structure* those features of Heidegger's own reflections on the "work of art" so appar-ent in his 1935–1936 lecture "The Origin of the Work of Art"—perhaps the most accessible statement of his view of art that we have—which leave him vulnerable to charges like those leveled against him by Adorno, Jaspers, and Löwith.[10] The second thesis is that it would be a serious mistake to use Heidegger's philosophy as an exclusive guide to reading Kuki's *Structure*, since such a reading can cause us to ignore significant features of the work that cannot easily be reduced to Heideggerian categories.[11]

Prior to considering the issues central to a defense of either of these two theses, I must, however, first offer a brief account of the problem referred to in recent Heidegger scholarship as *l'affaire Heidegger* and comment on the circumstances surrounding the composition of Heidegger's 1935–1936 lecture. These first two, preliminary tasks are completed, respectively, in the first two sections below. A third section is devoted to an all-too-brief discussion of Kuki's *Structure* in which significant differences between Kuki and Heidegger concerning their methods and views of art are clearly identified. These three sections are followed by a short conclusion.

L'affaire Heidegger

To speak of an *affaire* in this case is to refer to the international uproar, or scandal, that erupted following the publication, in 1987, of the French edition of Victor Farias' sensationalistic book *Heidegger et le nazisme* (Paris: Éditions Verdier, 1987).[12] That Heidegger, unlike Kuki, actively supported the fascist regime that came to power in his country during this period has long been known.[13] But partly as a consequence of Heidegger's own efforts after the war "to explain away" this part of his life, and, until recently, the widespread acceptance, to some degree or other, of his own account of the events of this period, his involvement with the Nazi regime was very often ignored by scholars concerned with his thought. Heidegger the philosopher, or, as he would prefer to be designated, "the thinker," was, therefore, frequently separated from Heidegger the man, who, according to this view, assumed the post of rector of the University of Freiburg on April 15, 1933, only two and a half months after the Nazis came to power, more as a matter of chance and not by conscious design. This easy separation of Heidegger the philosopher from Heidegger the Nazi sympathizer has, however, become increasingly difficult to make in recent years, even by philosophers who are still wholly committed to the view that Heidegger remains one of the central figures of twentieth-century philosophy.[14]

So how did Heidegger account for his involvement with National Socialism in the period from the early 1930s to the end of the Second World War? The account of these years promoted by Heidegger and his sympathetic followers is typically referred to as the "official story."[15] According to the "official story," Heidegger, like most Germans, was greatly disturbed by Germany's political instability in the period following the end of the First World War, but he was never seriously "engaged" politically except during the brief ten-month period when he served as rector of the University of Freiburg. Claiming that he displayed great political naïveté in taking this post, he later insisted that his support for the National Socialists during this brief period was indicative only of his desire to protect the academic world from being completely co-opted by politics. He also insists that he forbade the posting of anti-Jewish posters on university grounds during the period when he served as rector, that he resisted party demands to fire anti-Nazi professors, that he resigned from his post in February 1934 because he could no longer tolerate political interference in the university, and that he subsequently withdrew into a kind of "inner emigration" that lasted until the end of the war in 1945. Further, Heidegger also claimed that he was, during the war years, subjected to scathing criticism by party ideologues, that his classes were watched and even shut down by the Gestapo, and that he was, in 1944, declared one of the "most expendable" professors and sent to work repairing the Rhine dikes. However, even though Heidegger claimed that he never actively supported the regime, he was, after the end of the war, forced into retirement and not allowed to lecture again until the year 1951; and he might have been subjected to even worse punishment had it not been for the intervention of his old friend Karl Jaspers, even though Jaspers' judgment of Heidegger was, as previously noted, not very sympathetic.[16]

The inconsistencies between the "official story" and the accounts of Heidegger's political involvement provided by others have been discussed at length by many commentators and need not be examined here.[17] More significant for this discussion of Kuki's relationship to Heidegger is whether there is any specific textual evidence in Heiddegger's 1935–1936 lecture that offers any clear indication of his political views during this period, and, if such evidence can be found, whether the views expressed reflect core elements of his philosophical project that link both him and this project conceptually to his initial support for the National Socialist "revolution" of the early 1930s.

The Cultural/Political Origins of Heidegger's "Origin of the Work of Art"

According to Michael Zimmerman, a sympathetic but critical commentator, Heidegger had planned, prior to resigning from the rectorate, to offer a course on politics and the state during the 1934–1935 academic year, but

after his resignation, he instead offered a course in which he publicly medi-
tated on two of the most well-known longer poems, or "hymns," of the German poet Hölderlin (1770–1847), *Germany (Germanien)* and *The Rhine (Der Rhein)*
(HCM, 113).[18] *Origin* was then first presented shortly thereafter at a colloquium co-organized by Heidegger and given the title "Overcoming Aesthetics in the Questioning of Art" *(Die Überwindung der Ästhetik in der Frage nach der
Kunst)* on November 13, 1935.[19] Zimmerman further suggests that "[i]t was
no accident that Heidegger read the first version of the essay . . . in 1935,
not long after Hitler's Nuremberg speech about art and architecture," entitled
"Art and Politics," in which the German führer called for the "revival and
resurrection of German art" (HCM, 99).[20] However, whether or not Heidegger was responding in his 1935 lecture, either sympathetically or critically, to
Hitler's Nuremberg speech, his work from this period clearly marks a shift
of interest away from the priority that he had previously placed on "(philosophical) science" *(Wissenschaft)*—that is, the development of an *hermeneutic*
phenomenology in contrast to the *transcendental* phenomenology of his mentor Husserl—in works such as *Being and Time* and the lecture that he gave
on the occasion of being named rector, "The Self-Assertion of the German
University," toward a new concern with "art" *(Kunst)* and the "work of art"
(Kunstwerk).[21]

By the years 1934–1936, Heidegger seems, in other words, to have turned
away from "(philosophical) science," including, therefore, his interest in the
development of a distinctly hermeneutic form of phenomenology, to "art,"
particularly the poetry of Hölderlin, as the means of realizing a new "self-
disclosure of Being" to the late modern world that could be regarded as "primordial" as that, which in his view, had been given to the ancient Greeks.[22]
Thus, even though *Origin* has been ignored by some scholars in their accounts
of Heidegger's political development during this period,[23] it is regarded by
others as an important text that marks a key "turn" *(Kehre)* toward Heidegger's
later thought.[24]

Remarks in Favor of a Less "Heideggerian"
Reading of *The Structure of Iki*

Certainly *l'affaire Heidegger* casts a long shadow over Kuki's *The Structure of Iki*.
Were this not the case, scholars such as Pincus would surely have never even
considered undertaking a project so monumental in scope as that of investigating Kuki's position in the "cultural formation" of Japanese fascism in the
1930s in the light of Heidegger's involvement with National Socialism.[25] But
does *l'affaire Heidegger* really serve as a good model for understanding Kuki's

case? Specifically, should we expect, in reading *The Structure*, to encounter passages that indicate Kuki's political views as clearly as do some passages in Heidegger's *Origin*—even if the commentators do not agree as to what significance is ultimately to be given to those passages? I believe that this expectation is unfounded. I believe, in other words, that the connection between the view of art that Heidegger sketches in *Origin* is both historically and conceptually consistent with his political involvement with the Nazis, while the connection between Kuki's view of art and whatever political tendencies he may have actually held is hardly so evident in *The Structure*.

What is it, then, that commentators have found to be so objectionable about the view of art developed in Heidegger's *Origin*? Central to Heidegger's argument in this text is his view that the "work of art" expresses itself most fully in the tension, or "strife" (*Riss*), between two contrasting functions of art: "setting up a world" (*das Aufstellen einer Welt*) and "setting forth of the earth" (*das Herstellen der Erde*). To "set up a world" does not, for Heidegger, mean simply to set up a "mere collection of the countable or uncountable, familiar and unfamiliar things that are just there" (*OWA*, 44). Nor is it a "merely imagined framework added by our representation to the sum of such given things" (ibid.). To "set up a world" might instead be thought of as "founding" an entire cultural landscape, or, as Heidegger states in that sort of language for which he is so well known, and so often harshly criticized: "World is the non-objective to which we are subject as long as the paths of birth and death, blessing and curse keep us transported in Being" (ibid.).²⁶

The notion of "setting forth of earth" is complementary to that of "setting up a world." This "setting forth of earth" occurs when actual material forms appear in the "worlding" of "setting up a world." Heidegger describes this "earth" as "that which comes forth and shelters. . . . In setting up a world, the work sets forth the earth. . . . The work moves the earth itself into the Open of a world and keeps it there. The work lets the earth be on earth" (*OWA*, 46). As significant as Heidegger's notion of "earth" may be, however,²⁷ it is, for our purposes, important only to emphasize that the two activities that Heidegger introduces in the second section of *Origin*, namely, "setting up a world" and "setting forth of earth," do not exist apart from one another but are instead reciprocally related aspects of a dynamic process. Heidegger even goes so far as to claim that "[t]he work-being of the work consists in the fighting of the battle between world and earth" (*OWA*, 49), for "[w]orld and earth are essentially different from one another and yet are never separated" (*OWA*, 48).

Consequently, one of the central problems for assessing the political significance of the view of art that Heidegger sketches in *Origin* concerns reconciling the fact that Heidegger's view of art both (1) sanctions identifying certain works of art or art movements as being of great historical significance precisely because they "set up" a new "world" for a people and (2) logically entails that no specific "disclosure" of such a "world" could ever be taken as complete or absolute, since all cases of "setting up a world" are held in check by the "setting forth of earth." A fully developed account of Heidegger's view of art must, in other words, surely emphasize both the importance and the limitations of any specific "worlding" work of art, for example, the poetry of Hölderlin. Heidegger, however, is more inclined in *Origin* to emphasize the importance, rather than the limitation, of such works.[28] Further, he is inclined to emphasize this aspect of the work of art in language that can easily be understood as giving "world historical" significance to the Nazi rise to power as part of the emergence of a new epoch of human history.[29]

To state, then, the two major weaknesses of the view of art sketched in *Origin*: (1) Heidegger too easily resolves the tension between "setting up a world" and "setting forth of earth" in his account of the way in which a work of art might foreshadow a new historical "founding" of German/world culture by suggesting—if only indirectly—that the new Nazi regime might be capable of directing the contemporary German response to the great art of a poet such as Hölderlin; and (2) Heidegger blurs the boundaries between aesthetics, history, and political philosophy as a result of his search for the full and complete "disclosure" of the ultimate, unifying ontological ground of all reality, which, like Kuki, he ultimately finds in an "aesthetic" mode of existence—although Heidegger, like Hegel (1770–1831), perhaps the greatest figure of nineteenth-century German philosophy, clearly eschewed the term *aesthetic*.[30] There is, however, another, simpler way to describe—albeit from a critical, non-Heideggerian perspective—the deficiency of the view of art that Heidegger develops in *Origin*. Heidegger's view of art gives no pride of place to the themes of "play" (*Spiel*) and referential indeterminacy that had previously been prevalent in German philosophical aesthetics since the publication of works such as Immanuel Kant's (1724–1804) *Critique of Judgment*, in 1791,[31] and Friedrich Schiller's (1759–1805) *On the Aesthetic Education of Man*, in 1795.[32] By contrast, Kuki's text is, if nothing else, surely very "playful," especially in his use of literary sources, as Rimer suggests in his contribution to this volume, while it is extremely difficult—but perhaps not entirely impossible—to find the "playful" elements in Heidegger's *Origin*.[33] But if Kuki's work should, as Rimer suggests, be viewed as "playful" in its use of literary and other artistic sources, why should we not also view Kuki's use of Heidegger's hermeneutic phenomenology as "playful"? However, when Kuki's text is viewed in

this manner it becomes far more difficult to make the same sort of direct—
or even indirect—connection between his view of art and his political sympathies that can be made when reading Heidegger's *Origin*.

Further, once we begin to read Kuki's text with an eye toward finding such
dissimilarities rather than focusing primarily on themes that might have originated with Heidegger, other differences between the views of Kuki and Heidegger become apparent. A second dissimilarity concerns core differences in
the two philosophers' use of the phenomenological method itself. A third
concerns significant differences in the way in which the two philosophers
give attention to—or, in the case of Heidegger, inattention to—details in
their respective descriptions of particular works of art.

Clearly, Heidegger's influence upon Kuki is, as Pincus and others have
rightly emphasized, most evident in the first three chapters and the conclusion of *The Structure*. But Kuki's actual use of hermeneutic phenomenology
differs significantly from that which Heidegger employed in his classic 1927
study *Being and Time*, as even Pincus ultimately recognizes. In fact, at the end
of her rather lengthy discussion of the history and development of the science
of hermeneutics in German and Japanese philosophy in the first several decades of the past century,[34] Pincus identifies at least six ways in which Kuki's
use of hermeneutic phenomenology differs significantly from that which Heidegger developed in the 1920s.[35] Following Pincus' own account, these differences may be summarized as follows:

1. Heidegger viewed hermeneutic phenomenology as a method for addressing the fundamental issues of the Western metaphysical tradition, that is
   to say "the question of Being," while Kuki was interested in describing
   the particularized Japanese cultural experience of *iki* (ACIJ, 170–172). More
   specifically, Heidegger wished to focus on the experience of particularized
   Being-in-the-world in order to address universal ontological issues, while
   Kuki focused on the particularity of Japanese aesthetic experience for the
   purpose of elevating Japanese culture to a stature whereby its uniqueness
   might be recognized by others (ACIJ, 173).[36]
2. "Heidegger introduced the working concept of 'Being-in-the-world' in
   hopes of overcoming the fateful dualities of Western metaphysics . . .
   [such as the duality] [b]etween subject and object, consciousness and
   world" (ACIJ, 175), while Kuki "situated desire in the center of philosophical inquiry and affirmed the priority of intersubjectivity [rather than authentic, resolute, monadic individuality] in the question of being" (ACIJ,
   174).

3. "Heidegger . . . felt it necessary to deconstruct . . . the metaphysical foundations of his own tradition, [while] Kuki was more concerned with (re)constructing the pillars of a Japanese tradition" (ACIJ, 175).

4. Heidegger's "notion of Being-in-the-world, along with its various permutations from inauthenticity to authenticity, is conspicuously absent from [*The Structure*]" (ACIJ, 175), and Kuki, like many of his contemporaries, even "criticized [Heidegger] for his preoccupation with the individual at the expense of sociality and community" (ACIJ, 177).

5. "In Heidegger's view, Dasein [that is, the "there-being" of human being, as described by Heidegger, the analysis of which he believed to be central to the project of fundamental ontology enshrined in *Being and Time*] bears a structure that is fundamentally temporal—a being stretched, as it were, between two voids: a rootless origin and a self-negating end. Only through a realization of temporality in this sense, in other words, of the nonbeing or nullity upon which it depends could Dasein come into its own" (ACIJ, 177), while Kuki believed that Heidegger had ignored the fundamental importance of spatiality and that this neglect, as Pincus describes his views, "translated into a disregard for the communal dimensions of existence" (ACIJ, 178).

6. Heidegger's vague remarks about an "authentic folk" in the final section of *Being and Time* led naturally to "his more practical association with National Socialism" (ACIJ, 176), while "the conspicuous absence of politics from Kuki's conception of community [only] defined a particular kind of political horizon for Japan" (ACIJ, 178).

Pincus' account of the differences between Kuki's and Heidegger's uses of hermeneutic phenomenology should perhaps not be taken at face value. What is at issue here, however, is not the complete accuracy of her account but the fact that it shows that even she must—before completing her book—have come to recognize that knowledge of Heidegger's philosophy is not as certain a guide to understanding Kuki's *Structure* as she suggests in the earlier chapters of her book.[37] If, however, Kuki's reliance upon Heidegger's hermeneutic phenomenology is as un-Heideggerian as Pincus suggests it is in the latter part of her study, why should we think that any of the other materials discussed in *The Structure* need to be understood exclusively in terms of Heidegger's hermeneutic phenomenology? For, as previously noted, yet another significant difference between the work of these two philosophers is that Heidegger seems relatively unconcerned with detail in his analysis of specific works of art, while Kuki, like his French contemporary Alain (Émile-Auguste

Chartier; 1868–1951), is, as Rimer also notes in his contribution to this volume, far more interested in aesthetic details in *The Structure* than Heidegger could ever have been in *Origin*.[38]

Stated more pointedly, the basic problem with attempting to bring a discussion of Heidegger's hermeneutic phenomenology to bear on Kuki's investigations of the phenomenon of *iki* is that insofar as Heidegger was concerned with hermeneutic phenomenology, that is, during the 1920s when Kuki was attending his lectures and seminars in Germany, he was not at all seriously concerned with art, or with philosophical aesthetics;[39] and insofar as Heidegger was concerned with art, or, more specifically, with the "work of art," he was not really all that interested in the detailed phenomenological description of aesthetic artifacts, as is evident from the descriptions he does in fact provide of phenomenon like Van Gogh's painting or the Greek temple in *Origin*.[40] Kuki, on the other hand, seems to take great pleasure in describing different examples and forms of art—especially in the fourth and fifth chapters of *The Structure*—that, in his opinion, exhibit *iki*. Further, the framework of these chapters departs entirely from that of the earlier chapters, since the distinctions that Kuki makes in setting up the discussion of the examples he considers have their source in issues that would have been of great concern to late eighteenth and early nineteenth-century German philosophers such as Kant and Hegel, but they would surely have been of no special concern to Heidegger, who was instead, as noted previously, primarily interested in "overcoming" the tradition within which distinctions such as these had become matters of great importance to, in his view, the detriment of the real "work" of the "work of art."[41]

The fourth chapter of *The Structure* is entitled "Natural Expressions of *Iki*"; the fifth is entitled "Artistic Expressions of *Iki*." The discussion in these chapters is clearly patterned after a distinction prominent in the aesthetics of Kant and Hegel, namely, the distinction, in Kant's terminology, between "natural beauty" (*Naturschönheit*) and "fine art" (*schöne Kunst*). Kant preferred "natural beauty" to "fine art," but Hegel thought that this preference was indicative of the limits of Kant's critical idealism.[42] Admittedly, after introducing this framework, Kuki seems, like Heidegger, not at all interested in taking sides in an arcane philosophical dispute such as this; but, unlike Heidegger, he also seems not particularly interested in developing a view of art that might be regarded as superior to the views of both Kant and Hegel.[43] He instead merely appropriates these categories for his own purposes and moves on to the next subject.[44]

Similarly, in the fifth chapter of *The Structure*, Kuki offers us something of what in the Western tradition is typically referred to as a "system" of the arts.[45] To construct such a system was a matter of considerable concern to nineteenth-century German philosophers such as Hegel—as well as to Kuki's twentieth-century French counterpart Alain.[46] Kant, on the other hand, like Kuki, does not ultimately place any great emphasis upon his "system" of the arts, since, after having made the effort to construct such a system, he notes in a footnote that "[t]he reader must not judge this sketch of a possible division of the fine arts as if it were intended as a theory. It is only one of a variety of attempts that can and should still be made."[47] Hegel, however, provides us with perhaps the most influential of all "modern" attempts to codify the various art forms and to identify their historical significance.[48] Further, Hegel's systematic account of the various forms of art is also a significant feature of his philosophy of history, and knowledge of Hegel's philosophy of history clearly plays a significant role in the sense of "historicity" that is such an important feature of Heidegger's *Origin*. Kuki, by contrast, clearly proceeds, in his playful account of the various forms of the "artistic expression of *iki*" in the fifth chapter of *The Structure*, as if he were totally unconcerned with the strong narrative, teleological—if not, in fact, eschatological—view of history that ultimately predominates in Heidegger's *Origin*, a view which undoubtedly also plays such a significant role in the connection that Heidegger makes between the "work of art" and contemporary political events.

Can we not now conclude, then, after even so brief a comparison of Kuki's text with Heidegger's *Origin* as this, that it is unlikely that we will ever find in *The Structure* the same—or even a comparable—underlying conceptual framework like that found in *Origin*, that is, a structure which might reveal at least as much about Kuki's political views as *Origin* reveals about the reasons Heidegger publicly supported—at least initially—the National Socialist revolution in German politics of the 1930s?[49]

Conclusion

The underlying purpose of these remarks has, admittedly, been primarily negative. I have not attempted to make a detailed, substantive contribution to the problem of providing a fair, defensible interpretation of Kuki's *Structure*. I have not even claimed that Kuki's text could not possibly have contributed in some way or other to the "cultural formation" of a totalitarian national aesthetics in imperial Japan, although, as others, including, in the final analysis, Pincus, have suggested, the historical evidence linking Kuki personally to such developments is hardly so convincing as is the historical and textual evidence that can be brought to bear against Heidegger.[50] I have instead been concerned primarily only with showing why efforts to understand Kuki's *Structure* primarily through his relationship to Heidegger can be seriously misleading—especially when such efforts are not based upon a thorough understanding of the complex issues that have emerged in the effort to understand Heidegger's view of art not only as it was first presented in *Origin* but in the light of his continued interest in this topic throughout the 1930s and 1940s as well as in the postwar period.[51]

I conclude, therefore, that to "make Kuki into a Heidegger" with regard to the conceptual role that he might have played in the formation of the Japanese cultural landscape of the 1930s, it would be necessary to show both (1) that his views of this "Edo aesthetic sensibility" played a similar role in his thinking as did the poetry of Hölderlin, beginning in the 1930s, in the development of Heidegger's thought and (2) that he held a view of history as strongly teleological—if not, in fact, as previously suggested, eschatological—as did Heidegger during the period when he seems to have viewed the advent of the National Socialist regime as marking the "founding" of a new epoch in history in which the German spirit could finally fulfill the destiny that had been given to it, which it has otherwise, in the course of modernity, been denied. I suspect, however, that anyone searching the text of *The Structure* to find views comparable to those of Heidegger on matters such as these will surely be searching in vain.

Notes

1. References to this text hereafter abbreviated *ACIJ*.

2. Heidegger accepted a position in Marburg in 1922 with the expectation that he would eventually return to Freiburg, where he had been a student or lecturer since 1909, to assume Husserl's chair when his mentor retired, as he did at the beginning of the 1928 winter term. See, for further information concerning Kuki's initial meeting with Heidegger and the topics of Heidegger's lectures and seminars during this period, Stephen Light, *Shūzō Kuki and Jean-Paul Sartre: Influence and Counter-Influence in the Early History of Existential Phenomenology* (Carbondale: Southern Illinois University Press, 1987), 6.

3. Pincus, for example, suggests near the beginning of *ACIJ* that it was primarily "Heidegger's version [of phenomenology], along with its hermeneutic heritage, [that] enabled Kuki to stake out the exclusive territory of the Japanese spirit" and that "Heideggerian philosophy and hermeneutics is . . . central to an analysis of [*The Structure of Iki*]" (*ACIJ*, 6).

4. Graham Parkes, in the translator's preface to Reinhard May's *Heidegger's Hidden*

Sources: East Asian Influences on His Work, translated and with a complementary essay by Graham Parkes (London: Routledge, 1996), credits Kuki with writing and publishing, in 1933, "[t]he first book length study of Heidegger" (*Haideggā no tetsugaku* [The philosophy of Heidegger]). Kuki has also been credited with inventing Japanese equivalents for some of the key German terms to which Heidegger assigned special meanings or that Heidegger himself invented throughout the course of his philosophical development, and the publication of Kuki's Kyoto University lectures on Heidegger, entitled *Ningen to jitsuzon* (Man and existence), in 1939, seems to have done much to solidify the central place that Heidegger's thought already held, since the early 1920s, in the history of modern Japanese philosophy. Cf. Nakano Hajimu, "Kuki Shūzō and *The Structure of Iki*," in *Culture and Identity: Japanese Intellectuals during the Interwar Years*, ed. J. Thomas Rimer (Princeton: Princeton University Press, 1990), 261–272.

5. The words "a dialogue on language" followed by the descriptive phrase "between a Japanese and an Inquirer" is the title given to the text in the English translation by Peter D. Hertz, "A Dialogue on Language," in Martin Heidegger, *On the Way to Language* (San Francisco: Harper and Row, 1971), 1–54. References to this text hereafter abbreviated ADL followed by the page numbers of this translation. As Graham Parkes points out, however, in a note to his translation of Reinhard May's *Heidegger's Hidden Sources*, the first half of the German title of this text, "Aus einem Gespräch von der Sprache," could also be rendered into English, more simply, but no less accurately, as "From a Conversation on Language" (*Hidden Sources*, xvii).

6. Light reports that Heidegger's remarks concerning his desire to write such a preface were said to have been made in 1957 (Light, *Shūzō Kuki and Jean-Paul Sartre*, 30–31, n. 16). The first complete German translation of Kuki's *Structure* did not, however, appear, as a master's thesis with a brief introduction, until 1984, well after Heidegger's death. See Emi Schinzinger, "Die Struktur des 'iki' von Kuki Shūzō" (master's thesis, University of Tübingen, 1985).

7. Adorno's criticism first appeared in a letter written, in January 1963, to *Diskus*, the Frankfurt student newspaper, in which Adorno was responding to criticisms that had been leveled against him on account of a review article that he had himself written in the 1930s of a song-cycle by a German composer that had been dedicated to "the Führer, Adolph Hitler"; Jaspers' comments appeared in the letter that he wrote in December 1945 to the Freiburg University's de-Nazification committee reviewing Heidegger's case after the war; and Löwith's remarks come from an essay he wrote while living in Japan in 1939—where he had obtained a position, possibly with assistance from Kuki, to whom he had written requesting assistance—for a competition sponsored by Harvard University for German émigrés on the theme of "My Life in Germany Before and After 1933." The circumstances surrounding the publication of Adorno's letter are discussed in Phillipe Lacoue-Labarthe, *Heidegger, Art and Politics* (Oxford: Basil Blackwell, 1990), 117–118; the texts from which Jaspers' and Löwith's comments are taken are reproduced in *The Heidegger Controversy*, ed. Richard Wolin (Cambridge: MIT Press, 1993), 144–151, 140–143, respectively.

8. See, especially, the second essay in May, *Hidden Sources*, "The Conversation" (11–20), which focuses explicitly on the circumstances surrounding the composition of Heidegger's "pseudo-dialogue," the fifth essay, "A Kind of Confession" (45–50), in which May argues that Heidegger's text can most profitably be read as Heidegger's confession of a "deeply hidden kinship" between his thinking and East Asian thought in general, and the translation of the renowned Japanese Germanist Tezuka Tomio's account of the conversation that he had with Heidegger, which is likely the actual inspiration for Heidegger's text, "Tezuka Tomio, 'An Hour with Heidegger'" (59–64).

9. May, in other words, regards the conversation of Heidegger's "dialogue" as an inspired fiction, and suggests (*Hidden Sources*, 18–19) that Heidegger actually based his account of *iki* on a mixture of Japanese and German aesthetic ideals discussed in Oscar Benl's 1952 monograph, "Seami Motokiyo und der Geist des Nō-Schauspiels: Geheime kunstkritische Schriften aus dem 15. Jahrhundert," *Akademie der Wissenschaften und der Literatur, Abhandlungen der Klasse der Literatur, Jahrgang 1952, Nr. 5.* (Wiesbaden: Franz Steiner Verlag GmbH, 1953), 103–249. May's reference to Benl's monograph—which he appropriately describes as an "inappropriate text," since it contains no references to the notion of *iki*—appears to be based largely on the research of Yoneda Michiko, *Gespräch und Dichtung: Ein Auseinandersetzungsversuch der Sprachfassung Heideggers mit einem japanischen Sagen* (Frankfurt am Main: Lang, 1984).

10. In Martin Heidegger, *Poetry, Language, Thought*, trans. Albert Hofstadter (New York: Harper and Row, 1971), 15–87. References to this text hereafter abbreviated *OWA* followed by page references to this translation, which is based upon the German edition of the text published in a separate volume under the essay's title, *Der Ursprung des Kunstwerkes* (Stuttgart: Reclam, 1960). However, although this text is often regarded as providing a definitive statement of Heidegger's view of art, a trend is emerging in recent scholarship to treat it instead as representative only of the initial stage of Heidegger's thinking about art. See, for example, Günter Seubold, *Kunst als Enteignis: Heideggers Weg zu einer nicht mehr metaphysischen Kunst* (Bonn: Bouvier Verlag, 1996).

11. Cf. *ACIJ*, 2–3: "The idiom of these [introductory and concluding] framing chapters [of *The Structure*] is heavily indebted to more recent developments in modern philosophy, most notably, a Heideggerian hermeneutics of Being."

12. An English-language edition of Farias' book, edited with a foreword by Joseph Margolis and Tom Rockmore and translated by Paul Burrell and Gabriel Ricci, has been published under the title *Heidegger and Nazism* (Philadelphia: Temple University Press, 1989). Also of interest is the German translation of Farias' book (*Heidegger und der Nationalsozialismus*, trans. Klaus Laermann [Frankfurt am Main: S. Fischer Verlag, 1989]), which contains an introduction by the prominent twentieth-century German philosopher Jürgen Habermas, now available in an English translation by John McCumber, "Work and *Weltanschauung*: The Heidegger Controversy from a German Perspective," in *Heidegger: A Critical Reader*, ed. Hubert Dreyfus and Harrison Hall (Oxford: Blackwell, 1992), 186–208. Farias' book is, however, widely regarded—even

by some of Heidegger's harshest critics—as one of the least reliable and most un-philosophical of the many recent works devoted to examining Heidegger's political views and political activities during this period. For a representative review of Farias' book, see Thomas Sheehan, "Heidegger and the Nazis," *New York Review of Books*, 16 June 1988, 38–47.

13. Pincus suggests that Kuki "refrained from political engagement" during this period and that he preferred instead to adopt "a stance of intellectual detachment" (*ACIJ*, 212). Cf. Nakano, who cites Kuki's "lack of social and political concern" as "another remarkable peculiarity" of his ("Kuki Shūzō," 271); see note 4.

14. The need to "come to terms" with Heidegger's political past has been a matter of special concern in particular among leading figures of recent French philosophy. See, for example, Jacques Derrida, *Of Spirit: Heidegger and the Question*, trans. Bennington and Bowlby (Chicago: University of Chicago Press, 1990); Luc Ferry and Alain Renaut, *Heidegger and Modernity*, trans. Franklin Phillip (Chicago: University of Chicago Press, 1990); Phillipe Lacoue-Labarthe, *Heidegger, Art, and Politics*, trans. Chris Turner (Oxford: Blackwell, 1990); and Jean-François Lyotard, *Heidegger and "the jews,"* trans. Michel and Roberts (Minneapolis: University of Minnesota Press, 1990). For two of the better, more general English-language discussions of Heidegger's political involvement in relationship to his philosophical development, see Miguel de Beistegui, *Heidegger and the Political: Dystopias* (London: Routledge, 1998), and Julian Young, *Heidegger, Philosophy, Nazism* (Cambridge: Cambridge University Press, 1997). Of these two studies, De Beistegui's is clearly the more "philosophical," focusing as it does on a critical examination of the meaning of the notion of the "political" in Heidegger's thought; Young, by contrast, seeks to "de-Nazify" the study of Heidegger's philosophy by responding primarily to the charges leveled against him by two of his harshest recent critics, Richard Wolin (*The Politics of Being: The Political Thought of Martin Heidegger* [New York: Columbia University Press, 1990]), and Domenico Losurdo (*Heidegger and the Ideology of War: Community, Death, and the West*, trans. Marella and Jon Morris [Amherst, N.Y.: Humanity Books, 2001]). Young's book can, therefore, also be read as a general introduction to the extensive body of critical literature that has been written on Heidegger in the decade and a half that has now passed since the publication of the French edition of Farias' book.

15. I follow, in these remarks, the brief synopsis provided by Michael E. Zimmerman in his excellent study, *Heidegger's Confrontation with Modernity* (Bloomington: Indiana University Press, 1990), 47; references to this text hereafter abbreviated HCM. For documents in which Heidegger provides his own account of his activities during this period, see Martin Heidegger, "The Rectorate 1933/34: Facts and Thoughts," in *Martin Heidegger and National Socialism: Questions and Answers*, ed. Günther Neske and Emil Kettering (New York: Paragon House, 1990), 15–32; "Herbert Marcuse and Martin Heidegger: An Exchange of Letters," in Wolin, ed., *The Heidegger Controversy*, 152–164 (see note 7 above); and the text of the interview that Heidegger gave to the German news weekly *Der Spiegel* on September 23, 1966, on the condition that it not be published

until after his death. The interview, considered "disappointing" by many commentators, appeared in the May 31, 1976, issue of *Der Spiegel*, under the title "Nur noch ein Gott kann uns retten" (Only a god can save us), 193–219, and is available in translations by Maria Alter and John D. Caputo, in *The Heidegger Controversy*, 91–116, and by Lisa Harries, in *Martin Heidegger and National Socialism*, 41–66.

16. See Karl Jaspers, "Letter to the University Denazification Committee, December 22, 1945," in Wolin, ed., *The Heidegger Controversy*, 144–151 (see note 7 above).

17. Cf. HCM, 40–44. For more detailed discussions of Heidegger's life, academic training, and career, including critical evaluations of the "official story," see Hugo Ott, *Martin Heidegger: A Political Life*, trans. Allen Blunden (New York: Basic Books, 1993); and Rüdiger Safranski, *Martin Heidegger: Between Good and Evil*, trans. Ewald Osers (Cambridge: Harvard University Press, 1998). For a concise account of the results of this research, see Young, *Heidegger, Philosophy, Nazism*, 2–4 (see note 14 above).

18. I would like to thank Frank Edler for pointing out several errors in Zimmerman's chronology for the period following Heidegger's resignation from the rectorate in April 1934. After Heidegger's resignation, he was scheduled to offer a course during the 1934 summer term entitled "The State and Science" (*Der Staat und die Wissenschaft*), not a course on "politics and the state," but he changed the course title at the last minute to "Logic as the Questioning of the Essence of Language" (*Logik als die Frage nach dem Wesen der Sprache*). He gave his first Hölderlin class during the 1934–1935 winter term and did not change the title of this course after it was first announced.

19. The specific date is given by Heidegger in the brief preface included with the Reclam edition of the text (OWA, 5). The lecture was given a second time, in January 1936, in Zürich and a third time, in Frankfurt, in three parts, in November and December of the same year. The Reclam text was prepared from the third version of the lecture, which did not appear in print until 1950. An unauthorized edition of the text of the Freiburg lecture accompanied by a French translation has been published under the title *De l'origine de l'oeuvre d'art. Première version 1935*, ed. Emmanuel Martineau (Paris: Authentica, 1987). An even earlier, preliminary draft of the text—which Friedrich-Wilhelm von Herrmann believes to date from as early as 1931 or 1932—is now also available under the title "Vom Ursprung des Kunstwerks: Erste Ausarbeitung," *Heidegger Studies* 5 (1989), 5–22.

20. Cf. Adolf Hitler, "Nuremberg Parteitag Address of September 11, 1935," in *The Speeches of Adolf Hitler*, ed. Norman H. Baynes (New York: Oxford University Press, 1942), 1:562; cited in HCM, 99.

21. Cf. HCM, 67–69. The text of Heidegger's rectoral address is available in English translations by William S. Lewis, in *The Heidegger Controversy*, 29–39; and Karsten Harries, in *Martin Heidegger and National Socialism*, 5–13 (see note 15 above). For a sympathetic and detailed discussion of Heidegger's development during this period, see Jacques Taminaux, "The Origin of 'The Origin of the Work of Art,'" in *Reading Heidegger: Commemorations*, ed. John Sallis (Bloomington and Indianapolis: Indiana University Press, 1993), 392–404.

22. Cf. HCM, 116: "Just as the Greeks initiated Western history by profoundly experiencing and responding to what was disclosed in their primordial mood (awe), [Heidegger believed that] . . . the Germans could initiate a new historical beginning if they experienced and responded appropriately to what was disclosed in their primal moods (horror and boredom). Hölderlin's poetry could enable the Germans to become accessible to the pain involved in the horror of modernity. . . . The 'saying' of the poet could help to transform the mood of horror into one of 'holy affliction, mourning but prepared' *(heilig trauernden, aber bereiten Bedrängnis).*" For a concise summary of Heidegger's relationship to Hölderlin, see HCM, 113–118; for more detailed discussions, see Jacques Taminaux, "The First Reading of Hölderlin," in *Heidegger and the Project of Fundamental Ontology,* trans. and ed. by Michael Gendre (Albany: State University of New York Press, 1991), 191–211; and, at a more introductory level, the second and third chapters of Julian Young's *Heidegger's Philosophy of Art* (Cambridge: Cambridge University Press, 2001), 69–119.

23. See, for example, Tom Rockmore, *On Heidegger's Nazism and Philosophy* (Berkeley: University of California Press, 1997).

24. See, for example, Christopher Fynsk, *Heidegger: Thought and Historicity* (Ithaca: Cornell University Press, 1986), esp. chap. 4: "The Work of Art and the Question of Man," 131–173. Cf. Taminaux, "The Origin of 'The Origin of the Work of Art,'" 392: "I remember Heidegger saying in passing during the Zähringen seminar held in September 1973 that the meditation on the origin of the work of art had played a decisive role in the *Kehre.*"

25. The subtitle of Pincus' book *Kuki Shūzō and the Rise of National Aesthetics* clearly borrows from the expression "national aestheticism" coined by the French Heideggerian Phillipe Lacoue-Labarthe in his attempt to come to terms with Heidegger's Nazism. (Cf. ACIJ, 210: "Phillipe Lacoue-Labarthe has given a name to this recruitment of cultural organicism for political ends, 'national aestheticism.'") The expression should, however, also be traced back to its source in the work of another German philosopher, Walter Benjamin, who, as Lacoue-Labarthe notes, together with Bertolt Brecht, "sometime around 1935 or 1936, during their period of exile in Denmark . . . coined [this] classic slogan: to the 'aestheticization of politics' one must respond with the 'politicization of art'" (*Heidegger, Art, and Politics*, 61). To "de-link" Kuki from Heidegger can, therefore, be viewed as an attempt—*contra* Pincus—to find a way to approach his text that does not frame it entirely within the terms of this debate and that also seeks to find an alternative between the extreme alternative uses of art ("fascist" or "communist") identified by Benjamin in the epilogue to his classic essay, "The Work of Art in the Age of Mechanical Reproduction," in Walter Benjamin, *Illuminations,* trans. Harry Zohn (New York: Schocken Books, 1968), 241–242. Further, when the problem of understanding Kuki's text is placed with the context of the larger history of competing Marxist and non-Marxist currents in twentieth-century Japanese and German intellectual life, it becomes apparent that much of this discussion has focused less on the actual interpretation of the text than it has on "ownership" of the

text, that is, on whether or not Kuki's text is to be used primarily to serve the interests of "progressive/Marxist" or "conservative/anti-Marxist" cultural/political forces.

26. For a helpful discussion of the degree to which Heidegger's discussion of the "work" of the "work of art," namely, the "founding" of an entire cultural landscape, must necessarily focus on "great" works of art—along with a nuanced discussion of the likely sources and political implications of this claim—see Robert Bernasconi, "The Greatness of the Work of Art," in Heidegger Toward the Turn: Essays on the Work of the 1930s, ed. James Risser (Albany: State University of New York Press, 1999), 95–117.

27. For a more detailed discussion of the importance of this concept, see HCM, 121–126.

28. Cf. HCM, 113–121.

29. See, especially, OWA, 61–62: "One essential way in which the truth establishes itself in the beings it has opened up is truth setting into work. Another way in which truth occurs is the act that founds a political state. . . ."; and OWA, 77: "Whenever art happens—that is, whenever there is a beginning—a thrust enters history, history either begins or starts over again. History means here not a sequence of time of events of whatever sort, however important. *History is the transporting of a people into its appointed task as entrance into that people's endowment*" (emphasis added). Commentators are, however, as previously noted, deeply divided over what significance is ultimately to be given to passages such as this. Few, if any, contest the charge that passages such as this help explain why Heidegger, in 1933, could have become politically involved with the Nazis and that he had aspirations in the period 1933–1935, in Otto Pöggeler's telling phrase, "to lead the leader." (Cf. Otto Pöggeler, "Den Führer führen?" *Philosophisches Rundschau* 32 (1985), 26–67.) They nevertheless disagree over whether Heidegger began, during this period and the following years, to move away from what might be referred to as a "Promethean" perspective in passages such as this to a more "meditative" perspective. Commentators who emphasize the Promethean tone of such passages typically think that Heidegger continued to support an active political—perhaps even militaristic—role for Nazi Germany at least through the 1930s, while commentators who find a meditative tone in such passages typically claim that he begins to look to art during this period as the source for a kind of deep cultural revolution that might free the modern world, including Nazi Germany, from its fascination with technology. Consequently, they typically also find evidence of tension with Nazi ideological themes in texts dating from the early 1930s. For sustained defenses of the second view, see Taminaux, "The Origin of 'The Origin of the Work of Art,'" the epilogue to *Heidegger and the Project of Fundamental Ontology*, 213–226; and Young, *Heidegger's Philosophy of Art*, 29–38, 52–60. For a statement of the "Promethean" view, see, for example, Hubert Dreyfus, "Heidegger on the Connection Between Nihilism, Art, Technology, and Politics," in *The Cambridge Companion to Heidegger*, ed. Charles Guignon (Cambridge: Cambridge University Press, 1993), 289–316.

30. See, for a general, introductory discussion of Heidegger's relationship to Hegel and his criticism of modern aesthetics, Young, *Heidegger's Philosophy of Art*, 6–15.

31. Immanuel Kant, *Critique of Judgment*, trans. Werner S. Pluhar (Indianapolis: Hackett Publishing Company, 1987).

32. Friedrich Schiller, *On the Aesthetic Education of Man, in a Series of Letters*, trans. Reginald Snell (New Haven: Yale University Press, 1954).

33. Cf. ADL, 29: "The expression 'hermeneutic' derives from the Greek verb *hermeneuein*. The verb is related to the noun *hermeneus*, which is referable to the name of the god Hermes by a playful thinking that is more compelling than the rigor of science. Hermes is the divine messenger. He brings the message of destiny; *hermeneuein* is that exposition which brings tidings because it can listen to a message."

34. To her credit, Pincus' discussion focuses as much on Dilthey's contributions to the science of hermeneutics as on Heidegger's (ACIJ, 140–181). Cf. Richard Palmer, *Hermeneutics: Interpretation Theory in Schleiermacher, Dilthey, Heidegger, and Gadamer* (Evanston: Northwestern University Press, 1969).

35. Cf. Martin Heidegger, *Being and Time*, trans. Joan Stambaugh (Albany: State University of New York Press, 1996), 30–34. For a brief, general discussion of Heidegger's hermeneutic phenomenology, including a critical assessment of his "later philosophy," see Rüdiger Bubner, *Modern German Philosophy*, trans. Eric Matthews (Cambridge: Cambridge University Press, 1981), 11–50.

36. Cf. Pincus, 173: "Heidegger spoke to fundamental philosophical issues, while Kuki merely addressed a single term in a local repertoire of taste. But it was precisely the historical and material particularity of *iki* that provided Kuki with an exemption from the expansive universalistic pretentions of Heideggerian philosophy and of European theoretical discourse in general."

37. I appreciate, in other words, the sentiments of an anonymous reviewer who suggested "dropping the paraphrase of Pincus's contentious and muddle-headed list" of differences between the ways in which Heidegger and Kuki employed what they each understood to be phenomenological methodology, but think it worth including because—whether entirely accurate or not—it aptly demonstrates how difficult it is to gloss over the significant differences between the two figures once we become engaged in the difficult task of actually comparing specific texts and claims of the two authors, and I find her discussion clearer and far more helpful than that of T. Botz-Bornstein, "'Iki,' Style, Trace: Shūzō Kuki and the Spirit of Hermeneutics," *Philosophy East and West* 47:4 (October 1997), 554–581.

38. See Light, *Shūzō Kuki and Jean-Paul Sartre*, 13–19, for a more detailed discussion of Kuki's interest in—and his possible contacts with—Alain. Cf. ADL, 42: "[Kuki] used the European rubric 'aesthetics,' but what he thought and searched for was something else . . ."

39. Cf. Taminaux, "The Origin of 'The Origin of the Work of Art,'" 393–395, for a very helpful discussion of why Heidegger likely did not take art very seriously in the period prior to his first lecture courses on Hölderlin. See, also, Hans Sluga, *Heidegger's Crisis: Philosophy and Politics in Nazi Germany* (Cambridge: Harvard University Press, 1995), 220–222. Sluga notes that Oscar Becker—another of Husserl's students and

one of the figures that Kuki had first come to Freiburg to study with—had, in 1929, sharply criticized Heidegger, claiming that a major deficiency of *Being and Time* was that it could not provide an adequate account of art. Cf. Oscar Becker, "Von der Hinfällig-keit des Schönen und der Abenteurlichkeit des Künstlers," *Jahrbuch für Philosophie und Phänomenologische Forschung Ergänzungsband: Husserl Festschrift* (Halle a. d. Saale: Max Nie-meyer Verlag, 1929), 27–52. Alternatively, Graham Parkes suggests—but does not pro-vide any evidence to support his view—that "[t]he original stimulation for [Heideg-ger's] engagement with [the] topic [of 'Origin'] may have been his conversations with Kuki in 1927 and 1928" ("Rising sun over Black Forest," in May, *Hidden Sources*, 99).

40. Cf. ADL, 28–29: "[M]y use of the word ['hermeneutics' . . . as an adjunct word to 'phenomenology'] is not arbitrary . . . [but I dropped both words] not—as is often thought—in order to deny the significance of phenomenology, but in order to aban-don my own path of thinking to namelessness." See, for a critical assessment of Hei-degger's use of a Van Gogh painting in *Origin*, Jacques Derrida, "Restitutions of the Truth in Painting," in *The Truth in Painting*, trans. Bennington and McLeod (Chicago: University of Chicago Press, 1987), 255–382.

41. Heidegger explicitly criticizes Kant's view of art at the beginning of *OWA*, 25–26. By contrast, Heidegger, in the epilogue to *OWA*, refers to Hegel's *Lectures on Aesthetics* as "the most comprehensive reflection on the nature of art that the West possesses . . . because it stems from metaphysics" (*OWA*, 79); Heidegger, however, focuses in this brief epilogue only upon Hegel's thesis concerning the "death" of art ("art is and re-mains for us, on the side of its highest vocations, something past") and not on those features of his philosophy of art which may have fascinated Kuki, who, by contrast, seems completely unconcerned in *The Structure* with this important element of Hegel's philosophy. For a more detailed discussion of Heidegger's relationship to Hegel than that provided in Young, *Heidegger's Philosophy of Art*, see Gerhard Faden, *Der Schein der Kunst: Zu Heideggers Kritik der Ästhetik* (Würzburg: Königshausen und Neumann, 1986), 139–155.

42. Cf. G. W. F. Hegel, *On Art, Religion, Philosophy*, ed. J. Glenn Gray (New York: Harper and Row, 1970), 78–80.

43. Kuki, in other words, seems not to find "aesthetics" objectionable, while a cen-tral theme of Heidegger's preoccupation with art, beginning with *Origin*, as has been noted repeatedly, was to "overcome" aesthetics. For a more detailed discussion of this theme than that available in Young, *Heidegger's Philosophy of Art*, see Faden, *Der Schein der Kunst*, 27–43.

44. Cf. Nara's translation of the passage in which Kuki sidesteps taking a stance on this issue (p. 34 in this volume):

> Grasping the meaning of *iki* depends on whether or not we can understand the objective form of *iki* on the basis of *iki* as a phenomenon of consciousness and, at the same time, on whether or not we can comprehend the structure in its entirety. Let us begin by categorizing objective expressions of *iki* in two ways:

natural expression, that is, expression through **natural form;** and artistic expression, that is, expression in **artistic form.** There may be some question of
whether these two categories will permit a clear distinction. It could be argued
natural form is, in effect, identical to artistic form. We must, however, put that
intriguing question aside and press on. Let us follow a common custom and
assume, for the sake of convenience, that natural and artistic form are distinct
enough to consider separately.

45. Cf. Paul Oscar Kristeller, "The Modern System of the Arts," in *Renaissance
Thought and the Arts* (Princeton: Princeton University Press, 1990), 163–227.

46. Cf. Light, Shūzō *Kuki and Jean-Paul Sartre*, 18; Light refers to Alain's *Système des
beaux-arts* as "perhaps the centerpiece in Alain's oeuvre."

47. *Critique of Judgment*, 190 n. 58.

48. For a recent discussion of this problem, see Richard Dien Winfield, *Stylistics:
Rethinking the Artforms after Hegel* (Albany: State University of New York Press, 1996).

49. Due to space limitations, little emphasis has been placed in these comments
on the fact that Heidegger's initial public support for the Nazi regime should not be
taken as an indication that he supported all facets of Nazi ideology, a point generally recognized by even his harshest critics, or on the fact that even those commentators who see a strong link between Heidegger's philosophy and his political views
differ widely on how they view the connection between the further development of his
philosophical and political views during the 1930s and 1940s. For a primarily historical treatment comparing Heidegger's political involvement with the Nazi regime with
that of other prominent intellectuals during this period, see Hans Sluga's *Heidegger's
Crisis.* For a representative collection of more advanced philosophical essays evaluat-
ing Heidegger's development during this period, including a preliminary analysis of
the differences between the first draft of Heidegger's *Origin* and the text of the lecture
delivered in Frankfurt at the end of 1936 by Françoise Dastur ("Heidegger's Freiburg
Version of the Origin of the Work of Art"), see Risser, ed., *Heidegger Toward the Turn* (see
note 26 above). For a representative defense of the view that Heidegger actually developed a serious critique of Nazi ideology during this period, Fred Dallmayr, "Heidegger
on *Macht* and *Machenschaft*," *Continental Philosophy Review* 34:3 (2001), 247–267. Finally,
for a defense of the view that Heidegger's support for the Nazi cause was always quali-
fied by philosophical concerns that transcended politics, see Frank H. W. Edler, "Philosophy, Language, and Politics: Heidegger's Attempt to Steal the Language of the
Revolution in 1933–34," *Social Research* 57:1 (spring 1990), 197–238.

50. For a more sustained criticism of the efforts of Pincus (and others) to make of
Kuki a "fascist accomplice" of comparable degree as Heidegger, see Graham Parkes'
review of *ACIJ* in *Chanoyu Quarterly* 86 (1997), 63–71, and the relevant sections of his
longer article, "The Putative Fascism of the Kyoto School and the Political Correctness
of the Modern Academy," *Philosophy East and West* 47:3 (1997), 305–336.

51. Further, even if one were to agree that a comparison of Kuki's views and those

of Heidegger was useful, it would clearly be necessary to distinguish more carefully the period of Heidegger's philosophical development from which his view of art is to be considered. To this end, three periods might be distinguished: (1) the period before the "turn" of the early 1930s, during which reflection on art seems to play no role whatsoever in his philosophical development; (2) the period dating from the "turn" through the end of the Second World War, which for the purposes of these remarks might be characterized as having been initiated by an intensified interest in the poetry of Hölderlin, sustained by an effort to formulate a "de-Nazified" interpretation of Nietzsche's philosophy, and the complete transition to what Heidegger refers to as "Ereignis-thinking"; and (3) the postwar period during which Heidegger's view of art tends—when judged by the standards set forth in Origin—to become clearly less Promethean and more trivially "aesthetic," or, in other words, of less historical significance and instead more "meditative" and subjectively personal. Cf. Young, Heidegger's Philosophy of Art, 3, who suggests dividing the development of Heidegger's thought into four periods: (1) pre-1930, (2) 1930–1938, (3) 1938–1946, (4) "postwar."

Kuki Shūzō Chronology

Information based on *Kuki Shūzō zenshū* (The complete works of Kuki Shūzō)

1888 (Meiji 21), birth year
Born in Tokyo on February 15. Fourth son of Kuki Ryūichi, who had studied under Fukuzawa Yukichi and begun his career as a Ministry of Education official. Kuki's father was chargé d'affaires to the United States when Kuki was born.

1896 (Meiji 29), age 8
Kuki's father was given the title of baron.

1905 (Meiji 38), age 17
Entered the First Higher School in Tokyo with the intention of specializing in German legal studies.

1905 (Meiji 39), age 18
Failed a history class. Became close friends of Amano Teiyū (philosopher) and Iwashita Sōichi (Catholic theologian). Ochiai Tarō, Kashima Kikuo, Tatsuno Takashi, Tanizaki Jun'ichirō, and Watsuji Tetsurō were among his schoolmates. Studied philosophy from Iwamoto Tei and changed his major to literature.

1909 (Meiji 42), age 21
Graduated from the First Higher School. Entered the Tokyo Imperial University and studied philosophy under Raphael von Koeber.

1911 (Meiji 44), age 23
Baptized at St. Francis Xavier Church as Franciscus Assisiensis Kuki Shūzō.

1912 (Meiji 45/Taisho 1), age 24
Wrote a graduation thesis on the relationship between mind and mat-

ter and graduated from the Tokyo Imperial University; admitted into the graduate program in the fall. Received a scholarship to study.

1913 (Taisho 2), age 25
Submitted a report to the graduate school entitled "Die geschichtliche Entwicklung des Problems von Glauben und Wissen im Mittelalter" (The historical development of the problems of belief and knowledge in the Middle Ages).

1917 (Taisho 6), age 29
Older brother Ichizō died.

1918 (Taisho 7), age 30
Married Ichizō's widow Nuiko.

1921 (Taisho 10), age 33
Withdrew from the graduate program at the Tokyo Imperial University and became affiliated with the Ministry of Education. Left for studies in Europe, with Nuiko, on the ship *Kamomaru*, via Singapore, Colombo, Suez, and Marseilles, arriving at Nice in late November. Stayed for a while in Nice.

1922 (Taisho 11), age 34
Studied at Heidelberg University, beginning in October. Attended Rickert's lecture entitled "Von Kant bis Nietzsche: Historische Einführung in die Probleme der Gegenwart" (From Kant to Nietzche: historical introduction to the contemporary problem). Studied Kant's *Critique of Pure Reason* privately with Rickert, beginning on November 10. Also engaged Eugen Herrigel as a tutor to study the introduction in Kant's *Transcendental Philosophy*.

1923 (Taisho 12), age 35
April: Traveled to Dresden, Leipzig, Weimar, and Munich. Returned to Heidelberg to meet his friend Amano Teiyū. Attended Rickert's summer class on Kant "Einleitung in die Erkenntnistheorie und Metaphysik" (Introduction to the theory of knowledge and metaphysics) and "Philosphie der Kunst" (Philosophy of art). Also attended a seminar "Übungen über der Begriff der Intuition" (Tutorial on the concept of intuition). June: attended Miki Kiyoshi's lecture "Wahrheit und Gewissheit" (Truth and uncertainty). Other students from Japan, besides Amano and Miki, included Abe Jirō, Ōuchi Hyōe, Naruse Mukyoku, and Hani Gorō.

August and September: Collected plant specimens in the Alps. December: Moved to Zurich.

1924 (Taisho 13), age 36
Traveled extensively in Switzerland. Moved to Paris in the fall.

1925 (Taisho 14), age 37
April: Wrote and published poetry "Parii shinkei" under pseudonym "S. K." in Myōjō. September: Published tanka "Parii shōkyoku" in Myōjō under pseudonym "S. K." October: Entered the Faculty of Letters, University of Paris. December: Published poetry "Parii no mado" under pseudonym "S. K." in Myōjō.

1926 (Taisho 15/Showa 1), age 38
January: Published a collection of poems "Parii shinkei" in Myōjō under pseudonym "S. K." October: Published a collection of poems "Parii no negoto" in Myōjō under pseudonym "Komori Rokuzō." December: Finished "Iki no honshitsu" (The essence of iki). Engaged Sartre as a tutor for French and discussed Heidegger with him.

1927 (Showa 2), age 39
Moved to the University of Freiburg and studied phenomenology under Edmund Husserl and Oskar Becker. April: Met Heidegger at the home of Husserl. November: Studied at the University of Marburg and attended Heidegger's lectures on phenomenological interpretation of Kant's Critique of Pure Reason. Attended Heidegger's seminar "Schelling's Essay on the Essence of Human Freedom."

1928 (Showa 3), age 40
Audited Heidegger's lecture on Leibniz's Logic and Aristotle's Physics. June: Moved back to Paris. August: Gave a lecture on the oriental notion of time and the expression of infinity in Japanese art. Visited Bergson in Paris. Nishida wrote his colleague Tanabe Hajime at Kyoto Imperial University, recommending Kuki for a teaching position at the university. December: Returned to Japan via the United States. In Washington, D.C., he met Paul Claudel to discuss Alain's aesthetics.

1929 (Showa 4), age 41
Returned to Japan in January on the ship Shun'yōmaru. April: Appointed assistant professor of philosophy at Kyoto Imperial University. Gave lectures on the problem of time and contingency. Taught class at Kyoto on

contemporary French philosophy and a class on Bergson using *Essai sur les données immédiates de conscience* (Time and free will: essay on the immediate data of consciousness).

1930 (Showa 5), age 42

January and February: Published "Iki no kōzō" in journal *Shisō* in two installments. The articles were published by Iwanami shoten as a book in November. Gave a lecture on metaphysics of time. Taught classes on the problem of contingency and on Boutroux's *De la contigence des lois de la nature* (Contingency of the laws of nature).

1931 (Showa 6), age 43

August: His father, Ryūichi, died. October: Published articles on the rhyming structure in Japanese poetry. November: His mother, Hatsu, died. Taught class on Heidegger's hermeneutical phenomenology and on Leibniz's *Discours de métaphysique* (Discourse on metaphysics), *Monadologie* (Monadology), and others.

1932 (Showa 7), age 44

November: Doctoral dissertation on contingency was accepted at the Kyoto Imperial University and he became a doctor of letters. Gave class on Heidegger and on Bergson using *Matière et mémoire* (Matter and memory).

1933 (Showa 8), age 45

March: Promoted to the rank of associate professor. Published an article on philosophy of existence. Taught class on contemporary French philosophy and on Descartes, using *Méditations* (Meditations), and on literary theory.

1934 (Showa 9), age 46

Taught the continuation of French philosophy. Gave a seminar on Husserl using *Méditations cartésiennes*, a French translation of *Cartesianische Meditationen* (Cartesian meditations).

1935 (Showa 10), age 47

March: Promoted to the rank of professor of philosophy. December: Published *Gūzensei no mondai* (Problem of contingency) with Iwanami. Taught a class on the history of modern philosophy, a special course on empirical metaphysics of Bergson. Taught class on Husserl using *Méditations cartésiennes* (Cartesian meditations).

1936 (Showa 11), age 48

February: Received a letter from Karl Löwith, who was under persecution by the Nazis, asking for his help to secure an exit visa to Japan. Helped him to find a philosophy position at Tohoku University. Published a number of articles for the general public. Taught history of modern philosophy, a special class on Kant and philosophy after Kant, and a seminar on Bergson's *La pensée et le mouvant* (The creative mind).

1937 (Showa 12), age 49

October: Published "Jikyoku no kansō" (Thoughts on the current state of affairs) in the monthly literary magazine *Bungei shunjū*. Published a number of other articles for the general public. Taught history of modern Western philosophy, a special class on Kant and philosophy after Kant, and a seminar on Bergson's *La pensée et le mouvant* (The creative mind).

1938 (Showa 13), age 50

Published a number of articles for the general public. Taught history of modern Western philosophy, a special class on nineteenth-century philosophy, and a seminar on Bergson's *L'Évolution créatrice* (Creative evolution).

1939 (Showa 14), age 51

August: Traveled to Manchuria and China. September: Published *Ningen to jitsuzon* (Man and existence) with Iwanami. Taught history of modern Western philosophy, a special class on recent trends in philosophy, and a seminar on Bergson's *L'Évolution créatrice* (Creative evolution).

1940 (Showa 15), age 52

Moved to Yamashina, outside of Kyoto. Taught classes on the history of modern Western philosophy, on contemporary philosophy, and on German neo-Kantians and French philosophy of science. December: his close friend Iwashita Sōichi died.

1941 (Showa 16), age 53

Died of peritonitis on May 6.

Contributors

JON MARK MIKKELSEN is associate professor of philosophy and humanities at Missouri Western State College. His primary research interests include the philosophy of Immanuel Kant and the history and influence of German philosophical aesthetics. He is currently preparing a collection of translations of late eighteenth-century German writings on the concept of race, including three essays by Kant, of which two have already appeared in print: "Of the Different Human Races," in *The Idea of Race*, ed. Robert Bernasconi and Tommy L. Lott (Hackett, 2000); and "On the Use of Teleological Principles in Philosophy," in *Race*, ed. Robert Bernasconi (Blackwell, 2001). He is also working on a survey of German philosophical aesthetics from Kant to Lyotard. He can be reached at the Department of History, Philosophy and Geography, Missouri Western State College, St. Joseph, MO 64507.

HIROSHI NARA is chair and associate professor of Japanese language and linguistics in the Department of East Asian Languages and Literatures at the University of Pittsburgh. His interests include semantics (tense, aspect, and modality), Japanese language pedagogy, natural language processing, and, more recently, intellectual history of modern Japan as it relates to art and aesthetics. He can be reached at the Department of East Asian Languages and Literatures at the University of Pittsburgh, Pittsburgh, PA 15260.

J. THOMAS RIMER teaches Japanese literature and theater at the University of Pittsburgh. He has written widely on a variety of literary, theatrical, and artistic aspects of modern Japanese culture. He can be reached at the Department of East Asian Languages and Literatures at the University of Pittsburgh, Pittsburgh, PA 15260.

Translation Index

Essay Index